FREE $TUFF
From the
World Wide Web

Patrick
Vincent

CORIOLIS GROUP BOOKS

Publisher	Keith Weiskamp
Editor	Ron Pronk
Proofreader	Michelle Stroup
Interior Design	Rob Mauhar
Cover Design	Keith Weiskamp and Bradley O. Grannis
Layout Production	Rob Mauhar
Publicist	Shannon Bounds
Indexer	Lenity Mauhar

Library of Congress Cataloging-in-Publication Data

Vincent, Patrick
    Free Stuff From The World Wide Web / Patrick Vincent
        p. cm.
    Includes Index
    ISBN 1-883577-27-6 : $19.99

Printed in the United States of America

10 9 8 7 6 5 4 3 2 1

To my father and biggest fan, John Vincent Sr., with all my love.
Thanks, Dad, for sharing in my dream.

Here are a few of the author's favorite E-mail messages from readers, who offer their opinions of *Free $TUFF from the Internet*. We even let Mr. Vincent include his responses, which might have been a mistake....

I just purchased the book today and cannot put it down. As a new Internet user, this is the first publication I read that I could totally understand. I am still fumbling my way around, but am learning more each day. If you have any suggestions, or are planning an update to this book, please reply —D.S.

Your wish is my Alt+Shift+Command. The next book is called FREE $TUFF from the World Wide Web*, and will be available mid-year, 1995. There are a few other titles lined up for publication soon after, but they hinge on whether I'm released from Happy Acres by then. The nurses finally let me have my computer back, and told me that next week I may even be able to have visitors.*

Your book makes sense of many confusing Internet topics. It is well organized and humorously written. I'd like to see your team tackle a book about Mosaic, including as much of the help/configuration files as possible. —Joe D.

I appreciate the comments, and have in fact recently gang-authored a book with PC Guru Jeff Duntemann and Mac Wizard Ron Pronk (their true full names) called the Mosaic EXplorer Pocket Companion. *If you're looking for my name on it, look way down at the bottom. Jeff and Ron told me it was a matter of listing the names alphabetically, though that's what they said about why I was given such a small office with no window.*

I just got your book.... This is absolutely incredible!!!!! This place [the Internet] is unlimited in getting any kind of info anyone wants to whenever!! —Duffy M.

Thanks Duffy!!!!! I know you're excited, but easy on the exclamation key!!!!! And save a little caffeine for the rest of us!!!!!

I feel that *FREE $TUFF from the Internet* will not only be helpful for education but also helpful...in personal endeavors.... I feel that there is just so much in this book that it is well worth the purchase. —R.H.

It's also guaranteed to freshen breath, whiten teeth, and generally make you more attractive to the opposite sex.

RE: "Let us know what you disliked, as well." THE INK! The stench that emanates from your book, the asthma attack it produces in people who are allergic, and the fact that it must be read contained in a sealed, metal-glass-topped box. —C. L. W.

Since FREE $TUFF from the Internet *is intended for recreational use, I guess I should have included a warning that it not be smoked, inhaled, snorted, or ingested in any way. Rest assured that this oversight will be corrected in future editions.*

Regards from Malaysia! Just a note to say I am thankful for the info you've written to enable people like me who're quite new to the Internet to surf it more easily. Do you mean that I can write to President Clinton and expect a reply? —L. H. W.

I guess that's between you and the President. All I can say is that if you are going to write him, make it fast. His address is subject to change— perhaps to something like former.president@nobody.appreciates.me.

Thanks to everyone who sent me mail. I've tried to respond to each note, but with two kids, two books I'm currently writing, and only 24 hours in a day, I may have missed someone. Thanks for the feedback!

Contents

(448)

Art 25 23

Books, Magazines, and Literature 49 21

Business and Careers

71 23

Computers and Software

Education and Teaching Tools

Food and Cooking   143   19

Games   163   13

Government and Politics

Health and Nutrition

History, Genealogy, and Fun Facts 221

Household and Family Finances 233

Language and Literary Pursuits   297

Law   313

Religion

371 /³

Science and Technology

385   25

Travel and Geography 447 | 5

Index 463

 # FREE $TUFF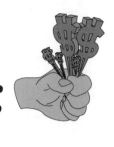

Introduction

News flash! The Internet and the Web are *not* the same!

What's the difference? *Hypertext*, the word of the '90s. Remember that word, because it helps define the difference between the Internet and the World Wide Web (Web, for short). It's a word you're likely to hear often over the next couple of years as the Web grows in both size and number of users.

It was the marriage of hypertext technology to the Internet that produced the Web, and with the recent availability of many free and easy-to-use Web browsers like Mosaic, Netscape, MacWeb, and WinWeb, millions of Internauts previously cut off from accessing the seemingly limitless wealth of Web freebies are now exploring this plethora of information, fun, and games.

The result? The Internet is taking its first giant leap forward in a decade. And surfing it will never be the same.

But what's all the fuss about? This hypertext thing's been around for decades. Why the sudden wave of interest? While it's true that the hypertext concept *has* been around since the late 1960s, and has been used on Mac and Windows PCs since the mid 1980s, using it to access computers across the globe has only been possible since around 1991. And the Web itself has been relatively easy for anyone to access only since 1993 when Mosaic was introduced. Even then, it was only accessible to computers running UNIX. PC and Mac users at the time were out of luck.

But all that's changed. Web browsers for Windows and the Mac were made widely available in late 1993 and throughout 1994, and are still freely accessible. Since the availability of Web browsers, millions of new Internet users have been getting their first taste of the World Wide Web. It's an exciting time in computing. Never before has so much information been available to so many for so little cost.

Welcome to cyberspace's answer to the Foreign Legion—the biggest rag-tag assembly of information warriors and free-stuff vampires ever to travel the globe—without ever leaving their computers. When you buy this book, *you'll be one of us*—if you're not already. Scary, huh?

Getting Started

Actually, the Internet can be pretty scary if you're not a fan of disorder. In fact, if you have any experience on the Internet, you know that it's just slightly less organized than Oscar Madison's desktop. The World Wide Web is not much different. Sure, one of the features of Web browsers and especially hypertext is their built-in capability for bringing some order to this chaos. (More details on the Web, Web browsers, and hypertext in short order.)

Even so, anyone with available time and resources can put anything on the Web. This makes for some of the wildest, most fascinating, bizarre, informative, and *creative* Web sites you can imagine—and some that, frankly, are beyond the realm of comprehension. It's a great place to browse, but when it comes to quickly finding exactly what you're interested in, the Web is easy to get tangled up in.

That's more or less the goal of *FREE $TUFF from the World Wide Web*— no, not to add to the confusion, but to tell you how to blow by it. In short, this book will point you to parts of the Web you didn't even know existed, and will help you to find the best of what the Web has to offer, regardless of your interests. And I promise to at least attempt to entertain you along the way. Another bonus: Nearly every Web site in this book contains links to related Web sites, so you'll be able to explore on your own with just a few clicks of your mouse.

And if you're new to the Internet or the Web, I suspect you'll find that the remainder of this *Preface* will answer a lot of questions (at least that's my goal), and will help you get started on that great travel adventure we affectionately call cyberspace. (Actually, I still gag on that word, but everybody else seems to love it.)

Birth of the Web

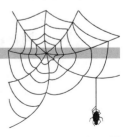

Veteran Net surfers get teary-eyed about the good old days (1991 and earlier—ancient history on the cyberspace timeline) in which finding your way around the Internet required more than a nimble index finger to point and click. *Real* Net surfers knew UNIX, a cryptic yet powerful operating system that users first had to tame to earn their wings and venture onto the Internet. Net surfing was not for the techno-challenged. No way.

But then, in the blink of an eye, the rules changed. Graphical interfaces and information servers like Gopher were created to make exploring cyberspace easier for the non-technical masses. Build it and they will come. And come they did—by the millions. No longer a research tool for the academic elite, the Internet soon became available to everyone. Theoretical physicists were rubbing elbows with high-school students, computer programmers were exchanging ideas with daycare volunteers. The Internet had become the great equalizer. All of Netdom had been roped and conquered as a communication tool for everyone, right?

Well almost. Not *all* of it.

One rapidly evolving corner of the Internet remained a mystery to the existing Net riff-raff: World Wide Web access. This ripe-for-the-picking cyber-niche was not so different in theory from some of the other tools being used to explore the Internet, save one very important distinction. Where other tools were character- or menu-based, the World Wide Web promised to combine sound, video, graphics, and text into a full-sensory cornucopia. Users no longer would need to remember long, cryptic commands to explore the Internet; they only needed to be able to point and click to tap into a whole new world in multimedia.

Strangely, many of the Internet old-timers were the last to hear about this brave new electronic world. The Web became the New World for hundreds of thousands of new cyberspace explorers. How did this mass techno-shift get started? Read on!

In the Beginning . . .

The World Wide Web traces its roots to the late 1960s, when a guy named Ted Nelson came up with the idea of attaching documents via *hypertext*, a system in which documents stored on computers contained links to

other documents. By having their documents linked together, users could more actively determine what to read or not read depending on the information they were looking for.

The concept of hypertext allowed users to break through the frustrating barrier of being forced to read a document linearly. Instead, readers could follow a seemingly infinite number of threads, changing paths and steering through documents depending on what information they were interested in finding.

An example of hypertext you're probably familiar with is the help screens used in Microsoft Windows and Macintosh applications. When you read a Windows or Mac help screen, you see words that are underlined and usually in a different color than the other text. By clicking on one of these words, you're instantly taken to another help screen. In this way, you can find the information you're looking for quickly and easily, saving you from having to pore through pages of superfluous documentation.

The basic concept behind the World Wide Web is no different, except instead of linking documents stored on your computer, it links millions of documents, programs, sound bites, movies, and more stored on thousands of computers around the world.

Vive le France

Tim Berners-Lee, working at the European Particle Physics Laboratory (known by its French acronym, CERN) in Geneva, Switzerland, took the concept of hypertext a step further. Instead of limiting the use of links to documents stored on one computer, he surmised, why not use hypertext to link documents on many different computers to provide researchers and academia with an easy way to search for and exchange data on ongoing projects?

The outgrowth of this idea was a set of hypertext tools, created by Tim at CERN and by others elsewhere, now called *browsers* because they made it possible to search through lists or other collections of information *links*, rather than sift through the information itself. It was an astonishingly simple approach to providing organized and extensive information access.

Early browsers were strictly character-based, with sound and video little more than an extension based on the kernel of a science fiction dream. Still, having a way to locate information quickly through hypertext was a tremendous step forward. The groundwork had been laid for the fun and free stuff you can explore and grab today with this book. But there's more to this tale.

Enter Marc Andreessen. An undergrad at the University of Illinois at Urbana-Champaign in 1992, Marc was working part-time at the National Center for Supercomputing Applications (NCSA) when he started toying with the development of a graphical interface to access the growing but relatively unknown Web. He quickly saw the potential for what he was onto, and the result of his resourcefulness, insight, and marathon all-nighters was Mosaic for UNIX, the first widely available point-and-click interface to the World Wide Web. Published in April 1993, versions for Windows and Macintosh soon followed.

Internet and the Web: the Difference?

This is a good point to take a breather and explain a few basics. For starters, a lot of people are confused about the difference between the Internet and the World Wide Web, understandably so. If you, too, are still scratching your head, you're in some heavily populated company, and I think I can remove the confusion pretty quickly.

Think of an automobile and its engine (stay with me for a moment even if you know nothing about cars). Conceptually, the difference between the two is the same as the difference between the Web and the Internet. You can wrap several different auto bodies around the same engine, but it's always the engine that makes the car go. Take the Ford Taurus and the Mercury Sable, for instance: different bodies and features, but underneath the hood they're the same car. And General Motors, as another big example, has built a billion-dollar business around the practice of putting different auto bodies around the same engine.

Now think about the Web and the Internet. The Web is essentially a great looking body wrapped around a high-performance engine—the Internet. You can use the Web to drive and control the Internet, but the Internet is still providing all the horsepower.

Actually, the Web as it exists today has been built by individual users who create *Web pages*—or Internet sites (auto bodies, of a sort) that all use the same technique to create graphics, text, and most important, the hypertext links that make it easy for you to leap from one Web page to another with the click of your mouse.

The use of the word "page" to describe a Web site is unfortunate, because each Web "page" actually can contain dozens or even hundreds of screens (or pages) of information. So think of a "Web page" as a "Web site" and you'll be better for the effort. In any event, the starting point for any Web site is called its *home page*. A Web site's home page typically contains the hypertext links to other pages, which in turn contain links to still other pages, and on and on.

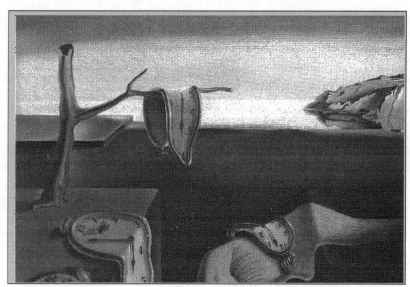

A page from the Salvador Dali Exhibit at the WebMuseum Web site.

7

The common organizational approach that all Web pages share is something called *HyperText Markup Language*, or *HTML* for short. HTML sounds complicated, but it's actually not much more than a glorified word processor that uses *tags* to format and define the text, graphics, and hypertext components that make up a Web page. For instance, if I want to put *something in italics* on a Web page, I just do this:

something in italics

Pretty simple, huh?

It really is almost that simple. In fact, everybody who creates a Web site uses the same set of HTML tags or codes like the italics tags that I've just shown; that's how all the thousands of Web sites are linked together seamlessly.

And guess what? For the purpose of this book, all you need to know about HTML is what you just finished reading in the previous paragraphs. In fact, you really didn't even need to know *that* much, but a passing knowledge of HTML can help you to conceptually understand how the Web works and how it's different from the Internet.

So What's the Role of a Web Browser

The bottom line is that Web sites are part of the Internet. But just because you have access to the Internet doesn't automatically mean you can access Web sites. With a few exceptions, *you can't access Web pages without a Web browser* like Mosaic, Netscape, WinWeb, or MacWeb. The reason is simple: A Web browser translates the HTML at a Web site into the graphical images, text, and hypertext links that you see on your screen. Without a Web browser, your computer doesn't know how to "see" a Web site's HTML, even though it knows how to "talk" to your Internet service provider.

The best part about Web browsers is that most of them are free—at least on a trail basis. Even the commercial Web browsers are typically distributed as a freebie by your Internet service provider or by Internet services

that want your business and want to provide an easy way for you to do business with them. Ain't life in the free lane great?

Mosaic, still the most popular Web browser, is not a commercial browser because technically it was created at NCSA. And because NCSA is funded by the National Science Foundation, the software tools it creates are considered public domain. Needless to say, computer users by the hundreds of thousands have been scrambling to download free copies of Mosaic.

But there's a catch with Mosaic—a small one, but a catch nevertheless.

Mosaic, even at this writing, is a work in progress. Technically, you could consider it to be "beta" software, an unfinished version. When you use Mosaic, you'll notice some inconsistencies in its features and, as you get more experienced, you'll quickly identify features that you think should be part of the software but aren't. Even so, Mosaic is a fairly stable piece of software. And most important, Mosaic has given birth to a litter of copycats.

Everybody Wants to Get Into the Act

The copycats are the commercial spin-offs of Mosaic that I wrote about in the previous paragraphs, and now include Netscape, WinWeb, and MacWeb, among others—many others. (I'll have more to say about the various browsers a bit later.)

The proliferation of Web browsers has led many people to conclude that conventional online services are going to be casualties—cyber-roadkill, if you will—on the information superhighway. In fact, recently some industry writers have been performing last rites on online service providers like Prodigy and America Online, calling Mosaic and its commercial clones the wave that will bury these companies in the sand.

I'll just say that reports of the demise of online services have been greatly exaggerated, mainly because these services have realized the potential of the Web and are scrambling to get onboard. Prodigy announced limited

---

Web access for its subscribers in December 1994, and America Online and CompuServe should have their own full-featured (more or less) Internet and Web services up and running by the time you read this book.

It might very well be that you're going to be accessing Web sites from one of these online services, rather than from a more "dedicated" Internet provider. That's just fine with me. Whatever it takes to get online; I don't care, as long as you're there.

Anyway, from a handful of sites in 1991, the World Wide Web has experienced an atomic explosion of growth in the past three years, with many thousands of Web sites rising from the cloud. And the growth is still mushrooming.

A Note about Addresses

There are a number of different "types" of sites on the Internet, each of which uses a different set of communications protocols for getting online. Some Internet sites are Gopher servers, while others are FTP servers, while others use Telnet, and still others (the most important category for you) require a Web browser. When you use a Web browser, you specify the type of site you're accessing by entering the *protocol* followed by its Internet address. This long, hieroglyphic-like statement, which you'll see a lot of in this book, is called a *Uniform Resource Locator* (or *URL* for short).

For this book, I'm assuming you're using a Web browser, in which case you initially access any Internet location by entering its protocol followed by the appropriate Internet address. For Web sites, the protocol is HTTP, which stands for HyperText Transfer Protocol. So a typical Web site address might look like this:

http://www.law.uc.edu/Diana

Here's an example of an FTP address:

ftp://ftp.einet.net/einet/mac/macweb

This Internet address will take you to an FTP site that provides the MacWeb browser for downloading.

Whatever your Web interest, you must enter the appropriate URL address in the dialog box that your Web browser supplies for this purpose. For Mosaic users, click on **File|Open URL**. For Netscape users, click on **File|Open Location**. If you're using some other Web browser, you'll probably find that the addressable dialog box is available by clicking on **File** and then some **Open** dialog box. After you've opened the appropriate dialog box, just enter the address that I've specified.

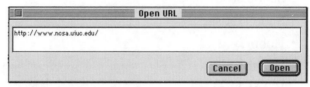

File|Open URL from Mosaic

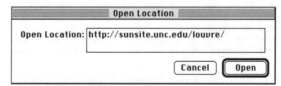

File|Open Location from Netscape

Watch Your Case

Most Web servers are located on UNIX systems, and UNIX is *very* case sensitive. So, if I tell you to type **http://curry.edschool.Virginia.EDU:80/**, type it *exactly* that way—with a capital "V" in Virginia and "EDU" in all uppercase. If you don't enter characters in the correct case, the URL will be about as useful to you as a Playskool phone.

How Much Does All This "Free Stuff" Cost?

Once you have access to the Internet and the World Wide Web, the programs, product samples, coupons, movie clips, newsletters, and other assorted freebies contained in this book are just that—FREE!

By accessing the Web sites detailed throughout this book, you and the rest of the army of bargain hunters will find loads of free stuff for your:

- Home
- Business
- Schoolwork
- Sports fetishes
- Hobbies
- Health
- Funny bone
- Sweet tooth
- Game addiction
- Love life
- Career

But don't get me started. This listing only scratches the surface of what you'll find waiting for you on the Web. So, what are you waiting for?

Who's in Charge?

Not too many years ago, when the number of Web sites could be counted on two hands and maybe a couple of toes, you probably could have actually pinpointed who was in charge of putting information on the World Wide Web. Those days have long since passed. Now the answer to the question, "Who's in charge?" is —drumroll please—*you*. Anyone with a direct link to the Internet (which probably includes yourself) and a minimal amount of HTML knowledge (which could include yourself with remarkably little effort) can create his or her own Web page for the rest of the world to see. Tutorials are readily available on the Web to help you create fun and interesting pages. A little HTML learning goes a very long way.

Is There Anybody Out There?

Formerly the domain of scientists and academicians, the World Wide Web has now become the newest craze for cyber-explorers looking for the best of the Internet. On the Web, you can:

- Get coupons, newsletters, software, product information, and other freebies from thousands of companies doing business on the Web.
- Read movie reviews and trivia from databases containing information on thousands of motion pictures, and even download pictures, clips, and sound bites of your favorite stars.
- Go shopping at hundreds of specialty stores.
- Confess your cyber-sins at an online confessional and be given penance (really).
- Dissect a frog without the mess (also really).

And you won't be alone. The latest count shows that as many as 40 million people are hooked up to the Internet through over 42 thousand computer networks in 160 countries. Another million hop onboard every month, and with recent announcements by both MCI and AT&T to begin offering Internet services in 1995, including Web browsers, easy-to-install software, and online shopping, these numbers are going nowhere but up.

Even IBM and Microsoft are getting into the act. IBM's new operating system, OS/2 Warp, comes bundled with a Web browser, and Microsoft Windows 95 will also include Internet access and a Web browser. The Internet and World Wide Web have finally hit prime time.

Don't Read This Book!

If the most you use your computer for is as a glorified typewriter or the world's most expensive paper weight, maybe *FREE $TUFF from the World Wide Web* isn't for you.

If the idea of getting something for free offends you ("I've never taken charity in my life!"), you might want to think twice about reading this book. If *ALF* reruns sound more exciting and intellectually stimulating than virtual travel through cyberspace to find the wildest, wackiest, most bizarre sights and sounds on the Internet, *please* don't read this book.

But:

If you're looking for excitement, fun, and bargains, bargains, bargains, *FREE $TUFF from the World Wide Web* will deliver. If you want to experience and take part in a revolution in communication as you explore the best of cyberspace, and even find out how you can access the Web *for free*, then *FREE $TUFF from the World Wide Web* is the book for you.

Plugging In

While there are certainly other books available that deal with the Web, only a few discuss more than a handful of the thousands of sites you can access, and none shows you the incredible array of freebies and bargains you can get your hands on with remarkably little effort. *FREE $TUFF from the World Wide Web* is the only book that shows you the incredible variety of sights, sounds, and freebies available to diligent Web surfers. So go ahead and join the rapidly growing club of freebie-seekers.

And while you're at it, ask yourself what you're looking for in a Web book. If wading through dry explanations of MOSAIC.INI, MIME protocol, and proxy servers is what really gets your heart pumping, more power to you. There's certainly a good supply of technical books dealing with these subjects. But I'm going to leave those discussions to the propeller heads who love that stuff, and their devoted following. My goal is far more basic.

I've got about 500 pages to tell you where to find the best in Webdom, so I'm not going to waste precious space trying to dazzle your synapses. This book has two goals: to show you how to get connected, and what to do once you're there. Okay? Enough said.

Tools of the Trade

You may have heard that getting on the World Wide Web can be a source of many headaches. It doesn't have to be. If your employer or university has a direct Internet connection, you're halfway there. You can also get connected at home relatively inexpensively through the countless local providers of Internet services popping up around the country, as well as major players like America Online, Prodigy, and CompuServe.

A word of caution: I did a radio talk show recently in which a caller told me about a great deal he could get with a company offering direct connections to the Internet—providing he pay a year in advance. Don't do it! Eventually, you'll be glad you have another provider you can call if and when it all goes up in smoke. Competition can be fierce among Internet providers, and many that are here today ain't gonna be around tomorrow.

So, shop around a bit, but remember that the best deal isn't always the one with the lowest price. Technical support is a biggie, and no system is perfect. Most service providers will also provide the TCP/IP (Transport Control Protocol/Internet Protocol, in case you're interested—you shouldn't be) connection software required to get you up and running, saving you the headache of finding and configuring this software for yourself. If your provider won't provide you with this level of assistance, I suggest you dump 'em fast. New, aggressive, customer-oriented providers are appearing every day. This can be a fairly technical business; don't settle for less than the best.

If, however, you're the kind of person who would rather do it all him/herself, go knock yourself out. You'd also probably prefer to build your own airplane in the garage on weekends than fly on a commercial passenger jet. Personally, I'd rather be in first class sipping a gin and tonic and leave the flying to the experts, but I'll be sure to wave to you from 30,000 feet.

As I mentioned earlier, most service providers will also provide you with the latest version of one of the more popular Web browsers available. If not, or if you'd prefer to try them all out (something I strongly recommend), here are some sites on the Internet you can access to FTP free copies of different browsers. Read the text files at each site to be sure you're getting the latest release.

FTP 101

File Transfer Protocol, or *FTP*, is a standardized method you can use to upload or download files stored on computers around the globe. FTP provides a standard interface for accessing files, regardless of what computer you're using to upload or retrieve the files. FTP rules make it possible for UNIX, Windows, Mac, and other computers to access the same files, provided the computer adheres to the same communications rules.

Many sites on the Internet are FTP sites, which means you must use an FTP-compliant utility to download files. Mosaic and most Mosaic clones provide FTP download capabilities by default—provided the FTP site allows users to log on as "anonymous," which means that all Internet users have unrestricted access to the files stored at this site. Anonymous FTP is far and away the most widely used method for accessing FTP sites.

For private FTP sites that require a logon name and password, you have to use a separate FTP utility, because you need to supply—before you can access the site—a logon name and password. Most Internet providers make available an FTP utility program that you can use to enter logon information to access non-anonymous FTP sites. Games, software upgrades, pictures, and documents are yours to download by using FTP, usually via anonymous FTP. In any event, check with your online service provider for documentation or help on using FTP.

Just Browsing

The following is a list of the most popular and powerful of the free browsers being used on the Web today. Drive as many as you can around the

block a couple of times to see which works best for you. I have my favorites, but your mileage may vary (see dealer for details).

NCSA Mosaic for Windows

The best known of the Web browsers, NCSA Mosaic for Windows, lets you access most of the major services on the Net, including HTTP, FTP, Gopher, and WAIS. It can be downloaded from NCSA at **ftp.ncsa.uiuc.edu/ Mosaic/Win**.

NCSA Mosaic for Windows requires an absolute minimum of an 80386SX-based machine with 4MB of RAM running Microsoft Windows 3.1 in 386-enhanced mode. The recommended configuration is a 33-MHz or faster 80486-based machine with at least 8MB of RAM, but even that's scraping bottom. The more memory the better, and the faster your processor, the better. In fact, the real key here is modem speed: A 9600 baud modem is a real crawler on the Internet. A 14.4K baud modem will do justice to the Internet, but you'll realize Internet nirvana only with a 28.8K baud modem or even a faster line, like ISDN or T1 access. You don't need to know what these designations mean; you just need to know whether your Internet service provider can offer these capabilities.

Netscape Navigator

Netscape Navigator 1.1 combines the latest in point-and-click interface design with lightning-fast performance. Developed by much of the same team that developed Mosaic, Netscape Navigator shows that these guys have learned a few things since then, like integrating all major Internet functions under one interface and improved performance at 14.4K baud. I give Netscape five stars for their design, and highly recommend this browser. And, by the way, some of my best Macintosh friends use Netscape for the Mac and are rip-thrilled by the prospect of using this software for their Internet explorations. You can download a free copy from **ftp.mcom.com/netscape/** for your Windows, Mac, or UNIX machine. Netscape 1.1 runs native on 68K and Power Macs.

EINet WinWeb

WinWeb is an excellent choice for Web browsing, and is provided free by many online services to their subscribers. To use WinWeb, you must be running Windows 3.1 or higher, have at least 4MB RAM, and 5MB free hard disk space. Note: Additional RAM and hard disk space, if available, is used for caching and improves performance. EINet WinWeb can be downloaded from **ftp.einet.net/einet/pc/winweb**.

Cello

Developed at the Legal Information Institute at Cornell Law School, Cello is a multi-purpose Internet browser that lets you access a wide variety of resources off the Internet, including HTTP, Gopher, FTP, Telnet, and Usenet sites. With Cello, you can view hypermedia documents containing images, text, and digital sounds, as well as online movies.

Cello runs under Windows on any 80386SX PC or better. While rumor has it that you can run Cello with only 2MB of RAM and a 386 16MHz machine, why would anyone want to test this theory? Leave those crazy stunts to the professionals. Access **ftp.law.cornell.edu/pub/LII/Cello** to download your copy.

EINet MacWeb

A full-featured Web browser, the latest version of MacWeb is now Power Mac native. To use MacWeb, your Macintosh must be running System 7 and at least MacTCP 2.0.2 (though MacTCP 2.0.4 or higher is recommended). Use StuffIt Expander (or an equivalent program) to de-BinHex and expand the archive. The EINet folder may be located anywhere on your hard disk. Get a copy from **ftp.einet.net/einet/mac/macweb.**

Mosaic for Macintosh

Developed at NCSA by the people who *know* Mosaic, Mosaic for the Macintosh is a full-featured Web browser that will run on any machine

using at least System 7, MacTCP 2.0.2 (though 2.0.4 or later is recommended), and 4MB of RAM. It also requires a partition of at least 2MB of hard-disk space (though Mosaic itself takes less than 1MB).

While Mac Mosaic will run with earlier versions of MacTCP, bugs in those versions cause memory usage for each document loaded to increase by 12K. Eventually, memory will run out, and either Mosaic, your computer, or your heart will need to be restarted.

The latest version of NCSA Mosaic for the Macintosh can be found compressed with StuffIt and encoded with BinHex at **ftp.ncsa.uiuc.edu/Mosaic/Mac**.

Mosaic for X

Mosaic for X, the UNIX-based browser created by Marc Andreessen before he went on to fame and glory at Netscape Communications, is a Motif Web browser from NCSA.

Mosaic for X will run on X11/Motif, Sun4, RS6000, SGI, and DecStations, as well as VMS and other UNIX workstations. You can get a copy at **ftp.ncsa.uiuc.edu/Mosaic**.

MidasWWW

MidasWWW, a Motif/X-based Web browser, has been available since mid 1994. It features multifont hypertext display, a source code viewer, Motif Style Guide compatibility, and will run under either UNIX or VMS. Download a copy from **freehep.scri.fsu.edu/freehep/networking_news_email/midaswww**.

Chimera

Chimera 1.61 is a World Wide Web browser from the University of Nevada, Las Vegas, with an X/Athena graphical interface. Chimera can access HTTP, FTP, and Gopher information servers, as well as local files. Go to **ftp.cs.unlv.edu** to get a free copy.

NeXT Browser-Editor for NextStep/OpenStep

The original prototype for Web browsing, the NeXT Browser, is still the only totally WYSIWYG editor for the World Wide Web. NeXT Browser lets you make links with two hot-key strokes, as well as insert images and format text. While the new version 2.x is buggy, it's a definite improvement over the older versions.

The NeXT Browser requires NeXTStep 3.0 and has total Web capability (HTTP, FTP, Gopher, and so on). You can even copy and paste images into your documents, easily make hypertext links from your documents to anywhere on the Web, and more. NeXT users can download a copy from **info.cern.ch/pub/www/src**.

SpiderWoman

Brand-new (as of December 1994), SpiderWoman is a graphical browser for NeXTStep. I've never actually seen this one up and running, but with a name like SpiderWoman, I just had to include it. Get a copy from **sente.epfl.ch/pub/software**.

Other Ways to Access the Web

Yes, you can get on the Web without a true Web browser, though I'm not sure why you'd want to if you can avoid it. At any rate, for those who aren't faint of heart or who have some truly archaic computer equipment, consider the following alternatives.

Telnet

Telnetting to Web sites is possible on the Internet, and is preferred by many whose options are limited. Personally, I'd rather have hot daggers shoved in my eyes than deal with the headaches that go with telnetting to the Web. I'm probably just spoiled since I have several exceptional browsers at my disposal. If you want to try your hand at using some of the software designed for linking Telnet with the Web, here are a few places to check out, in no particular order (I don't like any of them). If you're

asked for a password when logging in, type **www**.
Good luck, and don't say I didn't warn you.

www.njit.edu
New Jersey Institute of Technology, USA

ukanaix.cc.ukans.edu
University of Kansas, USA

vms.huji.ac.il
Hebrew University of Jerusalem, Israel

telnet.w3.org
Geneva, Switzerland

info.funet.fi
Finland

fserv.kfki.hu
Hungary

sun.uakom.cs
Slovakia

E-Mail

If you don't yet have a Web browser and you took my advice in the previous section and avoided Telnetting like cats avoid large bodies of water, but you just can't wait to see for yourself what's out there, you can still access the World Wide Web, albeit indirectly (*very* indirectly). You can actually send E-mail to an automated E-mail browser that sends you the text from any Web page you request (sorry, no graphics). You'll certainly lose the impact of what the Web is all about, but desperate times sometimes call for desperate measures.... Send E-mail to agora@mail.w3.org, with no subject and the message **www** in the body for step-by-step instructions.

Just the Fax

About the only thing your fax machine has in common with your computer is that they both use a phone line. But that's all you need to access thousands of popular Web pages. Check out the *World Wide Web Fax of*

Life in the *Business and Career* section of this book to learn how to access Web sites with your fax machine.

Maybe You're Already Linked to the Web

If you subscribe to one of the more popular online services, you might already have access to the far corners of the Web. Prodigy recently announced Web access to its subscribers and connections for 14.4 baud modems. America Online assures me they will have Web access by the time you buy this book, and also has recently begun offering 14.4 baud connectivity—and even 28.8 baud in some areas. CompuServe, too, should be a reasonably complete Internet/Web provider by the time you read this. Check the help area of your online provider for more information.

Finding Your Own Free $tuff

I've worked pretty darn hard to find the best free stuff and most fun Web sites available out there in the Internet universe (just ask my wife about my 10-coffee-cup nights). But you can still best me if you're a bona fide cheapskate. You can't get a much better deal than free, so why not give it a try? Here are a few tips to help you find your own freebies on the Web.

Read the Fine Print

A lot of businesses are going online, and it's a quiet day when I don't hear from at least one new company joining the Web. Many of these businesses have begun including their Web and Internet addresses in their press releases, as well as their newspaper and magazine advertisements, right next to their 800-numbers. Pay attention and you're sure to pick up a few goodies.

Watch the Newsgroups

There are newsgroups and mailing lists devoted to discussions of all-things Web related. Check out a few of these, as well as newsgroups that

discuss topics you're interested in and you're bound to run across lots of great Web addresses. A great place to start is **alt.internet.services** for the latest news and happenings on the Web.

Read Your Mail

Subscribe to the net-happenings mailing list for daily updates on new Web sites and other Internet events delivered right to your virtual mailbox. To subscribe, send E-mail to **majordomo@is.internic.net** with the message *subscribe net-happenings* in the body.

Another great mail service to subscribe to is Net Surf, an online magazine detailing the best of what the Internet has to offer. Each week you'll receive a new issue by E-mail with articles formatted for viewing on your Web browser. The magazine contains stories and features about the Web, and contains hyperlinks that connect you to Web sites around the world. To subscribe, send E-mail to **nsdigest-request@netsurf.com** with the message *subscribe nsdigest-html* in the body.

The More Things Change . . .

Experienced Net surfers know that three words never used to describe the Web are *concrete*, *stagnant*, or *static*. Web pages that are here today may very well be gone tomorrow—only to be back the next day with an entirely new look and feel. While this makes for the occasional frustrating exploration, it's also part of the Web's charm. Like surfing the Pacific, when you surf the Web no two rides are the same.

Keep these points in mind as you browse this book. I've checked and rechecked the Web sites, but don't be surprised if the page that appears on your screen doesn't always match the one shown in this book—or if the site isn't even available. Many of the sites are constantly being updated, improved, and even given complete facelifts. These are actually a few of the advantages to online publishing. If something's not right, it's usually easy to fix.

And here's a neat trick: My publisher (Coriolis Group Books) was foolish enough to lend me some space on their Web server. I'll post any address changes, deletions, and other interesting web info at this site, on a weekly basis or as time permits. Go to **http://www.coriolis.com.coriolis** and click on the Free $tuff from the World Wide Web link.

Support Your Local Shareware Programmer

Throughout this book you'll find games, utilities, and other software for your business, home, kids, and so on that you can download and try out for free. These are called *shareware* programs. Shareware costs nothing—zippo—*unless* you decide to keep it. This try-before-you-buy approach to merchandising is a great deal, and not one you're likely to find with most other merchandisers.

Basically, it's the honor system at work here, so play fair. If you like their programs, most programmers ask that you send a little something to keep 'em from having to work for a living. And once you've registered your software, many programmers will send you an upgraded version of the program with extras not included in the shareware version. Look for registration information when you load the program.

Feed a Cold, Starve a Fever

As Dennis Miller of *Saturday Night Live* fame so aptly put it: "When you link up to another computer, your're linking up to every other computer that that computer has linked up to." While many of the files you can download off the Web have already been scanned for computer viruses by diligent practitioners of safe computing at the sites the files are stored, practice safe computing yourself by using your own virus checker to make sure anything you download has not been tampered with. The odds are extremely slim that you'll be a victim, but if you're one of the unlucky few, you could be in for some major headaches—from weird messages flashing on your screen to having your hard drive reformatted. Take the extra time to scan your hard drive before running anything you download.

 # FREE $TUFF

Interpretation is the revenge of the intellect upon art.

Susan Sontag

Immature artists imitate. Mature artists steal.

Lionel Trilling

Art

The Children's Hospital of Philadelphia Gallery

Someone (probably my mother) once told me there is no greater compliment to an artist than to display his or her work on your refrigerator door. Now you can turn your computer screen into something resembling a refrigerator door with these works of art from some of the most talented artists to be found on the Web.

The Children's Hospital of Philadelphia's Cancer Center has commissioned some of its patients, ranging in age from 6 to 14, to create these wonderful drawings. Check this site for some of the most touching and upbeat works of art you're likely to find on the Web.

Where

http://cancer.med.upenn.edu/0h/docs/images/child/gallery1

Links

Gallery 2

Many GIFs for you to download

 This site is part of OncoLink, the University of Pennsylvania's multimedia oncology repository, arguably the best place on the Web to find the latest information and resources on cancer research. Look for more about OncoLink in the *Health and Nutrition* section later in this book.

Art Treasures from around the World

The World Art Treasures project is a collaboration between the J. E. Berger Foundation and the Swiss Federal Institute of Technology. Created with the hope of spreading the love of art, this project's marriage to the Web was a natural. Now Internauts have access to an incredible wealth and variety of art from all corners of the globe.

Available in both French and English, this online art exhibit includes works you can browse through from China, Japan, India, Burma, Laos, Cambodia, Thailand, and Egypt.

Where

http://sgwww.epfl.ch/BERGER/index.html

Links

Burma

Japan

Laos, Thailand, and Cambodia

Just a few of the many thumbnails you can click on to learn more about the culture and art of Laos.

 This site is supposed to be bilingual (French and English), and for the most part it is. But if you're reading the English version, you're likely to run into a couple of links that didn't seem to get the message. Don't worry, though. A picture's worth a thousand words. You won't have any trouble with the Web's universal language—pointing and clicking—to negotiate this site.

Stimulating the Senses

OTIS (Operative Term Is Stimulate), according to the literature, "is a place for image-makers and image-lovers to exchange ideas, collaborate, and, in a loose sense of the word, meet." Sounds more like a singles bar than an art gallery. All I know is that OTIS is one of the largest, most active galleries running in cyberspace, and for good reason. OTIS is as diverse as it is fun. Where else on the Web can you find art covering the spectrum from collages to collectibles, paintings to puppets, architecture to animation?

From its origins as a small FTP site in 1993 to its enormity today, OTIS is another example of something that by its sheer size can only exist in cyberspace.

Where

http://sunsite.unc.edu/otis/otis.html

Links

Gallery

FineArt Online

Online Museum of Singapore

Shot

Children's Hospital of Philadelphia Gallery

Horror, Madness, and the Grotesque in Art

If you're looking for upbeat and optimistic examples of art, this site would be so far back in the pack you'd need a telescope to get a glimpse of anything of interest to you. However, if it's pathos you want, this site's for you.

This collection explores the angst and anxieties of modern man. Intended for mature audiences, some of the content is graphically violent. While the work displayed here is often disturbing (the War link, for example), don't let the name of this sight turn you *completely* off. This collection contains some of the most famous paintings from some of the most prestigious museums in the world, including New York's Museum of Modern Art, Belgium's Royal Museum of Fine Arts, and Moscow's Tretyakov Gallery, by such renowned artists as Dali, Munch, and Grosz.

Where

http://www.ugcs.caltech.edu/~werdna/grotesque/grotesque.html

Links

Fear

Religion

Paranoia

Madness

Torture

Edvard Munch's Scream, downloaded from the Horror, Fantasy, and the Grotesque in Art Web site.

As with many art-related sites, some of the links here can be quite slow. It's well worth the wait, though.

The Writing's on the Wall

There's graffiti and then there's *graffiti*. What's the difference? Well, surf over to this site and take a look. The Art Crime's Webmaster has compiled a virtual gallery of, shall we say, unauthorized murals from around the world. Using only spray cans and whatever wall was handy for a canvas, these painters have created a rich and diverse exhibition not likely to be found in your local uptown gallery.

Here are examples of art created with no consideration given to their commercial viability. After all, who's going to buy a painting that must be cut into 30-pound bricks just to get it home? These works of wall art are meant to entertain as well as provoke. But then, I wouldn't want to be the one who had to clean them up.

Where

http://www.gatech.edu/desoto/graf/Index.Art_Crimes.html

Links

Prague, Czech Republic

Vancouver, Canada

Amsterdam, Netherlands

Munich, Germany

Art Crimes: The Writing on the Wall

Welcome to Art Crimes

This is a gallery of graffiti art from various cities. It's called "Art Crimes" because in most places, painting graffiti is illegal. Many of these pieces no longer exist in the real world. Each little picture in the gallery is a link to a bigger, better picture. If you want to see one, just click on it with your mouse.

Ain't it a crime? Graffiti artists from around the world are showcased at the Art Crimes Web site.

A Treasure Trove of CyberArt

Art junkies will have no trouble satisfying their cravings on the Internet. Through the Web, you'll find hundreds of sites, with every kind of art imaginable (and some that is, frankly, unimaginable—and I've got a pretty good imagination). ArtMap, a multimedia cultural information service, is a collection of links to art-related sites for all media and genre:

- Visual
- Mass media
- Literature
- Video
- Performance
- Design

Each site contains many, many links to other sites scattered around the globe, and the links are updated constantly. In fact, the word *collection* hardly does this site justice. This site is *voluminous*, *huge*, *really big*. Get the picture?

Where

http://wimsey.com/anima/ARTWORLDonline.html

Links

A lot more than *I* have room for. You're on your own here.

Picture This

Think of a picture, any picture. No I'm not going to pull it out of my magic hat, but I'll bet you'll find a copy of it—or something close— here. This archive contains thousands of megabytes of GIF and JPEG pictures for you to browse through, gawk at, talk about, and download. There are enough pictures here to satisfy anyone: famous faces, 'toon characters, lots of computer-generated stuff, and more.

Where

http://olt.et.tudelft.nl/fun/pictures/pictures.html

Links

Top 50 of Horny Geeks

Art

Comics

Computer Generated Images

Cars

Space

Max Headroom, the original cybernaut, is one example of the megabytes upon mega- bytes of art to download at the Digital Picture Archive.

If you're looking for porn, don't bother looking here. While you may still run across the occasional pinup, this site cleaned up its act a while back and is no longer carrying the smut. Also, this site gets so over- loaded that its Webmasters have invoked a very complicated and (some would say) bizarre quota system for downloading pictures. You might only be able to download one or two photos at a time before being booted out.

Online Art with Art on Line

Art on Line is a virtual gallery on the World Wide Web showing the best of artists from around the world. At the time this was written, the latest work of Dutch artist Herman van Valen was being showcased.

You'll also find an in-depth illustrated biography of the current artist to better understand the works displayed. For those who like to go Dutch, van Valen's page is in both English and his native language.

Where

http://www.xs4all.nl/~marvv/engels1.html

Links

More about the Artist

ArtVark

This Gallery Is Red Hot

The Cold War has become a memory. Now, in the wake of the breakup of the Soviet Union comes an outpouring of Russian art that in the past would never have been publicly displayed. Over 50 works of Russia's leading photographic artists can be viewed at this site.

These contemporary artists span the spectrum of photography, from the stark images of day-to-day Russian life to colorful landscapes and sophisticated computer-processed images. A must-see for anyone interested in getting past the Evil Empire rhetoric and learning more about the people of Russia.

Where

http://www.kiae.su/www/wtr/hotpictures/gallery.html

Links

FENSO

Alexander Kholopov

Boris Mikhailov

Avdei Ter-Oganian
Alexander Revizorov
Sky Commission
Alexander Slyusarev
Dmitrij Vrubel

This site (and many other Russian sites I've accessed) has a tendency to move about as fast as Cold War molasses. Be patient and try this link during off hours.

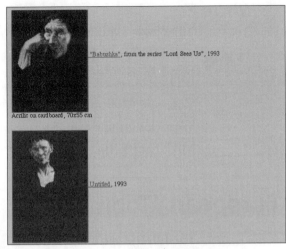

A sampling of featured artist Dmitrij Vrubel.

How Many Art Majors Does It Take...?

Art students at the Digital Art Gallery at Syracuse University collaborated on these computer-generated images, combining text, audio, and animation into strange and bizarre works of digital art. I'd expect nothing less from a bunch of aspiring graphic artists, and at least it keeps them off the streets. Visually stun-

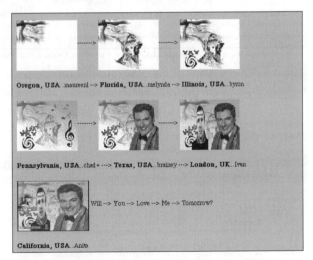

Liberace becomes another piece of art in this online collaborative effort.

ning, creative, and amusing, these images will give you a glimpse into the future of computer graphics and design.

Where

http://ziris.syr.edu/home.html

Links

OTIS

Carnegie Mellon Genetic Movies

Web Playground Gallery

M.C. Escher Images

European 'Toon Town

The European Cartoon Arts Network (CartooNet) provides news and information about cartoon events and examples of some of the best political and contemporary cartoonists in Europe.

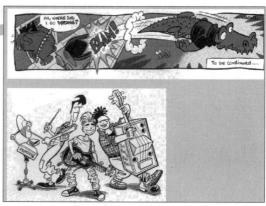

Tons of 'toons are yours to view at CartooNet, including these by Geo Parkin.

Works by such cartoonists as Roland Fiddy (winner of over 25 international awards in Japan, Brazil, Canada, Italy, Holland, and Belgium) and political cartoonist Martyn Turner (syndicated in over 200 newspapers and magazines, including *Time* and *Newsweek*), are two of the many cartoonist featured at this site.

Where

http://www.pavilion.co.uk/cartoonet/

Links

Cartoonery

Cartoon Arts Network

Fanny - Womens' Cartoon Network

Exhibitions

The Mother of All Museums

Museum Web, a project to make museums more accessible to a world-wide audience, is an exciting and fun way to see the treasures displayed in museums around the world. But don't define the word "museum" too narrowly. This site not only includes paintings of landscapes, it includes the actual *landscapes* as well.

In addition to museums, this site includes links to botanical gardens, zoological gardens, planetariums, and other fascinating hot spots on the Web. So now, rather than just admiring masterpieces like Van Gogh's Starry Night, you can check out the starry night he painted. There's also information about each institution, such as:

- Address
- Phone number
- Hours of operation
- Current exhibits
- Calendar of events
- Directions and maps

Where

http://www.primenet.com/art-rom/museumweb/

Links

Museums
Botanical Gardens
Antique Web

Vive Le WebMuseum!

Formerly known as Le WebLouvre in honor of one of the worlds greatest and most famous art troves in the world (though apparently one of the most paranoid as well), the WebMuseum offers two virtual exhibits for your visual feast: art of medieval France and more modern paintings by such masters as Van Gogh, Cezanne, and Dali.

After a day browsing Le WebLouvre—I mean the WebMuseum—you'll be ready for something a bit less cerebral—say, a little wild and crazy French night life. Try out the virtual tour of Gay Paris, complete with a trip to the Eiffel Tower. *Bon voyage!*

Where

http://sunsite.unc.edu/louvre/

Links

Famous Paintings

Auditorium

Les très riches heures du Duc de Berry

Monet's LA PROMENADE, courtesy of the WebMuseum.

 The address I've provided for the WebMuseum is actually a mirror to the real Web site located in France. For speed's sake, Europeans should access the true site at:

http://mistral.enst.fr/louvre/

Or if you're in Japan, you'll have a speedier link by pointing your browser to the Tokyo mirror at:

http://SunSITE.sut.ac.jp/louvre/

Also, while most of the text at this site is in English, it does have a tendency to fall back into French occasionally, so keep your dictionary handy.

Entropy Studio Online

I'm certainly not an art critic, and the extent of my creative abilities with a brush go little beyond a couple of coats of paint on my son's dresser, but I do know what I like. Artist Chris Rigatuso has created several digital masterpieces you can enjoy on the Web. These "paintings" were created with Fractal Design's Painter 2.0, which may or may not mean much to you. In short, his brush is a mouse, his canvas is his monitor. And the overall effect of his work is terrific.

Where

http://www.art.net/Studios/Visual/Rigatuso/rigatuso.html

Links

Various Works

Art on the Net

Breathtaking Beauty from Ansel Adams

No photographer has better captured the tranquil beauty and rugged power of the West's natural wonders than Ansel Adams. Arguably the greatest photographer of the 20th century, Adams captured the monumental beauty of America's mountains, rivers, and landscapes without benefit of even a hint of cyan, magenta, or yellow.

A staunch environmentalist, Adams helped preserve much of America's wilderness through his photographs. Now Adams' photographs are available to you on the Web. You can download copies of his famous images of Yosemite, Mount McKinley, the Snake River, and many more.

Mt. Resplendent, Canada, photographed by Adams in 1928.

Where

http://bookweb.cwis.uci.edu:8042/MuseumGraphics/LandsMount.html

Links

Ansel Adams Home Page

Ansel Adams Chronology

Ansel Adams: Fiat Lux

Digital Tie Dye

Once you get over the sensation that you're inside a lava lamp when you view these images, they get to be very soothing. Computer artist Mike Brutvan used various color/intensity adjustments, zooms, croppings, and blurrings to manipulate images downloaded from different Internet newsgroups to create these dreamy, mind-altering pictures. Most look like they could have come from alt.bad_acid.trip, but of course I wouldn't know. The point is, they're fun to look at and you don't need to worry about any lingering effects (such as flashbacks 20 years from now).

Can you say Rorschach?

Where

http://www.art.net/Studios/Visual/brutvan/mike.html

Links

The Display

Art on the Net

Features

Gallery

Studio

New Guinea Comes to California

Stanford University may seem a long way from New Guinea, but only in miles. The outdoor sculpture garden of New Guinea Art at Stanford University has brought to California the beauty and artistry of the rain forests of this tiny Pacific island. Jim Mason, a graduate student in anthropology, brought 10 artists from the Middle Sepik River Region of Papua New Guinea to Stanford as part of a project designed not to re-create a traditional New Guinea environment, but, according to Mason, "to experiment with and reinterpret New Guinea aesthetic perspectives within the new context of a Western public art space."

Judging by the images available at this site, Mason has succeeded. The pieces were carved from woods similar to mahogany and birch, and the trees used for these carvings were shipped directly from New Guinea to the United States. Some of these pieces were completed in three days or less.

Where

http://fuji.stanford.edu/icenter/png/ngp.html

Links

The Site

The Works

The Artists

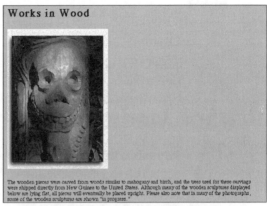

Works in Wood

The wooden pieces were carved from woods similar to mahogany and birch, and the trees used for these carvings below are lying flat, all pieces will eventually be placed upright. Please also note that in many of the photographs, some of the wooden sculptures are shown "in progress."

Here's looking at you. One of many New Guinea sculptures in wood you'll find at this Stanford site.

Many of the statues and carvings shown here are works in progress. And some of the photos were taken before the statues were erected, which is why you'll see many of them lying on their sides. Maybe in the future we'll see what the final exhibit looks like.

ArtServe Is Here to Serve You

Looking for the art of architecture on the Web, are you? Careful what you ask for because you're bound to get it. When it comes to compiling some of the most beautiful examples of classical, medieval, and renaissance architecture and sculpture in cyberspace, Michael Greenhalgh, professor of Art History at Australian National University, has outdone any other site I've visited.

You'll find over *8,000* images of prints in his database, from the 15th through 19th centuries, Classical architecture and architectural sculpture, and Classical European sculpture. What does this guy do in his *spare* time?

If that's not enough art for you cybergluttons, there are links to many other sources. By the time you're done here, you'll have culture coming out of your ears.

Where

http://rubens.anu.edu.au/

Links

Triumph of the Will (1934)

Olympiad 1936

EXPO Ticket Office

Warhol Meets the Web

Arguably the most influential American artist of the second half of this century, Andy Warhol and his art have never seemed more in their element than when viewed on the Web, a perfect marriage of media. Take a virtual tour of the Andy Warhol Museum, which features extensive permanent collections of art and archives. Temporary exhibitions, which may include the work of other artists, are also presented on a regular basis.

In addition to being an ideal way to learn of the power and influence wielded in Warhol's art, this site is a tremendous resource for anyone wishing to gain insight into contemporary art and popular culture.

Where

http://www.warhol.org/warhol/

Links

A Tour Through the Museum

Art Samples

Exhibits

Films

Museum Shops

This site is still a work in progress and will occasionally give you access problems and delays. Being able to view these Warhol prints, however, makes it worth the wait.

The Art of Fashion

If the extent of your fashion sense is "never mix plaids with stripes unless you're absolutely sure no one will see you," *The Fashion Page* couldn't have arrived too soon. Okay, so it's not Cosmo or Vogue, but fashion *has* arrived on the Web. This online magazine contains news on the latest fashion trends, styles, faux pas, and people. You'll also get plenty of online movie and book reviews, as well as style tips for men and women.

Where

http://www.charm.net/~jakec/

Links

Lots of different links for each issue

A Revolution in Internet Art

Artists for Revolution through Technology (ART, for the acronymically challenged) is a group of rabble-rousing cyberartisans propelled by the belief that music, art, and literature have become "vacuous, disposable, commercial entities." To correct these creative atrocities, they've established a music, art, and literature museum on the Web: the Internet Arts Museum for Free, or IAMFREE (what *is* it with these acronyms?).

IAMFREE exhibits a fine collection of contemporary art in a variety of media, including:

- Music
- Photography
- Video/Film
- Computer art
- Literature

But here's where this site gets truly revolutionary. We're not talking about music samples or thumbnails of artwork. The art showcased here is complete, downloadable, and *free*. Cybernauts are invited to view, listen, read, and respond to the films, music, literature, and other artwork available here, including a complete music album created exclusively for the Internet: *The Slowest Train in the World* by A Western Front. They may not be the Fab Four from Liverpool (then again, I haven't downloaded the album, so maybe they are), but I don't remember anyone ever offering me any of *The Beatles* albums for free.

Where

http://www.artnet.org/iamfree/index.html

Links

Sound

Words

Photo

Lectro-Art

Motion

Archive

 While you can start at the home page of IAMFREE, it might take you a while to get to the meat of this site. Some of the images are big, so navigating this site can be slow. A shortcut is to go directly to:

http://www.artnet.org/iamfree/IAMFREE/html/mappg.html

This bypasses a couple of the big images and takes you right to the good stuff.

Eskimo Art Exhibit

Most people have had little or no exposure to the beauty and craftsmanship that plays such a prominent part of the Eskimo culture and heritage. But here's a site that is helping to end the neglect. The Isaacs/Innuit Gallery exhibits sculptures, drawings, wall hangings, and more by internationally celebrated Innuit (Eskimo) artists.

The Innuit art featured here represents an extended community of artists located throughout the vast Canadian Arctic. Pieces are available for you to view online and even to purchase through the Web.

Where

http://www.novator.com/UC-Catalog/Isaacs-Catalog/Isaacs-Internet.html

Links

Original Drawings and Limited Edition Prints

Wall Hangings

Baskets

OUR JOURNEY BY SEA, a limited edition print by Innuit artist Pitseolak Ashoona, is one of the dozens of works displayed at the Isaacs/ Innuit Gallery.

Out of Africa

This fascinating exhibit of African masks, statues, headdresses, and other examples of African art and culture was designed to exemplify the aesthetic and moral principles of the African culture. While I can't say whether the exhibit accomplishes its goal, it certainly succeeds at showcasing some of the finest pieces of African art available on the Web.

Most of the pieces in this exhibit come from West African societies and each includes an in-depth discussion of its relevance and purpose in African culture, such as religious, sexual, marital, and other social customs and mores.

Where

http://www.lib.virginia.edu/dic/exhib/93.ray.aa/Exhibition.html

Links

Bibliography

Elements of the African Aesthetic

This site contains a lot of images that may take a while to load depending on your modem speed and the time of day you're connected. Try accessing the site after peak hours (sage advice for many of the Web sites you'll encounter).

Random Acts of Photography

Who *are* these people and what do they have to smile about? You won't find the answers here, but I can tell you that the Random Portrait Gallery contains pictures of Web users from around the world downloaded from their home pages. Each page at this site contains nine portraits to make viewing these images a little more manageable.

You may think this is frivolous and a waste of time, and you'd be right, but then that's what they said about Silly Putty. Frivolity aside, it's fun. Who knows, you may see someone you know.

Where

http://oz.sas.upenn.edu/Portraits/portraits-gal.html

Links

Different "rooms" you can enter to view portraits of people on the Web— sort of a virtual cocktail party.

Not all the portraits in a room may be visible at the same time, depending on whether the machines the portraits are stored on around the world are up and running.

Mummies in Memphis

No, this isn't another Elvis sighting. The Institute of Egyptian Art & Archaeology at the University of Memphis is dedicated to the study of the art and culture of ancient Egypt through teaching, research, exhibition, and community education. And what better way to learn about ancient Egypt than through these priceless relics, some over 5,000 years old?

The Institute's collection of over 150 Egyptian artifacts ranging from 3500 B.C. to 700 A.D. includes mummies, religious items, jewelry, and objects from everyday life. This site even includes a short tour of Egypt

Just a sample of the artifacts displayed at the Egyptian Art and Archaeology home page.

for those of you out there who just haven't gotten around to going yet.

Where

http://www.memphis.edu/egypt/main.html

Links

Egyptian Artifacts Exhibit

Color Tour of Egypt

A couple of times when I've connected to the Tour of Egypt link at this site, it seemed as though it would be quicker to just travel to Northern Africa and see it all myself. The wait, however, *is* well worth it for anyone with an interest in Egyptian culture and history.

Kaleidospace Eyes

Formed to promote art on the Internet, Kaleidospace is giving online artists their 15 minutes in the spotlight à la Andy Warhol. After viewing some of the works displayed here, I'd say many of the artists are destined for even more fame and fortune, while others are destined for a long stay at the Sunnyville Happy Farm. Either way, the artwork is fascinating, disturbing, and thoroughly enjoyable to view.

Where

http://kspace.com

Links

Screening Room

Newsstand

Spotlight

Tool Shop

Free Headaches (and 5-D Stereograms)

When I see crowds of people huddled around the stereograms in the malls and bookstores I can't help being reminded of *The Emperor's New Clothes*:

"Do you see it?"

"Of course I do. Do you?"

"Of course...What do you see?"

"What do *you* see?"

And on and on. Basically, stereograms contain two slightly different views of the same scene. Your brain, while slowly turning to jelly, tries to make sense of this seemingly jumbled mess and is fooled into combining the two images into one three-dimensional picture.

See for yourself in the privacy of your own home by downloading the samples available here from Blue Mountain Arts. There's also information on how to order books and prints of enough different stereograms to turn you into a slobbering idiot by the time you're finished. Get 'em while they're hot. (Remember the Pet Rock?)

Art

Where

http://www.ais.net/netmall/bma

Links

Links to several stereograms you can view and download

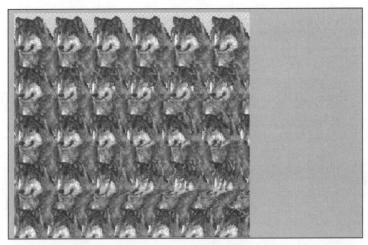

Do you see what I see? Stephen Schutz's 5-D stereograms turn hidden multi-dimensional images into beautiful pictures of interactive art—in this case, a lone wolf howling on a rocky outcropping.

Say Cheese

Tired of stuffing your photos into shoeboxes, waiting for the day you've got the time to sort through them and put them into albums? By the time you get around to that, the babies in those pictures will be graduating from college. Why not keep your photo album online instead? It's easy to do, and Seattle FilmWorks gets you started right.

Seattle FilmWorks will develop your film onto disks in GIF format, and they'll even give you two free rolls of film for trying their service. Then download a complimentary copy of PhotoWorks software to put your own photos on your PC and convert them to your favorite file format.

Where

http://Fine.net:80/New_FilmWorks/html/First.disk.Free.html

Links

Pictures on Disk

2 FREE Rolls of Film

PhotoWorks Software

Get Converted

So you've been browsing some of these online museums and would just love to take a little piece of them home with you. Once you've gotten past all the copyright legalities of reproducing these art treasures, here's a handy program you can use to convert GIFs into bitmaps so you can display your favorite Picasso in the way that Pablo—visionary that he was—no doubt intended: as wallpaper for your Windows computer.

Where

http://www.acs.oakland.edu/oak/SimTel/win3/convert.html

Download

gif2bmp.zip

This program is a dinosaur in computer years, but it works as good as any you'd buy off the shelf. Open up a DOS window within Windows and type in the command **gif2bmp** and the name of the GIF you're converting. Copy the BMP file it creates to your \WINDOWS directory and you'll be able to display it as Windows wallpaper.

Where to Find More Goodies

You'll find online museums and GIF/JPEG files mentioned throughout this book, including art resources in *Kid Stuff*; album art in the *Music* section; beautiful landscapes, sights, and sounds in *Travel and Geography*; and a gallery of cave art "20,000 years in the making" in *History*.

FREE $TUFF

You see, I don't believe that libraries should be drab places where people sit in silence, and that's been the main reason for our policy of employing wild animals as librarians.

John Cleese of Monty Python fame

Books, Magazines, and Literature

It's All Greek to Me

Whether you're looking for fascinating insights into ancient Greek culture or you just love a good tale, this entertaining collection of stories from Greek mythology will more than satisfy you. This introduction to the stories from ancient Greece includes an extensive collection of hyperlinks to help you keep all the characters straight.

Some of the stories included are:

- The Creation
- Creation of Man by Prometheus
- Zeus's Lovers (and take it from me, this is one god who got around)

Where

http://info.desy.de/gna/interpedia/greek_myth/greek_myth.html#GreekMythIntro

Links

The Gods

Heroes

Creatures

Stories

Family Trees

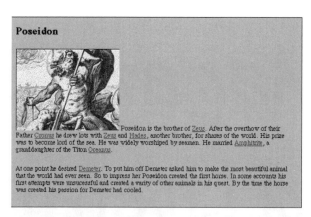

Poseidon

Poseidon is the brother of Zeus. After the overthow of their Father Cronus he drew lots with Zeus and Hades, another brother, for shares of the world. His prize was to become lord of the sea. He was widely worshiped by seamen. He married Amphitrite, a granddaughter of the Titon Oceanus.

At one point he desired Demeter. To put him off Demeter asked him to make the most beautiful animal that the world had ever seen. So to impress her Poseidon created the first horse. In some accounts his first attempts were unsucessful and created a varity of other animals in his quest. By the time the horse was created his passion for Demeter had cooled.

Another Poseidon adventure for you to read about at this Greek mythology home page.

Time for World News

Time magazine online? Why, it's about time! But get this one while it's still free for the browsing because it won't be *gratis* forever. With *Time* online, not only do you have access to the latest issue on the newsstands, you also get back-issues and daily updates to breaking stories (can you say O.J.?).

You'll get more than news, though. There's also an Internet gateway that provides you with links to lots of other great places on the Net, including FAQ archives and places to find great shareware. You can even send a letter to the editors (which I strongly recommend; let 'em know that *you* know about this site). So have a good *Time* (sorry)!

Where

http://www.timeinc.com/time/universe.html

Links

This Weeks Time
Today's News
Internet Gateway
Library

All the News That's Fit to Download

Extra! Extra! Read all about it from these online news sources. Commercial newspapers have been dabbling with electronic versions of their publications for a while, but now they're finally realizing the distribution and readership potential that cyberspace offers. And what's good for cyberspace is good for you.

To keep up with which newspapers are now online—if that's even possible, since they're coming on in increasing numbers—check out the University of Florida's College of Journalism and Communications list of publications. This hotlist of hot rags links you to many daily and weekly news sources for your reading pleasure—and you'll be spared the black ink smudges on your fingertips. The list includes online campus newspapers as well as a list of journalism, media, and communications colleges that maintain Web servers of their own. Stop the presses!

Where

http://www.jou.ufl.edu/commres/webjou.htm

Links

Detroit Free Press

GNN News

The Electronic Newsstand

An Eclectic Electric 'Zine

Here's a theme-oriented online magazine that's as eclectic as it is electric. Each issue focuses on a specific topic, such as favorite authors or travel, which is then explored in a lively, interesting way by a collection of exceptional writers.

Winner of the Best of the Net award for '94, *Teletimes* originates from Vancouver, Canada. Though that doesn't mean a lot in cyberspace, it does explain a leaning toward Canadian topics. Still, there are plenty of articles to please the international crowd. Browse some of the back issues and if you like what you see and want more, it's easy to subscribe.

Where

http://www.wimsey.com/teletimes/teletimes_home_page.html

Links

Links to back issues are but a mouse-click away

Read Me a Story

This site arguably offers some of the most enjoyable modern children's literature you'll find on the Internet. Concertina, a rising star in Canadian children's book publishing, is committed to traditional and electronic publishing.

And while most sites offer text-only versions of their hardcopy counterparts, the books you can access at Concertina are identical to the ink and paper versions. And your kids will love the stories. With wonderfully drawn artwork and imaginative stories, you'll love them too.

One of the stories available, *Waking in Jerusalem,* by Sharon Katz, follows a young child who awakens before his parents and in the early morning hours watches the city of Jerusalem come to life.

I Live on a Raft, by Jerzy Harasymowicz, is a collection of haiku-like verse that your children will love. A well-known poet in Poland, Harasymowicz is noted for his unique personal mythology and the spontaneous fantasy of his works.

Where

http://www.digimark.net/iatech/books/intro.htm

Links

Hard Copy Versions

My Blue Suitcase

If you're new to the Internet, you may not fully appreciate the importance of sites like Concertina that provide these try-before-you-buy offers of their products. Sort of a literary version of shareware, these books can be purchased

A page from WAKING IN JERUSALEM, **copyright 1994 by Sharon Katz.**

directly from the publisher by those who enjoy them. So be sure to support publishing on the Internet and order a copy of one of these books.

Hot Wire Your Computer

The hottest magazine *about* the Internet just became part of the story. Now, not only is *Wired* about cyberspace, it's *in* cyberspace, albeit in a slightly different format and title. Each issue of *Hot Wired* shows you the latest happenings and developments on the Net with a slightly subversive yet always entertaining collection of articles and features.

Read about where to go and what to see on the Net, get the latest industry gossip, and read about communications technology's latest leaps forward—and giant steps backwards—in every issue.

You also get online access to back issues, direct connections to the editorial staff, job info, and even writers' guidelines. So get *Hot Wired* while it's free, because something this hot won't be given away forever.

Where

http://www.wired.com/

Links

Back Issues

Promo Video

Wired/Roadside America Hypertour '94

To Log On or Not to Log On?

William Shakespeare, unrivaled playwright of the 17th century, is still surviving the test of time—realtime, that is. I even read about one of old Bill's plays recently being "acted out" on the Net through the magic of IRC (Internet Relay Chat)—complete with scenery. I'm still trying to figure out how *that* was accomplished. No word on how it went or the audience it drew, but with a potential "audience" of millions, it *is* a novel choice of media.

In any event, here's a site where you'll find the complete works of William Shakespeare, including *Hamlet, Henry VI, Henry VI Part 2* (Henry's Back), *Henry VI Part 3* (Henry Won't Leave), *Twelfth Night*, and more, with the promise that his sonnets are soon to follow.

Where

http://the-tech.mit.edu/Shakespeare.html

Links

All the plays of Shakespeare (stay tuned for the sonnets)

 What makes this site especially interesting is a nifty hyperlinked glossary that acts as a sort of Cliffs Notes to the manuscript. The hyperlinks, scattered throughout the plays, will help you keep the plethora of characters straight and are just a mouse click away.

Browsers Won't Be Shot

Hey! You gonna buy that? At the Electronic Newsstand (motto: "browse for free, subscribe for less!"), it doesn't matter. Read your fill from these free samples of the most recent issues of some of the world's most popular publications. There's also an extensive archive of past issues.

Since 1993, the Electronic Newsstand has provided Internauts with free access to a huge collection of interesting articles and features on computers, technology, science, business, foreign affairs, the arts, travel, medicine, nutrition, sports, politics, literature, and many other areas from the world's leading magazines, including:

- *Field and Stream*
- *Atlanta Review*
- *Blue & Gold Illustrated - Notre Dame Football*
- *Business Week*
- *Dr. Dobb's Journal: Software Tools for the Professional Programmer*
- *Guitar Player*
- *Inc. Magazine*
- *Internet World*
- *The Sporting News*

Where

http://www.enews.com/

Links

Magazines, Periodicals, and Journals

Electronic Bookstore
Electronic Car Showroom

This Library Is Virtually Enormous

Bookworms and wormettes will think they died and went to heaven (or should that be earthen topsoil?) after checking out this site. Started in 1971 by Michael Hart when he attempted in one swoop to send the Declaration of Independence to every human being wired to the Net (even then this guy thought big), Project Gutenberg—whose namesake invented the movable type printing press—has grown into an electronic library of hundreds of classical novels and reference books. Hart's goal is to make 10,000 titles available by 2001. I say he'll make it.

The Gutenberg project's army of volunteers take books whose copyrights have expired, convert them into text files, and make them available to the general public for free. Ranging from light to heavy literature and reference works, some of the books encompassed in the Project Gutenberg library include *Alice in Wonderland*, *Peter Pan*, *Aesop's Fables*, *Moby Dick*, *Roget's Thesaurus*, and various almanacs, encyclopedias, and dictionaries. You don't even need a library card!

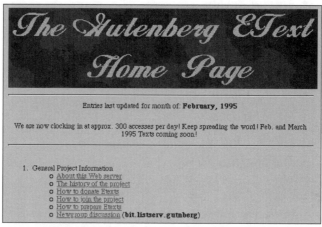

The Gutenberg Etext Web site is a great example of volunteer Internauts at work to make the Web better and just a bit classier.

Where

http://med-amsa.bu.edu/Gutenberg/Welcome.html

Links

Hundreds of links to classical literature

The Gutenberg Project volunteers have made it as simple (translated, idiot-proof) as possible to download and read files, by providing each of the files in plain-vanilla ASCII, which ensures that the files are compatible for everyone running anything more powerful than an abacus. You can also get the files compressed for the PC or Mac, and can even download the decompression software from here. What's next, valet parking?

E-Zine Into Electronic Publishing

The Internet is about information in it rawest form, and the Web is no different. Anybody with a hard drive and a modem can create his or her own electronic publishing empire—sort of a cyber-version of Rupert Murdoch, without the labor problems.

Mom and Pop electronic magazines have been cropping up on the Web faster than they can be read, covering a broad assortment of topics—certainly more than you're likely to see at the corner newsstand. Here's a great site that's done a good job bringing some order to the publishing chaos invading the Web. John Labovitz has compiled the most comprehensive list of E-zines available on the Net.

Started in the summer of 1993 when it covered just 25 electronic publications, John's list has since grown to over 250, which should give you some idea of the popularity of this explosive grassroots Web niche. These 'Zines definitely cover the spectrum from the mainstream to the bizarre, but then variety is the spice of the Net. Check out a few and you'll see what I mean.

Where

http://www.ora.com:8080/johnl/e-zine-list/

Links

250+ links to the best E-zines on the Web and the rest of the Net

At this point, some of you might be scratching your head wondering just what the devil is an *E-zine*. Since union rules require that I answer just this type of question, let me explain: *Zine* is short for *magazine*, or sometimes *fanzine*, though I've never actually heard it called the latter. I'll let you guess what *E* stands for, but if you said *electronic* you're right. The mark of a true E-zine is that it's published by a small group whose primary goal is to do something worthwhile and interesting, not to make a lot of money. That kind of publishing mission works out great for readers, since E-zines are usually distributed for free and don't contain advertising.

Also, no points are deducted for being bizarre. In fact, it seems to be an unwritten rule that the more bizarre the E-zine, the better. When in doubt, remember that, while *Time* is distributed electronically, it is not a *true* E-zine; *The Neon Gargoyle Gazette*, *Notes of a Dirty Old Woman*, and *Pete and Bernie's Philosophical Steakhouse*, however, are.

Keeping Up with the Joneses

If you like your politics served from the left, you'll appreciate *Mother Jones* magazine. If you prefer the right, hold your nose and keep on moving. Billed as a "magazine of investigation and ideas for independent thinkers" (which apparently assumes that those on the right prefer to have their politics spoon-fed à la Rush Limbaugh), *Mother Jones* is on a self-appointed mission to "inspire action towards positive social change by exposing abuses of power, challenging conventional wisdom, redefining stubborn problems, and offering fresh solutions." And that's just before lunch.

Be sure to catch some of the spicier articles rehashed from back issues on that "pillar of moral leadership," House Speaker Newt Gingrich. They definitely make for some good reading.

Where

http://mojones.com/motherjones.html

Links

Mother Jones Interactive

Current Issue

Extras

Make a hard left turn in cyberspace to head for the MOTHER JONES home page.

Surfing Safari, Web Style

The Web has been described as a community of anarchy, difficult to navigate, and easy to get lost in. *Netsurfer Digest* serves as a compass to help guide you through the muddle and lead you to interesting online news, places, and resources.

Delivered each week to any mailbox in cyberspace, *Netsurfer Digest* is fully hypertexted so that you not only read the notices, reviews, and snapshots of what's happening in the weird wired world, but by loading the file into your Web browser, you are instantly able to travel with the click of a button to the Web and Net sites you're reading about. There are even special features, letters to the editor, and special bulletins about significant breaking stories.

Where

http://www.netsurf.com/nsd/index.html

Links

Back Issues

Netsurfer Marketplace

The ClariNet e.News

Once you've subscribed to *Netsurfer Digest*, be sure to read the FAQ file to learn how to load your mail files onto your browser (nothing tricky here, but it makes for a great way to read a magazine).

Banned in Boston

What do *Little Red Riding Hood, Tom Sawyer,* and *The Merchant of Venice* have in common? Each was banned in the U.S. at some point—*Little Red Riding Hood* because of its use of alcohol in the story (the Hooded One, as you might recall, is taking food *and* wine to Grandmother's house), *Tom Sawyer* was deemed racist, and *The Merchant of Venice* was considered anti-Semitic.

This special exhibit is made up of books, broadcasts, and artwork whose sole commonality is that each has been the object of censorship or censorship attempts at some point in history. The books featured here range from the obscure to the widely known, from the obvious to the ludicrous.

This mural is one of the more ironic examples of censorship ever. The mural was created by elementary school students in San Diego, and, in its original form, included the titles of once-banned books on each stairstep. The principal objected and hired an artist to remove the names of the books.

Where

http://www.cs.cmu.edu:8001/Web/People/spok/banned-books.html

Links

Most Frequently Challenged Books of the 1990s

Banned in the U.S.A.

Keep the First Amendment alive and read these books before someone else tries to ban them. The terminally repressed and humorless will probably try to ban the Constitution next because it *promotes* violence (Second Amendment) and drinking (Twenty First Amendment). The Declaration of Independence could be in danger, too, because it's *so* subversive.

A Great Review

The Morpo Review is an E-zine covering all forms of literature, including poetry, essays, and fiction. Published bimonthly, *The Morpo Review* includes an impressive variety of pieces by an excellent collection of up-and-coming talents. In short, it's what many of the mainstream hardcopy literary journals claim to be between their pages of advertisements but don't quite live up to: refreshing, thought-provoking, shocking, and sometimes disturbing. Hopefully, *The Morpo Review* will keep its edge.

Where

http://morpo.creighton.edu/morpo/

Links

Back Issues

Non-Fiction

Fiction

Poetry

Discover DISCOVER Magazine

It doesn't take a rocket scientist to recognize a good deal. *Discover* magazine, *the* monthly magazine of science and technology, is available for free in cyberspace. Providing the layman with a lively look at science, technology, and a universe full of wonder, *Discover* offers colorful and entertaining insights into a world where new ideas and new products are emerging at an astounding pace, and at the same time is helping to unwrap the secrets of science.

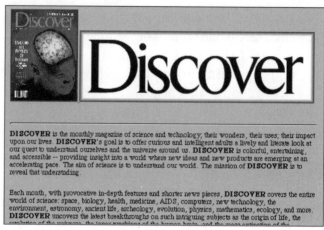

DISCOVER **magazine's home page.**

Each month, *Discover* covers the entire world of science, including:

- Space
- Biology
- Health
- Medicine
- Computers
- Physics
- Mathematics
- The appeal of *Beavis and Butthead*

With *Discover*, you can read about the latest breakthroughs in medicine, the evolution of the universe, the inner workings of the human brain, and the mass extinction of the dinosaurs. Not bad for a freebie!

Where

http://www.enews.com/magazines/discover/

Links

Current Issue

Archive

How to Subscribe (Special Offer to Internauts)

Go Ask Alex

What to read, what to read? You'll find the answer at this site. If you can't find something to capture your attention after browsing here, you're probably illiterate. (Then again, how could you be reading *this* book?) Alex, a catalog of electronic texts available on the Internet, includes over 1,800 entries for online books and shorter texts. It's an understatement to say that Alex is well read.

Even searching for the right book is a breeze. You can find what you're looking for by author, date, host, language, subject, or title.

Where

http://www.lib.ncsu.edu/stacks/alex-index.html

Links

On-Line Books Page

Search

Browse

Christian Literature

The Christian Classics Ethereal Library offers religious seekers a huge assortment of classic Christian books to help them along their electronic pilgrimages. With nearly a billion Christians scattered throughout the world today, what better way to distribute the historical teachings of Christian leaders and thinkers—from St. Alphonsus to John Calvin—than on the Internet?

Where

http://www.cs.pitt.edu/~planting/books/

Links

Recommended Readings Bookshelf

Hymn and choral music archive

Writing Poetry on Seventeen Syllables a Day

Nearly everyone who is exposed to the Japanese poetry of Haiku quickly develops an appreciation for its simple, yet elegant, form. Matsuyama University in Japan has provided this Internet forum to help spread Haiku throughout the world.

Haiku typically takes the form of three lines consisting of five, seven, and five syllables, usually evoking a deep spiritual insight into nature and other intangibles. Sound easy? Try it, then compare your work with some that you'll find here.

Where

http://mikan.cc.matsuyama-u.ac.jp:80/~shiki/

Links

Pleasure of Haiku

How you can compose and appreciate HAIKU

The English Server's Poetry Page

Dogwood Blossom's Haiku Server

Can You Say "Newbery Award Winners?"

Once upon a time, in a bygone era when the world was still new and innocent (1922), the American Library Association created the Newbery Medal to award the writer of the most distinguished American children's book published that year. But our story doesn't end there, boys and girls. Since then, this prize—named for the eighteenth-century English bookseller John Newbery—has become the best known and most discussed children's book award in America.

This site provides you with the history of the Newbery award, along with cover photos and abstracts of the winners. There are even bios of the authors of these classics and classics-to-be. And they all lived happily ever after.

Where

http://ils.unc.edu/award/nhome.html

Links

Caldecott Award Books

More Information in WWW

Medal Description

Number the Stars/ Lois Lowry

Abstract

"How brave are you, little Annemarie?" Uncle Henrik asks his ten-year-old niece. It is 1943, and to Annemarie Johansen, life in Copenhagen is a complicated mix of ordinary home and school life, food shortages, and the constant presence of Nazi soldiers. Bravery seems a vague virtue-one possessed by dragon-slaying knights in the bedtime stories she tells her younger sister, Kirsti. Too soon, she herself is called upon for courage.

The Newbery Award site includes cover images and abstracts for several award-winning books—a great resource for parents and children alike.

Dial a Book

Maybe *you* can judge a book by its cover, but I still prefer to thumb through mine before buying. Here's an online bookstore that lets you browse first chapters, tables of contents, and other excerpts of its books for free before you decide to buy.

What's more, Dial-A-Book's Download Bookstore makes current in-print trade books available over the Internet in Adobe Acrobat 2.0

 Acrobat™ Exchange

Portable Document Format (PDF), so you can purchase and download the
books directly to your hard disk. Even Federal Express isn't *that* fast!

With PDF, books can be viewed, searched, and printed—for personal
use only, of course—from DOS, UNIX, Macintosh, and Windows computers. Books available for downloading include:

- Children's books
- Chess books
- Bible translations
- Computer books

Where

http://www.psi.net:80/DialABook/

Links

Chess books selected by the U.S. Chess Federation

Excerpts from eleven Bible translations

Ziff-Davis and Albion Books computer books

In Search of the Perfect Book

What would a library be without some kind of cataloging system to point
you to just the book you're looking for? Total anarchy! It would be a lot
like my den, actually. Though I've always considered the Dewey Deci-
mal System to be the enemy, I've softened my opinion of it and now
think of it merely as a necessary evil. Until they devise a system in which
I can follow a trail of bread crumbs right to the book I'm searching for
and be able to follow it back to where I began, I'll continue to fumble
along with Dewey.

My digression aside, here's an easy-to-use index of hundreds of online
books scattered across all corners of the Net. It also points you to some
of the more common repositories of online books and other documents.

It's easy to search through the over 450 English works by author or title, or you can browse by subject or by new books. *You'll* have to supply the bread crumbs.

Where

http://www.cs.cmu.edu:8001/Web/books.html

Links

Reference Works

Bibliographies

Journals

On-line Catalogs

Electronic Libraries

Ode to a Poet

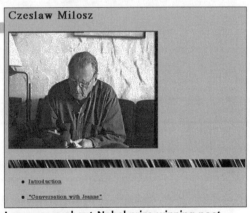

Czeslaw Milosz

- Introduction
- "Conversation with Jeanne"

Learn more about Nobel-prize-winning poet Czeslaw Milosz and his work at the Internet Poetry Archive.

The goal of the Internet Poetry Archive is to make the works of a number of contemporary poets accessible to a new audience and to give teachers and students of poetry new ways to present and study these modern-day masters.

Still a project in progress, this archive is putting the works of living poets from around the world onto the Web, making it much easier for those never exposed to modern poetry to gain an appreciation for this genre. The initial unit will feature eight poets, including Seamus Heaney and Polish poet Czeslaw Milosz, a Nobel Prize winner in poetry.

Since poetry is meant to be read *and* heard, audio clips of many of the poets reading their works will be included, as well as the poet's comments on the works. There are also biographies and short bibliographies, and poems are presented in their original language, as well as in English translation, if necessary.

Where

http://sunsite.unc.edu/dykki/poetry/about.poetry.html

Links

Czeslaw Milosz

Seamus Heaney

 As I said, this site is a work in progress, but holds a lot of promise. Check back occasionally to see how things are progressing.

The Good Reading Guide

What better place to read about the science fiction genre than on the Sci Fi come-to-life world of the Internet? This site gives you reviews of dozens of some of the best and most popular science fiction authors, including Isaac Asimov, Robert Heinlein, L. Ron Hubbard, and Douglas Adams, as well as many other lesser-known SF authors. The reviews are written not by the pros, but by the real people who buy these books, so you're likely to see less of the "works well as a higher metaphor to the assertion that man is ultimately controlled by blah blah blah..." kind of reviews and more of the "I liked/didn't like" kind.

If you're new to science fiction, you'll also be pleased with the many suggestions of books to read, though I'm not quite sure what Jean M. Auel (*Clan of the Cave Bears*) is doing here.

Where

http://julmara.ce.chalmers.se/SF_archive/SFguide/

Links

Links to dozens of reviews of famous and not-so-famous SF books.

The Garden of Etext

The Eden Etext archives, located in Australia, doesn't have the volume of books found at other sites, but for sheer variety you can't beat it. While the archivers here warn of the site's total subjectivity to what they consider to be the cream of Internet electronic texts, they seem to share my tastes as well, so I didn't mind too much.

You'll find nearly two dozen classic novels, a large collection of Edgar Allen Poe, and the complete works of Shakespeare, as well as historical, political, and religious documents, a library of FAQs, and much more. As a bonus for sports fans, you'll find lots of great NBA basketball info here. This site is definitely a browser's Eden.

Where

http://www.cs.rmit.edu.au/etext/etext.html

Links

Inaugural Speeches of US Presidents

NBA Draft Picks

Twilight Zone Episode Guide

Warner Brothers Complete Cartoon List

This is one of those sites you'll want to include on your Hotlist or Bookmark menu. It's only a slight exaggeration to say that it's got something for everyone.

Alice in Webland

Lewis Carroll's birthday marked the official kickoff of this Web page on January 27, 1995. If you were hoping to make the ceremony in time, you're late for a very important date. Still, you're not likely to find a more comprehensive collection of Carroll-related links elsewhere on the Net.

The Lewis Carroll Home Page provides links to Carroll's books online, including *Alice in Wonderland, Through the Looking Glass,* and *The*

Hunting of the Snark. You'll also find links to graphics from some of his books, as well as photographs of Carroll and Alice herself.

There are even links to events, lectures, and exhibits related to Carroll around the U.S., and related organizations.

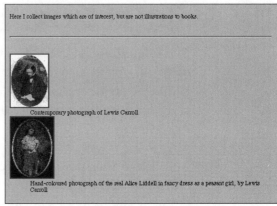

Here I collect images which are of interest, but are not illustrations to books.

Contemporary photograph of Lewis Carroll

Hand-coloured photograph of the real Alice Liddell in fancy dress as a peasant girl, by Lewis Carroll

Through this looking glass on the Web, you can get a glimpse of the real Lewis Carroll along with the real Alice.

Where

http://ux4.cso.uiuc.edu/~jbirenba/carroll.html

Links

Lewis Carroll Society of North America (LCSNA)

Carroll Texts On-line

Graphics

Where to Find More Goodies

Words, words, words. If you haven't had enough of them yet, here are a few places to go to get your fill:

- For children's literature, check out the *Kid Stuff* section and the *Language and Literary Pursuits* section.
- Magazines in the *Business and Career*, *Movies*, *Travel* sections, as well as that Book of Books, the Bible, can be downloaded for free—see the *Religion* section.
- Hip hop over to the *Movie* section to find lots of links to online 'zines.
- Reading about it may not be as fun as doing it, but armchair tourists can read about other peoples globetrotting adventures in the *Travel* section.
- The *Language and Literaty Pursuits* section includes a few additional literary sites that I frankly uncovered too late to include in this section.

 # FREE $TUFF

The key to success is unknown,
but the key to failure is trying
to please everybody.

Bill Cosby

Business and
Careers

Don't Make a Career Out of Looking for a Job

Looking for a job is hard work, and the pay isn't that great, either. But the Web has a wealth of resources to ensure that beating the pavement is only temporary. One valuable site is *Career Magazine*. This interactive resource features:

- Openings for professional, technical, and managerial jobs, updated daily
- Employer profiles
- Jobnet Forum, an interactive discussion group that allows job seekers and employers to meet online
- News and articles relevant to the job search and the workplace environment
- Classifieds

Whether you're looking for a new job or just expanding your professional network, *Career Magazine* will help you get the job done.

Where

http://www.careermag.com/careermag/

Links

Job Openings
News Articles
Career Forum

Start your job search right with Career Magazine on the Web.

Hey, I Wish I'd Thought of That!

When it comes to brainstorming, most of us end up discussing the weekend's Big Game rather than coming up with ways to build better mouse traps. Paramind can help change that. A unique brainstorming program, Paramind helps you get your ideas on paper, expand them, and even come up with new, fresh ideas.

Equipped with a database of 200 related word chains that you can expand *ad infinitum*, Paramind works as a kind of free-association program to help spark your thought process, changing your 40-watt ideas into floodlight-level business plans.

Where

http://www.acs.oakland.edu/oak/SimTel/win3/educate.html

Download

paramd15.zip

Best Bets for Job Hunters

No two job seekers are alike. *Best Bets from the Net*, an exciting new online guide to help job seekers navigate the Net's growing arsenal of employment and job-related information, recognizes the diverse needs of individual pavement pounders.

Created by information resource and career development professionals, *Best Bets from the Net* is designed to meet the career needs of the people who use the Internet. Check out the job postings, learn how to submit resumes electronically, and locate online career information resources. Good luck!

Where

http://asa.ugl.lib.umich.edu/chdocs/employment/

Links

Best of the Best

Career Development Resources

Other Internet Job Guides

When It's All Said and Dun

If you're in business for yourself, you know the value of gaining the edge on your competition. Get that edge with information from Dun & Bradstreet, right off the Web. In addition to valuable data on economic trends, you can get lots of great business how-to's, including:

• Predicting slow payers

• Finding a job

• Managing vendors

In addition, you'll get the latest data on regional growth worldwide, industry profitability, market segment growth, and business failure statistics. Take advantage of this free educational business information and gain an advantage *before* the other guys do.

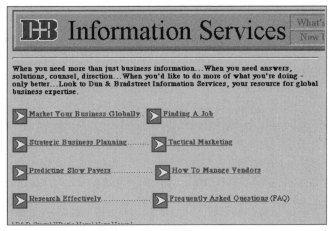

When it's all said and Dun, this is one of the best business sites you'll find on the Web.

Where

http://www.dbisna.com

Links

Market Your Business Globally

Finding a Job

Predicting Slow Payers

How Much Did You Earn While Reading This?

Here are a couple of programs that, when used together, complement each other nicely. SalaryMeter displays the amount of money you're earning while you work (or play, but that'll be our little secret). Now you'll know not only how much *time* you wasted competing in the big office Doom competition, but you'll instantly know how much *money* you made while you were doing it.

Once you've totaled things up, it's time to pass the buck—or bill—to the patron with the deepest pockets. Client Biller and Tracker, an easy-to-use program for keeping track of your clientele, makes it easy for you to bill customers for all your hard labor.

Where

http://www.acs.oakland.edu/oak/SimTel/win3/finance.html

Download

cbill13.zip

salry101.zip

Hong Kong Business Directory

Hong Kong has become a cash machine for companies located around the globe. Exciting and fast-paced, Hong Kong has emerged as a booming manufacturing and exporting mecca.

The Hong Kong Business Directory can connect you to over *123,000* firms dealing in textiles, clothing, electronics, plastics, tourism, and more on Hong Kong island and the New Territories. Once you've located the companies you want to contact, this site lets you fill out a form that will be faxed automatically to them to get more information. Find out why *The Pearl of the Orient* is also called the Far East's "most vibrant commercial center."

Where

http://FarEast.Com/HongKong/directory.html

Links

Thousands and thousands of links to companies throughout Hong Kong

The Hong Kong Business Directory puts you in touch with the Orient's mecca of manufacturing.

The World Wide Web Fax of Life

You've been reading about some hot Web site on your lunch hour and can't wait to see it for yourself. But the boss hasn't been willing to spring for that company SLIP account, so Web access is still out of your reach. What's a junior executive to do? Why, just pilfer some company resources, of course (namely the fax machine and a couple of minutes of long-distance telephone time), just like the cyberspace gods intended. All kidding aside, this site will show you a great way to access the Web via your humble fax.

Here's the deal: The Universal Access WebFax server lets you retrieve World Wide Web documents using just a fax machine. Simply pick up the handset on your fax machine (or whatever the drill at your office), dial the number listed at this site, follow the voice instructions, then push the start button on your fax machine. The selected document will be automatically transmitted to your fax machine.

Although not every Web site can be accessed, this server has a database of several thousand commonly referenced URLs. Some might call this petty larceny, but you can call it creative resourcefulness at your next review. Besides, everybody else is doing it, so it must be okay (remember trying to pull that one on your mother?).

Where

http://www.datawave.net/wf_instructions.html

Links

Not much in the way of links here, but you will get instructions on how to link your fax machine to thousands of Web sites. That's worth something, isn't it?

The Web Is Open for Business

No power-lunch yuppie who's survived the drug-induced '60s would dare claim that cyberspace is a paragon of organization and sensibility—in fact, navigating the Web sometimes seems like the supreme hallucination. It's a great place to go browsing if you've got a lot of time to kill, but if you're looking for something in particular, the Web can quickly seem like a demon bent on hiding the proverbial cyberneedle in a virtual haystack.

That's why you'll appreciate sites like this one at the University of Houston's College of Business Administration. They've compiled all the known Web business sites into this comprehensive listing of links to who's doing business on the Web.

From the megabuck conglomerates to the doing-business-in-the-garage types, they're all here—or at least almost all. Business is booming in cyberspace, and moving forward at a pace even Michael Eisner would find tough to keep up with. But this site, organized by category, is updated regularly, and makes it easy for you to keep abreast of business sites on the Web. Just check in from time to time to see who's hung their shingle here.

Where

http://www.cba.uh.edu/ylowpges/ylowpges.html

Links

Nearly 200 listings of businesses on the Web

The Ups and Downs of Wall Street

Buy! Buy! Buy! No, wait—Sell! You'd better decide for yourself. But you'd also better decide fast. And if you want up-to-the-minute news of the Wall Street roller coaster, you're not going to get it from your afternoon newspaper. Hop on the Web for free electronic quotes and graphs of the Dow Jones Industrial Average and S&P 500.

All information posting is delayed a few minutes to satisfy the SEC, but that's definitely more current than you'll find anywhere else. You can even get historical data and graphs of stock performances spanning the past 25 years.

Where

http://www.secapl.com/cgi-bin/qs

Links

Ticker Search

Dow Jones Industrial Average

S&P 500 Index

Will Work for Internet Access

Are you ready for a job change, or do you already change jobs the way others change their socks? Maybe you're ready for a whole new career. Maybe your *boss* thinks you're ready for a whole new career. In any event, check out CareerMosaic before you hit the pavement. Named "Best Commercial Site on the Web" by PC Week Labs, CareerMosaic gives you the latest information about the best companies to work for. It's like having a buddy on the inside feeding you the best and worst of working for some of the hottest companies, like:

- US West
- National Semiconductor
- Hewlett-Packard
- Sybase
- Union Bank

You'll get the latest scoop on benefits and employee programs, opportunities for college students, company profiles, career opportunities, and more. Arm yourself with the information you need to make those can't-turn-back-now career decisions.

Where

http://www.service.com/cm/cm1.html

Links

Fifth Annual Los Angeles Daily News Women's Career Conference

Strictly Personnel Seminar Series

Employment Directory Guide to North American Markets

Make It Your Business

Starting your own business is a big step—sometimes off a high cliff. There are a thousand hazards and even more pitfalls when you're starting out, and no single person has the business-savvy to identify them all. And no one needs to tell *you* about your chances of "making it." But you *can* with the right product—and the right information.

Did you know that more businesses fail from not taking risks than from trying to be innovative? Arm yourself with the knowledge that will strengthen the odds *your* business will be the one to succeed where others haven't.

If you're looking for information about starting, running, marketing, advertising, or expanding your business, Business Sources on the Net is *the* place to start. This hotlist has links to some serious business resources so scattered across the Net you couldn't find 'em even if you *had* a net. You'll get information on business accounting, finance, management, marketing, and more.

Where

http://kiwiclub.bus.utexas.edu/wwwlecture/businesshotlist.html

Links

Too many to list. Make it your business to start browsing 'em.

Who's the Boss? You Are!

The entrepreneurial spirit is alive and thrashing on the Web. If you're one of the little fish, you'll want to check out the tons of resources available to help you succeed and make a splash in the big pond.

Entrepreneurs on the Web provides lots of useful business information, gathered specifically with adventurous venturers in mind. Take a quick look at some of the offerings:

• Your business listed in national directories for *free*

• Free publicity for your newsletter or magazine

• Information on laws concerning unsolicited telephoning or faxing

Plus, you'll get the latest *entreprenews* with *A-ha! Monthly*, the newsletter for and about entrepreneurs from The IDEA Association, a support group for people starting their own businesses.

Where

http://sashimi.wwa.com/~notime/eotw/EOTW.html

Links

The Internet Business Center
Advertising on the Internet
IDEAbase

A Patently Good Web Resource

Okay, so you've built a better mouse trap and are ready for the stampede. But before the world beats a path to your door, make sure somebody else hasn't built your invention already.

The Source Translation & Optimization's (STO) Internet Patent Search System provides Web users a way to perform patent searches, as well as to access information on the patent process. STO provides free patent information, and at the time of this writing is in the process of developing a free patent-search service on the Internet. Currently, you can retrieve all patent titles since 1970 by class/subclass code, as well as get information on filing fees, archives of stories from the Internet Patent News Service, and the latest info from the IPNS, an excellent source for patent-related news bulletins and lists of new patents.

Where

http://sunsite.unc.edu/patents/intropat.html

Links

US Code Section 35 - federal patent laws

IPNS Internet Patent News Service

A shopping mall for patent services

The designers of this site could have made it more intuitive to use. As is, it falls a little short in the tutorial/documentation category. But it's a work in progress and has the potential for being a fantastic Web resource. Keep checking back for new features.

Belly Up to the Bar

Wbar, a bar-code-generating program, makes it a snap to create many different types of bar codes to insert into any Windows program that accepts bitmaps or metafiles.

Follow the comprehensive documentation to get up to speed quickly, then simply position the cursor in the window where you want to place the barcode and click. You'll be prompted for the type of bar code you want, and you're done.

Where

http://www.acs.oakland.edu/oak/SimTel/win3/barcode.html

Download

wbar19.zip

Nothing But Networking

The three most important words in job searching are network, network, and network (in that order). The Interactive Employment Network (IEN to those who prefer the alphabet soup) will help you land that job you'd kill or die for (an approach that seems kind of self-defeating to me, though).

IEN, sort of an online employment agency without the long line, provides job listings for professionals, technicals, and human servicables. You'll also find tips from job-advice columnists Joyce Lain Kennedy and Marilyn Moats Kennedy.

Great for job seekers, recruiters, and human-resource managers, IEN provides information on the latest trends and resources for potential employees and employers. You can even post your resume online and get invaluable tips on how to land the perfect job—or job applicant.

IEN has employee listings, salary guides, career fair calendars, and more. Plus, if you need to polish your interviewing skills (and who doesn't?), there's an interview simulator to help you practice your answers to the tough interview questions. Now get to work!

Where

http://www.espan.com/ienhome.html

Links

Career Manager

Job Library

HR Manager

Welcome! E-SPAN's Interactive Employment Network (IEN) provides current, authoritative resources for the job seeker and--in the near future--for the employer.

E-Span's Job Library is the best you'll find.

● 1700 employers, 2500 job openings, all paid!
● All less than four weeks old--the most up-to-date on the net!
● Searchable by keyword, region, industry, date posted and job title.

Rumor has it this is the site The Donald used to get his start.

It All Adds Up

You may think your pocket calculator has all the features you need to keep track of your billables and payables, but try out a couple of these programs and you may never go back. These calculators will keep an electronic tape transcript of your calculations that you can then print; they also convert dimensions and even calculate wages. It's like hiring a new bookkeeper, except these programs won't demand their own office.

Where

http://www.acs.oakland.edu/oak/SimTel/win3/calc.html

Download

10key301.zip

addease1.zip

calcpd12.zip

dimcalc1.zip

pclc20.zip

wwages1a.zip

Security Blanket for Investors

Investing is a tricky business, and smart investing can be downright night-marish—assuming you can sleep at all. Luckily, there's help for the newbie who wants to do something more with his/her money than stuff it under his/her mattress—or flush it down the toilet. Security APL provides free stock quotes instantly (minus 15 minutes—there's that pesky SEC rule again) and even has a stock-symbol lookup service and charting function.

In addition, Portfolio Accounting World Wide from Security APL (PAWWS) has many free (as well as fee-based) services, including a financial library that includes loads of links to other Web and Internet resources to help you learn as much as you can about investing and the companies you're betting on.

And if you think you're ready to start investing, but aren't *quite* sure, take the PAWWS Portfolio Management Challenge. This contest gives you the chance to test your money management skills against competi-tors from around the world, using (almost) live security prices, at no risk: because it's all play money.

Where

http://www.secapl.com

Links

Industry Classifications

PAWWS Portfolio Management Challenge

Dow Jones Industrial Average

Market Watch

Personal Investment and Tax Information

Interesting Business Sites on the Web

Before you start investing, invest a little time at Security APL—time well spent.

At over 150,000 accesses per day, this site might give you some minor delays, but it beats fighting it out on the trading floor.

Mining for Moola

If you're ever one of the lucky ones to strike gold on the Internet, make this your first stop. The Mining Channel is the Web's most comprehensive online exploration and mining site.

From gold exploration to diamond mining, the Mining Channel has the most up-to-date information to assist you with your investment decisions, including company profiles, news releases, the current closing quotes, industry data, and related investment news.

Where

http://www.wimsey.com/xr-cgi-bin/select?/116@/Magnet/mc/cover.html

Links

Mining and Exploration Companies

Vancouver, British Columbia

Newsletters and Newsgroups

Time for a Reality Check

Reality Online, developers of the nation's leading online personal investment service, operates Reuters Money Network, the largest online service dedicated to personal investing. Reality also publishes WealthBuilder, a financial planning software program for individuals.

For $10 a month, you can get unlimited stock quotes, investment news, and information about companies you're thinking of acquiring in your next takeover (friendly, of course). Even if you don't subscribe, you'll still get a free copy of the newsletter *Reality Investor,* *"The Insider Newsletter For The Computer-Savvy Investor."*

Where

http://www.rol.com

Links

WealthBuilder

Reuters Money Network

Premium Research Reports

The Feeling Is Mutual

Mutual funds are the hottest ticket in town these days. They make it simple to get started, simple to make money, and simple to lose your shirt if you're not sure what you're doing. NETworth can help you get up to speed and have you wheeling and dealing like a Rockefeller in no time.

Featuring in-depth information on thousands of mutual funds, NETworth helps you get information straight from the managing companies, including prospectus and performance figures.

You'll get prices quoted direct from the markets via dedicated S&P real-time data, access to a database featuring information on over 5,000 mutual funds, a comprehensive listing and samples of financial newsletters, and access to question-and-answer forums with some of the industry's most knowledgeable professionals.

In addition, NETworth's Mutual Fund Market Manager offers loads of information on how to pick the best mutual funds to fit your needs. There are also company profiles, fund descriptions, and an option that lets you order more information on the funds you choose.

Where

http://networth.galt.com

Links

The Mutual Fund Market Manager
NETworth Market Outlook
Bull & Bear

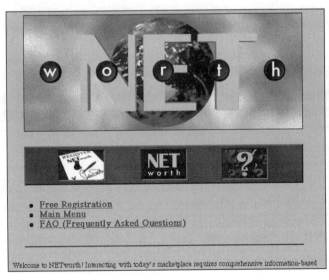

Know your NETworth before tackling the tricky business of mutual funds.

Follow the Money

If you're looking for business information, the Internet is a great place to start. And this server at Stanford University offers everything you need to get comprehensive business information. With hundreds of hot links to business-related sites and services, this one will keep you busy for a while.

You can also get comprehensive analyses of brokerage houses, tips on dividend reinvestment programs, historical commodities quotes, current prices of vegetables, business magazines and newsletters, and more.

This is a great site for small business information, tax advice, and links to business-related newsgroups.

Where

http://akebono.stanford.edu/yahoo/Business/

Links

Corporations

Marketing

Indices

Know the SCOR

One of the biggest hurdles that growing businesses have to overcome is the need to raise capital. But new or growing companies have a difficult time gaining access to the stock markets. And unless you're rich, or if Aunt Barbara leaves you the family fortune in her will, or if you've somehow managed to attract the attention of an investment banker, you and your company are dead in the water.

But now there's help for small businesses on the upswing. The Small Corporate Offering Registration (SCOR) provides a new avenue to help small companies raise up to $1 million without the need to find an investment banker or expensive securities law firm. Shares issued are freely tradeable and may be listed on various stock exchanges, and the registration forms are designed to be used by companies, attorneys, and accountants who are not necessarily specialists in securities regulation. Find out if your company is eligible.

Where

http://www.cei.net:80/jeaton/

Links

List of states allowing SCOR offerings

Qualifications to use SCOR

Complete copy of Form U-7 with instructions

List of Required Exhibits

Financial Statements Requirements

Pacific Stock Exchange Listing Requirements for SCOR Companies

Plug In to the Global Business Network

Where's the global market headed in the 21st century? No one knows for sure, but the Global Business Network is using its experience to peer into the future.

Trend spotters at GBN are trying to predict the future.

Though not equipped with a crystal ball, GBN does use a unique membership network that brings together strategic thinkers from over 50 leading companies, as well as individuals from the sciences, arts, business, and academia. Its objective is to explore the driving forces and critical uncertainties in today's business environment to come up with scenarios and insights into the global economic future. Its results will help businesses to plan more effectively for an uncertain economic world. Check out some of the early results here to help you plan *your* future.

Where

http://www.well.com/www/gbn/index.html

Links

Scenarios

WorldView

Own-ly You

Employee ownership of companies is an idea whose time has come. More and more companies are starting to realize the benefits of higher productivity, increased morale, and getting employees to think like owners by giving them a personal stake in the profit margin.

FedNet is helping companies implement some form of employee ownership to achieve their business objectives. Currently, nearly 12,000 U.S. companies of all sizes and industries have some level of employee ownership encompassing more than 11 million participants and $120 billion in stock. Check this site out for more information.

Where

http://www.fed.org/fed/

Links

Equity Compensation Methods

Employee Motivation and Empowerment

International Employee Ownership

Case Studies of Successful Companies

Government Policy & Legislation
F.E.D. Publications

Can I Quote You on That?

You're only as rich as the bottom line on your portfolio. And it's too late to sell if there's nowhere to go but up. So stay on top of the markets via QuoteCom. With QuoteCom, Webheads can get the most up-to-the-minute financial market data available, including:

- End-of-day portfolio updates detailing the performance of your stocks during the day
- Portfolio alarm monitoring to help oversee your stocks
- Notification of news items concerning your stocks
- Profiles of over 1,200 of the largest, most influential, fastest-growing companies around the world
- Canadian, London, and European market data

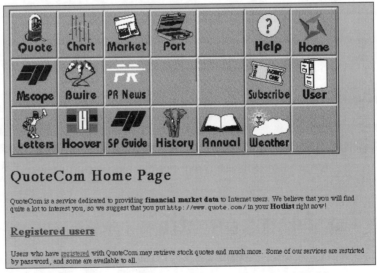

Stock quotes, company profiles, and lots of market-related freebies are yours for the taking at QuoteCom.

Trying the service is free—not a bad deal. If it's critical that you have the most up-to-date financial data, QuoteCom is your free ride to Wall Street.

Where

http://www.quote.com/

Links

Free Stock Quotes

BusinessWire

Hoover Company Profiles

Other Links for Investors

Can You Change a Twenty?

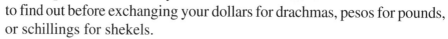

How's the dollar doing against other currencies around the world? Don't ask, you say? C'mon, it's not *that* bad. Try this simple-to-use currency converter to find out before exchanging your dollars for drachmas, pesos for pounds, or schillings for shekels.

With the Koblas Currency Converter, you just select the desired currency and all other currencies are instantly recalculated to the current exchange rate. Over 50 countries from Argentina to Venezuela are represented.

Where

http://www.ora.com/cgi-bin/ora/currency

Links

Dozens of links to currency exchange rates around the world

The Tax Man Cometh

According to this site, "all the money that the average U.S. taxpayer makes for two hours and 41 minutes of each workday goes to pay federal, state, and local taxes," so use that time wisely by browsing around this site and its related links.

You'll get up-to-the-minute information on state and federal tax issues, hundreds of tax forms (no, you don't have to fill them *all* out), links to many great tax-related Net sites, including the IRS itself, and much more. There's even help for Canadian filers. Happy returns!

Where

http://www.scubed.com/tax/tax.html

Links

Federal tax forms and instructions in different formats

State Tax Forms and Instructions

Public Domain Tax Software via FTP

Canada Taxation Forms

Tax Forms via E-Mail

The ENTIRE Tax Code

The IRS Online

Conquer Your Calendar Confusion

When it comes to organizing your office, the first step is to get out from under the clutter. Let your computer take some of the load off your desk by installing one of these calendar programs.

I won't promise that you'll never miss another appointment or meeting, but these calendars will help take some of the burden off of your tracking efforts. Try out a few of these calendars to find out which one is best for you. Some of the features of the different programs include automatic reminders, day planners, weekly schedulers, and other bells and whistles to help you get the office organized.

Where

http://www.acs.oakland.edu/oak/SimTel/win3/calendar.html

Download

3dvcp20.zip

am_cr10.zip

dw4win10.zip
sew200.zip
stdc10.zip

Track It Down

When your package absolutely, positively has to be there, but isn't, you can use the Web to track it down, saving yourself—and your boss—a world of worry and aggravation. At Federal Express's Web site, you can track your package anytime of day, anywhere in the world.

You'll get up-to-the-minute information on your shipment, and you'll even see who signed for it once it gets where it's going. Just type in your FedEx package tracking number to display the information for the package, then select Send Request. It's that easy!

Where

http://www.fedex.com/cgi-bin/track_it

Links

FedEx Home Page

CommerceNet

When entering a tracking number, be sure to include any dashes that appear in the number (international numbers begin with 400- and COD shipments begin with 300- or 320-).

Where to Find More Goodies

For more business links, try these sections:

- Look for business-related software in *Computers and Software* for both PCs and Macs.
- Get business help from government agencies in *Government and Politics*.

 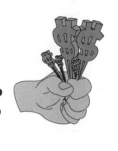

FREE $TUFF

There are two major products that come out of Berkeley: LSD and UNIX. We don't believe this to be a coincidence.

Jeremy S. Anderson

Computers and Software

Surfin' on Silicon

Silicon Graphics, Inc. is a leading developer of applications to create three-dimensional graphics, and is a major corporate booster of and participant on the Internet. As the world's fastest growing supplier of visual computing workstations and high-performance servers, SGI has produced some exceptional accomplishments in a broad range of technical, scientific, corporate, and entertainment applications.

But even more important, they've got a Web site that's fun and loaded with information and free software. You can download *Silicon Surf*, SGI's online industry newsletter. Read the latest SGI news, learn about training courses, see videos, and get free software and graphics.

Where

http://www.sgi.com/ss.home.page.html

Links

Surf Sites

Awesome Products

Cool Freeware

Surf's up at Silicon Graphics' home page

Zip-a-Dee Doo Dah

Programs designed to run on today's computers often take advantage of graphics, sound, and multimedia capabilities. The result: much more impressive programs. The tradeoff: Much bigger files to download. Do you want to burn valuable Web time on a free program that takes forever to download?

Me neither. That's why nearly any program worth its megabytes has been run through some form of compression software before being made available on the Web. By far the most common format you'll come across consists of files that have been "zipped," technolingo for the PKZIP compression program that gives a file the extension .ZIP.

Here's a site where you can download your own shareware version of many popular compression programs including PKZIP/UNZIP, ARJ, LZH, and UC2. They're downloadable as self-extracting programs, so these are some of the few programs on the Web that you don't need a compression package to use. Let me recommend the latest version of WinZip.

Where

http://www.acs.oakland.edu/oak/SimTel/win3/archiver.html

Download

zippro10.exe

winzip55.exe

dz50.exe

Let's Start Where It All Began

Home to some of the country's most talented scientists, engineers, and all-around propeller heads, the National Center of Supercomputing Applications (NCSA) is a high-tech research facility that uses computational science on a high-performance computer to simulate natural phenomena that can't be investigated outside of the laboratory.

And don't let the pretty graphics fool you—this site is loaded with great Web info and links to other sites. Picked as the 1994 Best Overall Site on the Web, NCSA is most famous for being the spawning ground for Mosaic, the grandfather to all other Web browsers.

The National Center for Supercomputing Applications' super Web site.

You'll find great information on what's new in cyberspace and many documents helpful in using and contributing to the Web, including:

- Excerpts from NCSA's latest CD-ROM, which contains 250 megabytes of scientific images and animations
- Software tools
- Access Online, NCSA's general interest magazine

Where

http://www.ncsa.uiuc.edu/

Links

Multimedia Exhibits

Software Tools

Publications

Software 'R' Us

Unless you bought your computer with the intention of using it as the world's most overpriced door stop, you've probably got an insatiable appetite for software. Let's face it, go past the word processor and spreadsheet programs—you know, *work stuff*—and what have you got? A couple of hundred megabytes of unused disk space all dressed up and no place to go.

What better way to use all that free space than by gorging your hard drive's sectors at this all-you-can-eat roadside restaurant of free-to-try software? The SimTel Software Repository is a software junkie's paradise. You'll find hundreds—no, *thousands*—of programs and utilities for astronomy, business, cooking, all the way to zoology and beyond.

Where

http://www.acs.oakland.edu/

Links

PC/Blue Disk Library

SIMTEL-20 Macintosh Archives

SIMTEL-20 Unix&C Archives

SIM-ply the best site for **DOS** and **Windows** software you're going to find on the Net.

You'll notice a gaping hole in the SimTel directories where games should be, but fear not! Look under "education," and you'll find some great ones hidden away. Who are they trying to kid?

Have Computer, Will Travel

Every blessing comes with its own curse, and laptop computing is no different. Like a godsend, laptops freed itinerant business people to work on the road, making them more productive and less dependent on the home office. Right. And some of you probably still believe in Santa Claus, too.

Laptop computers can certainly be a blessing, but they also create as many problems as they solve, especially if the user's knowledge goes little past knowing how to turn it on. The Road Warrior Outpost, an Internet resource for portable computer users, contains lots of information and tips that can help, including laptop accessories and ordering information.

Where

http://warrior.com/

Links

Laptop News Group

Mac Portables News Group

Business News

Travel Information

Open Up Your Windows

If you're looking for great Windows programs to make computing just a little easier—or at least a lot more fun—you'll want to try a few of these programs. You'll find programs to launch your applications faster, monitor your system resources, customize your desktop, and more.

There are also programs for randomizing your wallpaper, converting your GIFs and JPEGs to bitmaps, posting notes on your desktop, even changing your cursor to display as an eye, a pencil, or a slice of pizza. You can even create your own custom cursor icons.

Where

http://www.acs.oakland.edu/oak/SimTel/win3/desktop.html

Download

Too many to list. Browse through these and you'll find some terrific programs to make your computing easier and fun.

OAK Repository

**SimTel, the Coast to Coast Software Repository Windows
Primary Mirror
Directory SimTel/win3/clock/**

You may need to set your software to load files to disk first.

barclk24.zip (Image)
     WIN3: BarClock:Caption bar alarm clock w/timer
     11/07/94, 76230 bytes

cman-10b.zip (Image)
     Intelligent alarm clock for Windows3, w/alarms
     12/30/91, 156169 bytes

cuckoo11.zip (Image)
     Cuckoo Clock for Windows
     02/03/95, 22734 bytes

digclk12.zip (Image)
     DigiClock: Win3.1 digital clock replacement
     09/27/94, 48437 bytes

All work and no play makes your hard drive very dull. Liven things up with some of these free utilities right away.

Not Just for Newtons

It's not just the auto industry that comes out with the occasional Edsel. Computer manufacturers have had their share, too. (Can you say PC Junior? And how about that Lisa?) The Newton was no exception. Before its time? Perhaps. Buggy as all get out? Without question. But just as you can still get parts for a '74 Pinto, so it goes with the Newton.

If you're among the small band of semigullible users who bought the Newton (and you know who you are), here's the place to go for a one-stop

Newton software shopping experience. Even better, there are hundreds of Mac and PC programs available here as well, including online books, games, and programs for business or pleasure.

Where

http://newton.uiowa.edu/

Links

Applications

Books

Code

Games

Utilities

 If you're a PC or Mac user looking for software, you'll find plenty at this site. Just click on PC or Mac, then browse the directories. Happy hunting!

C'mon, Clean Up Your Desktop!

Remember when you first got that computer? You felt as though the amount of disk space available was limitless. Fat chance. Next thing you knew, those hundreds of megabytes of free space were filled up with spreadsheet programs, flight simulators, and bitmaps of supermodels Kathy Ireland and Audrey Taflinger. Now it feels like half your RAM called in sick this morning and you wonder why you keep getting all those error messages.

Hmm. We need to start doing just a *little bit* better in the disk management department, don't we? Here's a site that can help. Within this large collection of Windows utilities are disk compression and file search programs, utilities to display the amount of disk space available, programs to copy and format disks in the background, and other disk management add-ons.

Where

http://www.acs.oakland.edu/oak/SimTel/win3/diskutil.html

Download

epwffv1.zip
wfree101.zip
windru14.zip
wndc111.zip

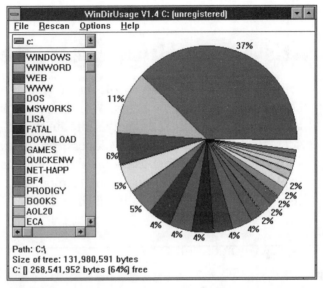

WinDirUsage, a shareware utility that displays a pie chart of
your disk space usage, is one of several disk management
utilities you can download here.

Share and Share Alike

You grabbed your Web browser for free and now you're probably using
the company telephone to tap into the Internet. So none of this Internet
stuff's costing you a penny, but you're still not satisfied. What else do
you *want?* Well how about some *more* free software?

Here's the place to go for hot Windows software available for the right
price: *free* (at least on a trial basis). Shareware, the best marketing idea
since free samples at Cinnabons, is by far the best way to decide just

what kind of software you need. You'll find hundreds of programs here to satisfy your software appetite.

Where

http://coyote.csusm.edu/cwis/winworld/winworld.html

Links

Newloads

Screen Savers

Microsoft's Mega Huge Web Site

Computer-age Goliath Microsoft has a Web site for the rest of us Davids to access. You'll find the latest information about the company's products and services, up-to-date news for developers, product announcements, fixes for bugs (or are those features?), employment information, and more. Rumor has it the Justice Department spends a lot of time here.

Where

http://www.microsoft.com/

Links

Windows News

Employment Opportunities at Microsoft

Microsoft Sales Information

Microsoft Network

You can find lots of information here on Microsoft Network (formerly code-named Marvel), Microsoft's very own online service to be bundled with the release of Windows 95. Network reportedly will allow users access to the Internet and World Wide Web, and unlike most online services, it will be "transaction based," which means you pay only for what a particular vendor on the Network charges—there are no connect-time charges. With a potential user base in the tens of millions, Network could become the reigning champ overnight in the online services prize fight.

Break de Code

Odds are that you'll run across files in some archives on the Internet that have been uuencoded (nno, tthat's nnot aa ttypo). Basically, uuencoded files are binary files such as pictures or word-processing documents that have been converted to ASCII to make them easier to transfer through cyberspace, since many newsgroups and mailing lists are unable to handle binaries. Once a file has been converted to ASCII, it can be sent just like any other mail message. Besides, you haven't *really* earned your cyberwings until you've decoded this mass of hieroglyphic mumbo jumbo, and the programs at this site will get you through flight school.

These decoders offer a variety of options, but they all share the common trait of being shareware:

- UUdecoder for Windows
- WIN3
- WinCode 2.61
- XFERPRO

Give 'em each a try to find out which you prefer. My choice? WinCode.

Where

http://www.acs.oakland.edu/oak/SimTel/win3/encode.html

Download

extrct34.zip
uucod314.zip
wncod261.zip
xferp100.zip

The Fax of Life

You've got the hardware, but your fax program's been nothing but trouble. The line forms to the right, and it's a long one. Computers these days are usually mixes and matches of square pegs and round holes that software unites to make it all work in harmony. Unfortunately, all too often the gap between what should work and what actually does rivals the distance across the Grand Canyon.

SimTel has lots of programs you can use to try and bridge that gap. If these don't help, I've found that a large rock and a blowtorch can work wonders. The results aren't great, but you can imagine the satisfaction....

Where

http://www.acs.oakland.edu/oak/SimTel/win3/fax.html

Download

faxsu2b.zip

faxsu6a.zip

faxwin34.zip

Infobahn Roadside Assistance

When you pull off the fast lane of the Information Highway for a quick pit stop and look under the hood, take a few minutes to check out PC Lube and Tune, an online information service station to keep you humming smoothly in cyberspace.

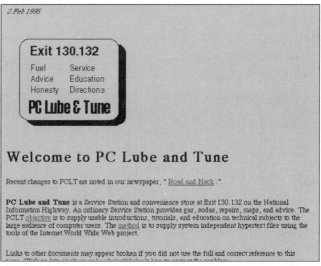

Fill 'er up at PC Lube and Tune, and don't forget to have the tires checked.

While you won't get your windows washed by a snazzy guy in a white uniform and bow tie, and there are no balloons for the kids, you *will* get valuable information about how your PC works and how to troubleshoot it when it doesn't (or just plain shoot it). You'll learn more than you ever wanted to know about ethernets, partitioning your hard drive, com ports, and the next trend in operating systems. Now, back on the highway!

Where

http://pclt.cis.yale.edu/default.htm

Links

Windows on the World

Surviving the Next OS

Introduction to TCP/IP

Let Me Talk to the Manager

Mac users sometimes have a hard time making the switch to using Windows. Here are some add-on utilities to make the transition a little smoother. This site has some Mac-like trashcans that let you drag and delete, copy, move, and rename files, conversion programs to move your Mac files over to the PC and—if it doesn't work out—to move them back again. You'll also get some great file finder utilities and programs to convert your Mac and PC files to UNIX so that when you get called up to the show, you'll be ready.

Where

http://www.acs.oakland.edu/oak/SimTel/win3/fileman.html

Download

dragfl20.zip

dragvu12.zip

dropdesk.zip

dumper10.zip

fmedit.zip

fmgrd120.zip

Tips for the Computationally Challenged

Stupid OS/2 Tricks, created by Melissa Woo, is a collection of tips and secrets to get you quickly up to speed on IBM's OS/2 operating system. Far from being stupid, the tricks in this hypertext document will turn you into an OS/2 guru, enabling you to espouse OS/2 wisdom and philosophy like a prophet returning the lost souls of the Microsoft masses to the IBM flock. Hallelujah, brother!

Where

http://index.almaden.ibm.com/nonibm/tricks/tricks.html

Links

System Tips

Command Line Tips

Warp Tips

In Search of . . . Redundancy

Obsolete files on a PC are like roaches in your apartment (stay with me on this one): For every one that you actually see, there are 10 more you weren't even aware of, waiting to lick the chicken you left thawing on the kitchen counter overnight. I probably lost you there.

Still, you'd be amazed at how many duplicate files a PC can contain. Many programs that you install contain the same files as other programs, and when you delete a program it's almost impossible to wipe it completely clean. The result? Wasted disk space.

Here's a program on a mission from the PC gods. It'll search and destroy—with your permission, of course—duplicate files that it locates on your PC. This cyberbounty hunter can save you tons of disk space that would be better served storing love notes from your cybersweetheart.

Where

http://www.acs.oakland.edu/oak/SimTel/win3/fileutil.html

Download

spcmk150.zip

The University of Texas Big Mac Archive

Everything's big in Texas, but you can't beat the prices—at least not at this site. The University of Texas Macintosh archive contains lots of shareware and—even better—*freeware*. Talk about your blue light specials!

You'll find virus detectors, graphics converters and viewers, compression/uncompression software, games, and lots more. Shop till you drop, then rest the keyboard on your belly and shop some more!

Where

http://wwwhost.ots.utexas.edu/mac/main.html

Links

Anti-Virus Software & Information

Internet Software & Services

Sound

Desk Accessories

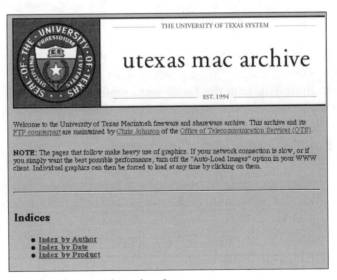

Bargain software at bargain prices.

These pages tend to go heavy on the graphics and can get pretty memory intensive. You may want to turn your image loader off if the connection is too slow for your liking.

Robert Lentz Goes Home

I don't know where Robert finds the time to keep track of what's new (in terms of software) for the Mac and the Power Mac, but I guess I don't really care—as long as he keeps this Web site around for a few more years.

Robert Lentz's home page is a good source for up-to-date versions of Web browsers, graphics viewers, file converters, and other utilities for the Mac. You won't actually find an extensive collection of shareware here, but you *will* find links to just about every good Mac shareware program available on the Web.

Where

http://www.astro.nwu.edu/lentz/mac/net/mac-web.html

Links

HTML/World Wide Web Resources

MacHTTP

Internet Server Cookbook

 There are many, many dozens of other links to shareware and shareware sites. This is a great place to start if you're looking to load your Mac's hard disk with the latest and greatest software.

The Mac Goes to College

This repository at Stanford University arguably contains the largest collection of Macintosh shareware and information of any site on the Internet and Web. If you don't find what you're looking for here, it probably doesn't exist (unless it's at the University of Michigan archives, which I'll get to next).

Current directory is /info-mac

Up to higher level directory

00readme.txt	Thu Oct 13 14:24:00 1994	Symbolic link
AntiVirus	Thu May 12 00:00:00 1994	Symbolic link
Application	Thu May 12 00:00:00 1994	Symbolic link
Communication	Thu May 12 00:00:00 1994	Symbolic link
Compress-Translate	Thu May 12 00:00:00 1994	Symbolic link
Configuration	Thu May 12 00:00:00 1994	Symbolic link
Development	Thu May 12 00:00:00 1994	Symbolic link
Disk-File	Thu May 12 00:00:00 1994	Symbolic link
Font	Thu May 12 00:00:00 1994	Symbolic link
Game	Thu May 12 00:00:00 1994	Symbolic link
Graphic	Mon Jun 6 00:00:00 1994	Symbolic link
Help	Thu May 12 00:00:00 1994	Symbolic link
Hypercard	Thu May 12 00:00:00 1994	Symbolic link
Information	Thu May 12 00:00:00 1994	Symbolic link
Newton	Thu May 12 00:00:00 1994	Symbolic link
Periodical	Thu May 12 00:00:00 1994	Symbolic link
Print	Thu May 12 00:00:00 1994	Symbolic link
Recent	Thu May 12 00:00:00 1994	Symbolic link
Science-Math	Thu May 12 00:00:00 1994	Symbolic link
Sound	Thu May 12 00:00:00 1994	Symbolic link
TextProcessing	Thu May 12 00:00:00 1994	Symbolic link
UserInterface	Thu May 12 00:00:00 1994	Symbolic link
Utility	Sun Jun 19 00:00:00 1994	Symbolic link

Here's a sampling of some of the categories of Mac software available at the Stanford University repository.

Where

ftp://sumex-aim.stanford.edu/info-mac

Links

None, really. Just select a folder to get a listing of shareware for that category.

This is a very crowded site, so try to access it in the evening, or even better, try during those wee hours inhabited mainly by burglars, 7-Eleven employees, musicians, and UNIX programmers.

The Awesome Ann Arbor Archives

If you can't find a particular Mac shareware or freeware package at the Stanford site (see the previous topic), try the University of Michigan archives, which rivals Stanford in sheer size and scope of software, and is updated regularly. Like Stanford, this site is frequently busy. Fortunately, though, most people use the FTP address into this archive, rather than the Web address I've given below. So, as a certified Webbie, you'll find it easier to get into the University of Michigan archive than those bottom-feeders still scrounging the Net with an FTP utility.

Where

http://www.umich.edu/~archive

Links

None really, just select the folder that represents the software category you want to view.

 If you're a Power Mac user, head straight for the powermac/ folder to access and download scads of megabytes of native Power Mac software.

Index of /group/itd/archive/Public/html/mac/

Name	Last modified	Size	Description
Parent Directory	17-Feb-95 14:35	-	
00help/	24-Feb-95 23:15	-	
00introduction	14-Feb-95 13:47	19K	
00ls-lRfile	23-Feb-95 22:32	514K	
00newfiles/	24-Feb-95 00:18	-	
development/	04-Jan-95 19:05	-	
game/	12-Jan-95 13:40	-	
graphics/	20-Nov-94 05:07	-	
hypercard/	18-Feb-95 10:17	-	
incoming/	24-Feb-95 23:34	-	
misc/	01-Nov-94 07:08	-	
powermac/	24-Feb-95 16:27	-	
sound/	18-Jul-94 12:07	-	
system.extensions/	31-Jul-94 21:01	-	

When Stanford and U. Michigan next meet on the gridiron, I suspect that U. Michigan will walk away with the victory and the ball. Their Web sites provide a much better, classic matchup.

Time Is On My Side

Probably one of the most underappreciated utilities that comes with Windows, the clock program sits in the background, always ready when you need it. Hardly the stuff movies are made about, but you can't beat it for dependability.

Still, the Windows clock hardly ever—if at all—makes the headlines, maybe because it's so, so...boring. Give your clock a wake-up call with these timeless dress-ups. There's a cuckoo clock that sounds every half hour, LED displays, fully configurable digitals, and lots more. There's even a talking clock—just don't talk back.

Where

http://www.acs.oakland.edu/oak/SimTel/win3/clock.html

Download

barclk24.zip

cuckoo11.zip

ledclock.zip

uclock12.zip

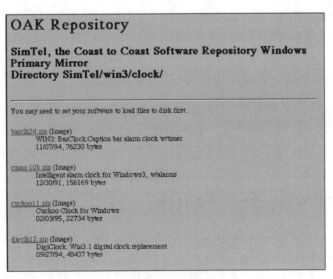

A great place to stop for all you clock watchers.

Do You Have Pretty Good Privacy?

One of the hottest issues on the Internet these days is privacy. Get 30 million people together in one place and, face it, personal privacy's bound to come up, along with where do they keep the virtual bathrooms. Now, with encryption programs like PGP (Pretty Good Privacy) you can at least be ensured that your E-mail is safe.

Without encryption software, nothing you write online is sacred. E-mail and other electronic communications are just as vulnerable—and in many ways more—than more conventional forms of communication.

PGP, created by Phil Zimmerman, lets ordinary people protect their electronic communications quickly and easily using strong encryption. PGP can also protect you from fraudulent E-mail—another big problem in cyberspace—by authenticating the originator of a message.

Slink over to this site to get more information about PGP, including the legal firestorm it has sparked. There's also lots of information about other encryption software and many organizations dedicated to protecting the rights of individuals on the Internet.

Where

http://rschp2.anu.edu.au:8080/crypt.html

Links

Cryptography, PGP, and Your Privacy

The cryptography FAQ

Crypto Rebels

The Cypherpunks home page

A Fondness for Fonts

Don't even think about checking this site unless unusual, strange, and wild fonts are a few your favorite things. You've got to have a love for fonts to appreciate the magnanimous volume of fonts available for downloading at the Internet Font Archive. If you're one of those who feel a font's a font, what's the big deal, the IFA will leave you only with a sense of overkill. With *thousands* of fonts of every style you can imagine, this is a typesetter's dream—or nightmare, I suppose. In addition, the database contains information about each font as well as a thumbnail containing a few sample characters.

Where

http://jasper.ora.com:80/comp.fonts/Internet-Font-Archive/index.html

Links

ftp.cica.indiana.edu

info-mac

The Wadalab Font Project

He Who Dies with the Most Software Wins

The Mac is back—and there's software out there to prove it. At the Nexor archive, you'll find hundreds of Macintosh shareware and freeware programs to satisfy all your software desires.

There are games, spreadsheets, word-processing programs, and utilities of all kinds to customize your Mac from the ground up. Are you paying attention, Microsoft?

Where

http://web.nexor.co.uk/public/mac/archive/welcome.html

Download

Lots of development, game, and graphics programs, as well as other utilities.

UNIX and C Archives

While the Net traces its roots back to UNIX users, that trend took a hard turn once PC users were introduced to cyberspace. The result is that, while there are archives of UNIX programs on the Net, in the big picture, pickings are slim when compared to the volume of DOS, Windows, and Mac programs available.

Nevertheless, UNIX programs *can* be found, and here's a site that will show you what's out there. SimTel's UNIX and C archive contains calendar generators, compression software, editors like EMACS and vi, as well as source code for many other C programs.

Where

ftp://oak.oakland.edu/pub/unix-c/

Download

Too many to list. Browse through them for some great graphics programs, editors, printer and modem utilities, and lots more.

Okay, I know that this site is actually an FTP archive, but I didn't want UNIX and C programmers to feel left out. Be sure to read the Index files in each directory for descriptions of the programs available for downloading.

Know When to Say When

How much software do you need? It sounds like a trick question: How much have you got? But rephrase it as "How much software do you want to pay for?" and the answer is "As little as possible."

The Express Meter Audit Kit will help you determine how many software licenses your company *really* needs and how many it's paying for that are going unused. Produced by the Express System's Software Management Resource Center, the Express Meter Audit Kit, available for free, provides a snapshot of up to 30 days of application usage for any number of users on any type of network, including the Internet. It gives users a no-cost way to assess how their company could benefit from proper management of its software assets.

Where

http://www.express-systems.com/

Links

A Guide to Software Management

Walt Disney's Home Page

You're Getting Warmer

So many home pages and so little time to explore them all. The last thing you need is to get slowed down because your Mosaic Hotlist is getting unorganized. Warmlist can help.

Warmlist is a UNIX software package to cache, search, and organize Web documents you access frequently. Easy to set up and use, Warmlist extends your Mosaic Hotlist, making it much easier to keep things organized. Download the source code and see for yourself.

Where

http://glimpse.cs.arizona.edu:1994/~paul/warmlist/

Links

University of Arizona

UAInfo

I know these links don't have a lot to do with the subject matter, but this *is* my alma mater, so I thought I'd show you around.

How's That Grab Ya?

Probably the most common use of personal computers is for word processing (okay, except for games that let you rip your opponent's spinal cord out of his head). But why not take those dry, boring-to-look-at and even-worse-to-read documents you're creating and dress them up with snapshots of whatever you're running on your computer? Why just write about the game your playing when you can grab a picture of it and include it in the document? Now you can grab it, snag it, or capture it; the choice is yours with these three screen capture utilities for Windows:

- Grabit Pro version 3.1
- SnagIt screen capture and print utility
- Multimode, an "advanced" Windows screen capture program

Where

http://www.acs.oakland.edu/oak/SimTel/win3/capture.html

Download

grabit31.zip

snagit22.zip

wcaptr31.zip

From C to Shining C

Though I never quite figured out who the "Captain" was at this site, I did leave satisfied that I had found a great compilation of C-related Net sites. Liverpool University's archive of C sites on the Web contains links to

Here's enough information about C programming to make anyone C sick.

newsgroups, FTP sites, documents, and other Web pages devoted to C and C++ programming. If you're interested in C programming and want to learn more, make this site your first stop.

Where

http://hpux.csc.liv.ac.uk/users/workexp/wk/c_arc.html

Links

Programming in C

C Lessons

OOP Information

See Here, You CAD

Computer-aided design has been around for over a decade, but as personal computers have become more versatile, these programs—once relegated to only the most demanding drafters and architects—have come into their own as powerful, fun, and easy-to-use design tools.

You can take out a second mortgage to buy the latest version of AutoCAD and spend the rest of your life trying to learn all its bells and whistles, and you'd still only scratch the surface. But if your needs are a little less demanding, you can find some excellent shareware CAD programs at this site.

To be certain, the programs available here won't give you the same versatility or options in the best-selling CAD programs available off the shelf, but then you *will* be much happier with the prices of the shareware versions.

A couple of the programs you'll find here are GammaCAD, a full-featured CAD program for Windows, and CAD/DRAW, which promises to be as easy to use as it is powerful (also for Windows).

Where

http://www.acs.oakland.edu/oak/SimTel/win3/cad.html

Download

gcad110.zip

tscad20.zip

Where to Find More Goodies

There are freeware and shareware programs mentioned throughout this book, as well as online resources for programmers. Here are a few:

- Turn your GIFs into Windows wallpaper with the conversion program mentioned in the *Arts* section.
- Find *Wired* magazine's online counterpart in the *Books, Magazines, and Literature* section.
- Doom, Descent, and many other shoot 'em ups are in the *Games* section.
- *Food and Cooking* contains several electronic cookbooks.
- The *Health and Nutrition* section includes software to help you eat right.
- Shareware programmers wanting to protect their interests will find lots of legal help in the *Law* section.
- Programs to keep track of your CDs, video collections, and sports cards can be downloaded—see the *Music, Movies and Videotapes* and *Sports, Recreation, and Hobbies* sections.

FREE $TUFF

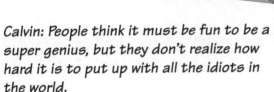

Calvin: People think it must be fun to be a super genius, but they don't realize how hard it is to put up with all the idiots in the world.

Hobbes: Isn't your pants zipper supposed to be in the front?

from CALVIN AND HOBBES

Education and Teaching Tools

121

Explore the Exploratorium

The Exploratorium, one of San Francisco's most famous museums, is not your typical gallery of art, but then again, San Francisco is hardly your typical city. The Exploratorium is more of an "educational center," and with a collection of over 650 interactive exhibits covering science, art, nature, and technology, this site provides students with a rich variety of hands-on education opportunies.

Welcome to ExploraNet!

The Exploratorium's World Wide Web server

internet@exploratorium.edu

The science of funology is studied extensively at the Exploratorium.

And with the World Wide Web, you don't have to brave the cable cars or even walk through the Exploratorium's front doors to enjoy what it has to offer. You can access many of the exhibits online, including an extensive collection of images and software.

Where

http://www.exploratorium.edu/

Links

The Palace of Fine Arts

How to Become a Member

Latitude 28 Schoolhouse

The Web is taking students out of the classroom (a place we know they just *love)* and sending them on virtual journeys around the globe to help them learn by experience. These hands-on lessons enable students to better understand the cultures, languages, geography, and history they

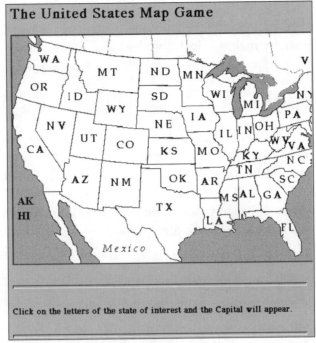

Who says learning can't be fun?

are studying. And best of all, parents don't have to spend a dime to send their kids abroad.

The Latitude 28 Schoolhouse is one such example. This site covers the basic three R's, but keeps going. There are educational games, online children's books, links to the United Nations and all the branches of the U.S. government, and a whole lot more. Field trips were never *this* much fun when I was in school.

Where

http://www.packet.net/schoolhouse/inside.html

Links

Art for the Student
United States Map Game
Mathematics
Reading
Science

The Latitude 28 Schoolhouse is one of many privately funded projects that are making electronic learning accessible to students of all ages.

1 + 1 = Fun!

Who says math has to be a drag (except for maybe 3 million school kids nationwide)? These computer programs help kids master the 'rithmetic part of the three R's before they even realize they're learning.

Among the multitude of math and reading programs available at this site for you to download are:

- Talking math games
- Flash card programs
- Hangman-like word and phrase quizzes
- IQ tests
- Programs to help teachers create and maintain printed tests

And that's just a fraction of what's available here. It all adds up: Your kids can discover how easy *and fun* math can be. In fact, tell them what I just said. After they stop laughing, send 'em into cyberspace math orbit. Then, revel in your ability to say "I told you so."

Where

http://www.acs.oakland.edu/oak/SimTel/win3/educate.html

Download

arith12.zip
cbmath15.zip
hngwn200.zip
iq150.zip
twwin15.zip

Some of these programs require you to have a Visual Basic DLL (Dynamic Link Library) file called VBRUN300.DLL loaded in your

WINDOWS\SYSTEM directory in order to run them. That's already more than you need to know about it and you probably already have it, but if not, you can download the zipped file from:

http://www.acs.oakland.edu/oak/SimTel/win3/dll.html.

Big News on Campus

College students tend to get a little isolated from the real world (except for Domino's Pizza and football betting pools), so it's easy for them to lose track of what's happening in real life. For many, their only source of news is their own college paper, which on the other hand is probably better than some of the tabloids many scandal-hungry adults read. Anyway, here's a site that provides links to dozens of college dailies, near dailies, and some experimental online college publications from across the country.

You'll find links to the University of Arizona's *Daily Wildcat*, Kansas State's *Collegian*, the University of Nevada's *Sagebrush*, and many more. There's also a comprehensive list of links to professional dailies and weeklies, as well as scores of magazines and radio stations. Sounds like big news!

Where

http://mixcom.mixcom.com:80/~qqddqq/#campus_daily

Links

Professional Newspapers

Other News Links

Get Your Kicks on Web66

The Web would have made Bobby Darrin proud, and this site would have made him sing. (If you don't know who *he* is and you're under the

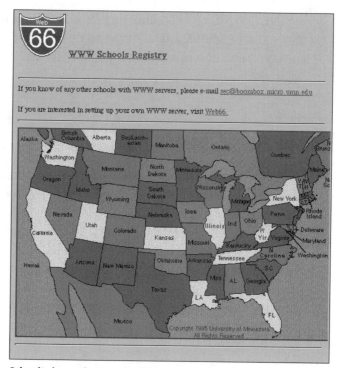

School's in session on the Web.

age of 18, you're the right candidate for this site. If you *do* know who he is, and you're a teacher, you too should take a pit stop here.) The Internet is helping to turn schools around the world into one big global school-house, thanks to Web sites like Web66. In addition to helping educators learn how to set up their own Internet servers, locate resources on the Web, and link up to other teachers and students around the globe, Web66 now includes an easy-to-navigate listing of online K-12 schools.

This clickable map of the United States links you to schools around the country that are wired to the Web. And from Australia to Turkey, you'll also find links to other schools around the world.

Where

http://hillside.coled.umn.edu/others.html

Links

Links to K-12 schools around the block and around the world.

Speech! Speech!

Okay, so you're not a kid any-more. Does that give you an excuse to stop learning? Of course not! There's too much happening in cyberspace alone to lose touch with the latest and greatest ways to learn about everything you didn't learn in school but wish you had. Now the Web makes it easy for your group or organi-zation to find just the right speaker for just the right en-lightening occasion. Speakers On-line lists biographies and contact information for speak-ers and entertainers from ev-ery area of specialty and in every price range.

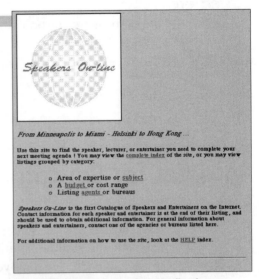

From Minneapolis to Miami - Helsinki to Hong Kong ...

Use this site to find the speaker, lecturer, or entertainer you need to complete your next meeting agenda ! You may view the complete index of the site, or you may view listings grouped by category:

- Area of expertise or subject
- A budget or cost range
- Listing agents or bureaus

Speakers On-Line is the first Catalogue of Speakers and Entertainers on the Internet. Contact information for each speaker and entertainer is at the end of their listing, and should be used to obtain additional information. For general information about speakers and entertainers, contact one of the agencies or bureaus listed here.

For additional information on how to use the site, look at the HELP index.

Will speak for food. Speakers On-line is your one-stop shop to choose from dozens of celebrity speakers for your next garden club meeting. I won't lie to you: These folks aren't free, but at least access to their site is.

Actually, this technically isn't free stuff, since most of these speakers charge way-big bucks for their services. But I'm a public-service kind of guy, so I thought you'd like to know who's available for your next Friends of Nature meeting....

Some of the speakers-for-hire include:

- Dr. Joyce Brothers
- Robert Fulghum
- Vic Sussman, Cyberspace editor for *U.S. News & World Report*
- Harvey Mackay, author of *Swim with the Sharks Without Being Eaten Alive*

Coming soon, sample audios and videos of the speakers will also be available—and those *are* free.

FREE $TUFF from the World Wide Web

Where
http://speakers.starbolt.com/pub/speakers/web/speakers.html

Links
Topics
Budget
Agents

Internet for Educators

School's in session on the Internet and virtual classrooms are bursting at their virtual seams. This site lists scores of education-related sites for teachers and students, with everything from course information on language, science, math, adventure (I don't remember *that* class—it must have something to do with detention), and many more.

You can also get information about departments of education around the country, policy and reform movements, special projects for education on the Internet, museums, planetariums, zoos, lists of schools plugged into the Net, and tons of other helpful links for anyone interested in improving the classroom experience.

Where
http://archive.phish.net/eos1/webs_image.html

Links
Free-Nets
Mars Missions
JASON Project Voyage 5
Early Instruments Museum

Home Ec. Was Never This Good

You can bet the students at the New England Culinary Institute are not your typical brown-bag-the-PB&J types found at other schools. According to the literature, this school in Vermont is staffed by an exceptionally

128

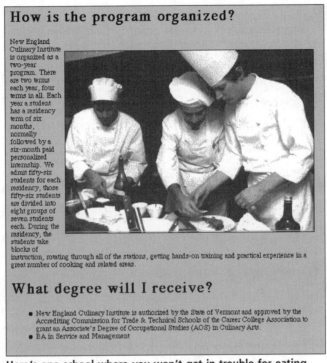

How is the program organized?

New England Culinary Institute is organized as a two-year program. There are two terms each year, four terms in all. Each year a student has a residency term of six months, normally followed by a six-month paid personalized internship. We admit fifty-six students for each residency, those fifty-six students are divided into eight groups of seven students each. During the residency, the students take blocks of instruction, rotating through all of the stations, getting hands-on training and practical experience in a great number of cooking and related areas.

What degree will I receive?

- New England Culinary Institute is authorized by the State of Vermont and approved by the Accrediting Commission for Trade & Technical Schools of the Career College Association to grant an Associate's Degree of Occupational Studies (AOS) in Culinary Arts.
- BA in Service and Management

Here's one school where you won't get in trouble for eating in class.

talented faculty of chefs committed to the philosophy that the best education takes place when students receive personal instruction in small classes. With a placement rate of 100 percent for graduates, it sounds like this school's philosophy is on the mark.

The New England Culinary Institute's two-year professional chef's program includes:

- A seven-to-one student/faculty ratio
- An advanced placement program
- Hands-on training in actual restaurants, bakeshops, cafeterias, and banquet/catering operations

While the $17,000+ tuition is hardly free, it won't cost you anything to browse around here. *Bon appetit!*

Where

http://www.cybermalls.com/cymont/culinary/culinary.htm

Links

CyberMont

Vermont Daily Ski Conditions Report

CyberWharf

Buddy Can You Spare a College Education?

Were it not for financial aid programs (or deep pockets from Mom and Dad), a college education would be only a dream to many. Here's a site that's making it easier for the college-bound of today to become the college grads of tomorrow.

Helping to cut through the bureaucratic red tape, the Financial Aid Information page will answer many of the questions needy students have about the application process, loan information, loan alternatives, and much more. This site is also great for financial aid administrators who need to keep abreast of the latest aid information.

Where

http://www.cs.cmu.edu:8001/afs/cs/user/mkant/Public/FinAid/finaid.html

Links

Scholarship and Fellowship Databases

Grant and Loan Information

Free Information from the US Government

Free Documents

University Financial Aid Offices

Coming to You Live from Antarctica

If you don't mind sharing a classroom with a penguin and can easily study through the din of chattering teeth, Live from Antarctica may be

School's in session at the coldest place on earth.

for you. This Passport to Knowledge project is designed to let students and teachers travel the Internet to experience what life is like in the coldest place on the planet, Antarctica.

This electronic trip uses interactive television, the Internet, and classroom activities to take students on a scientific journey to the bottom of the world. Live from Antarctica provides students and teachers the opportunity to exchange E-mail with scientists working in this polar region to ask them questions—and even help answer a few of the scientists' own. Participants can access scientists' diaries, logs, and other information, and link to international research centers to download color photos and computer images. Now *that's* cool.

Where

http://quest.arc.nasa.gov/livefrom/livefrom.html

131

Links

Teacher's Guide

Classroom Projects

National Science Foundation

www u.

Pick a college, any college. Chances are it's listed at this site, along with about 999 others—many of which you'll be hard pressed to pronounce. From Denmark's Aalborg Business College to Taiwan's Yuan-Ze Institute of Technology, the College and University Home Page is the most comprehensive listing of schools of higher learning available on the Web. And with nearly 1,000 links, the list continues to grow.

The Franklin Building, home of the University of Arizona's College of Journalism. Find out what's going on at the U of A, as well as at hundreds of other colleges and universities.

Many of the colleges provide student and faculty information, course descriptions, maps of the campuses, and much more. Definitely a great resource for both the domestic and the international college bound.

Where

http://www.mit.edu:8001/people/cdemello/univ.html

Links

Geographical Listing

List of American Universities

Geography Made GeoSim-ple

What do you get when you cross the Virginia Tech Geography and Computer Science departments? Excellent simulation software, for one. Project GeoSim, a joint research project between these two departments, has created simulation software to study population growth and migration, as well as a quiz program to make sure you were paying attention in the first place.

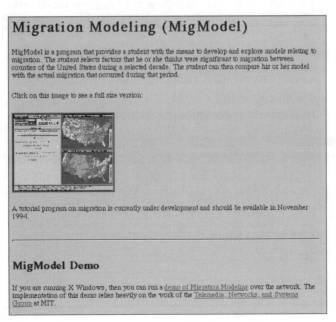

Find out who's going where with Migration Modeling version 1.0.

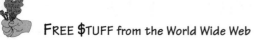

Intended to be used in introductory geography courses, these programs can be downloaded by anyone wanting to test their knowledge of topography, landforms, and climate—in short, geography.

Where

http://geosim.cs.vt.edu/index.html

Links

Virginia Tech

Blacksburg Electronic Village

Middle School, Cyberstyle

"It's not just a school, it's an adventure," or so claims the motto posted at the Cyberspace Middle School. That's a pretty significant promise to have to honor, but this site manages the task easily. Designed for students from 6th through 9th grade that are hooked into—and hooked on—the World Wide Web, Cyberspace Middle School (or CMS to the techno in-crowd) contains links to the home pages of middle school classes and schools around the country. It also includes a list of who's new to CMS and instructions on how your class can contribute.

Of special interest—at least to educators—is help for teachers who want to use the Internet in their classrooms. This link contains lots of introductory information on how teachers can get the most out of the Net to find information valuable to their classes.

Where

http://www.scri.fsu.edu/~dennisl/CMS.html

Links

Educational Resources for Teachers

Virtual Bus Stops

Surf City

The Forecast Calls for Fun

What do math, science, geography, and music have in common? At this home page, they're all used to learn about the weather. The Weather Unit makes climate watching fun by providing creative approaches to studying the workings of the atmosphere.

These lesson plans show teachers how to make studying the weather more exciting for students by using creative approaches to a subject that frankly has a 70-percent chance of being boring. This site does just that. Who knows, you just might plant the seed that will blossom one of your students into the next Hippy Dippy Weatherman.

Where

http://faldo.atmos.uiuc.edu/WEATHER/weather.html

Links

Reading & Writing
Social Studies
Art
Drama
Field Trips

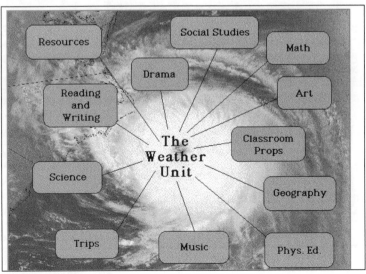

The eye of the hurricane.

It's All Academic

Created with the purpose of establishing a low- or no-cost international online educational resource for students, parents, educators, and administrators, Academy One provides information and online projects for schools wired to the Web. Students and teachers alike can participate regardless of their expertise (or lack of) with computers and the Internet. In short, Academy One is as easy to use as it is fun.

Sponsored by the National Public Telecomputing Network (NPTN), Academy One is a nonprofit organization dedicated to establishing and developing free, public access, computerized information, and communication services for the general public. Academy One's wealth of information includes projects on:

- Stock market and space simulation
- Science and foreign languages
- Bridge building
- Bird migration

Where

http://www.nptn.org/cyber.serv/AOneP/

Links

Learning Center

Government House

Science Center

You'll need to become an NPTN affiliate to get full access to Academy One. Send E-mail to Linda Delzeit at linda@nptn.org to find out how to get set up.

Global Grammar School

If you're a teacher (or even a parent), you know that this is true: Kids love to talk to each other. So why not put this natural desire to use on the

Internet? The Global Schoolhouse, funded in part by the National Science Foundation, helps K-12 schools around the country and around the world share information in a collaborative learning project. Students and teachers participate by using the tools available on the Internet (E-mail, video-conferencing, the Web, and so on) to assist each other in a virtual classroom.

Besides helping to shape the way kids learn, the Global Schoolhouse Project is demonstrating how the Internet can be used as an experiment in the future of education; I hope we'll see more projects like this in cyberspace. Kids love to experiment, and projects like this really give their creativity a jump start.

Where

http://k12.cnidr.org/gshwelcome.html

Links

GSH Objectives

GSH Site Reports

GSH Projects

Letter in Literacy

Opened in September 1994, the International Literacy Institute (ILI) provides scientific leadership in training and development of the basic skills of reading, writing, and calculating among kids and adults.

With a special emphasis on assisting developing countries, the ILI is helping to improve literacy through training, innovation, and technology. Follow the NCAL/ILI Gopher link to find some examples of great Mac freeware and software that make learning to read fun, including:

- Buzzword Bingo
- Fastball Fractions

- Math Tutor
- Story Starters
- Talking Spelling Bee

Where

http://litserver.literacy.upenn.edu/intro-ili.html

Links

U.S. Department of Education

Current Projects at the ILI

Recent Publications by the ILI

If You Don't Know the Answer, Go AskERIC

The Web isn't all fun and games (though it is mostly). Remember, the Internet's original purpose was as a tool to share research information among universities. The only thing that's changed is the number of players. Now millions of users can access educational resources.

AskERIC for the best in education-related information on the Web.

ERIC (Educational Resource Information Center) is a federally funded national information system that provides access to many education-related resources on the Internet, like:

- An online dictionary
- Electronic books through Project Gutenberg
- An acronym dictionary
- The *CIA World Fact Book*

Where

http://eryx.syr.edu/COWSHome.html

Links

Sunsite at the University of North Carolina

NCSA Mosaic Home Page

Electronic Exploration

Point your browser to this site and discover the wealth of information available to cyberexplorers looking for educational-related software and videotapes. The Explorer is part of an online research and development effort to establish a clearinghouse for a full range of information resources available to educators and students on the Internet.

Arranged by subject, each link at the Explorer leads you to information about videotapes you can order (free for Pennsylvania educators) or Mac shareware you can download (free to everyone on a trial basis) to help learn general math, measurements, geometry, and science for K-12 students.

Where

http://unite2.tisl.ukans.edu/

Links

Mathematics

General Science

Creepin' Critter Math

Seek and Ye Shall Find

With nearly 300 colleges and universities from around the world linked to this server, it's probably the most comprehensive and easy-to-use phone directory I've seen on the Web. Simply key in the name of the person you're trying to locate and select his or her college. The database will do the rest. With a little luck, you'll get a name and E-mail address. With a lot of luck you'll get a phone number and street address.

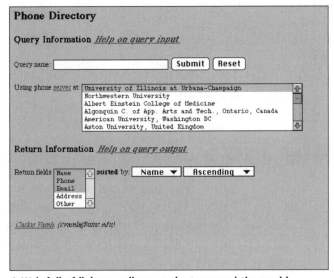

A Web full of links to college students around the world.

Colleges and universities from around the world are included here, including institutions in:

• Canada
• Turkey
• United Kingdom
• Israel
• France
• Hong Kong

- Switzerland
- Italy

And, of course, the U.S.

Where

http://fiaker.ncsa.uiuc.edu:8080/cgi-bin/phfd

Links

Links to college students around the world. If they're in school and you're looking for them, they're probably here.

Where to Find More Goodies

When do you ever stop learning? Try some of these sections to keep your brain firing on all cylinders:

- Look for online museums in *Arts* to help stimulate the senses.
- Learn to manage your money in *Business and Career*.
- Foreign language programs are available in *Language and Literary Pursuits*.

FREE $TUFF

If we can put a man on the moon, why can't we put metal in a microwave!

Dr. Frazier Crane, *Cheers*

Food and Cooking

The Electronic Gourmet Guide

If you're accustomed to placing your dinner order at a drive-thru window or having your food wrapped in Styrofoam, this may not be the site for you. But if you truly appreciate food and its preparation, welcome to the *Electronic Gourmet Guide*, an online magazine devoted to bringing you the best in fine dining.

You'll find excellent cookbook reviews, recipe ideas, and interviews with culinary gurus, as well as an extensive list of links to other food pages on the Web. Also, be sure to check out the great list of emergency backup substitutions for those dinner party preparations when all your cumin is goin' and all your thyme is used up. You just never know when this list might come in handy.

Where

http://www.deltanet.com/2way/egg/eggpage.html

Links

The links change with each issue.

Chef Boyardee, he's not.

If you'd like to be notified by E-mail about publication dates of upcoming issues and their content, click on **Comment** and fill out the form provided, or send E-mail to egg@2way.com.

Wake Up and Smell the Coffee

The Los Gatos Coffee Roasting Company is now available on the Web, which may or may not mean a lot to you, but if you're a true coffee aficionado, you're sure to appreciate it. Los Gatos provides loads of information on how to select the best coffee, the art of roasting and brewing, how to home roast, and other tips guaranteed to make your coffee taste its finest.

You'll also get plenty of help picking out the blend that's right for you through informative pages describing each of the coffees sold at Los Gatos.

Where

http://www.los-gatos.scruznet.com/los_gatos/businesses/los_gatos_coffee/storefront.html

Links

Our Coffees
Roasting and Cupping
Brewing

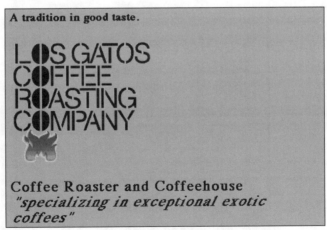

You can almost smell the beans roasting at Los Gatos.

145

All Things Herbivorous

The Vegetarian Resource Group, a non-profit organization dedicated to educating the public about vegetarianism, offers dozens of free pamphlets, brochures, electronic files, and more to vegetarians and those considering swearing off red meat and other critter fare.

Some of the information available includes:

- Vegetarianism in A Nutshell
- Vegan Diets in a Nutshell
- Vegetarian Nutrition for Teenagers

There's also a quarterly newsletter titled *Vegetarian Journal's Foodservice Update*, as well as excerpts from their bi-monthly magazine, *The Vegetarian Journal*. Haven't eaten your fill yet? There are also numerous articles to browse, as well as a hypertext list of restaurants, organizations, and other vegetarian-related sites around the world.

Where

http://catless.ncl.ac.uk/Vegetarian

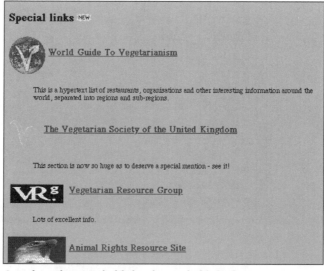

One cheeseburger—hold the cheese, hold the burger.

Links

Internet Vegetarian Resources

World Guide to Vegetarianism

Animal Rights Resource Site

Eat, Drink, and Surf the Web

Judging by this site, Amy Gale's two favorite things are cooking and computing. Maybe you don't think these two go together very well, but Amy's found a common denominator in the World Wide Web and created a comprehensive Who's Who, What's What, and Where's Where of culinary Net sites.

Regardless of your tastes, you'll find something here to satisfy your craving. From fat-free cooking to decadent desserts, this site has links to archives of ethnic recipes, restaurants around the world, recipe- and cooking-related software, links to coffee, tea, and beer pages, and much more.

Where

http://www.vuw.ac.nz/who/Amy.Gale/other-sites.html

Links

Too many to list. Browse around to find something that's sure to match your tastes.

Where Can I Plug In the Cookbook?

You have an electric oven, an electric can opener, and maybe even an electric potato peeler ("Only $9.95 and operators are standing by!"), so why not an electric cookbook? These DOS shareware programs will make life in the cooking lane go a little bit smoother by helping you keep your recipes organized, fine tune your diet, create shopping lists—even do the dishes! (Well, maybe when you register....)

Where

http://www.acs.oakland.edu/oak/SimTel/msdos/food.html

Download

dw_cook.zip

mcook136.zip

nutri321.zip

prm.zip

qbook100.zip

 This site has lots of other great cooking-related recipes. Unfortunately, lack of space keeps me from listing them all. Download a copy of the index to see what else is offered.

Take-Out of Africa

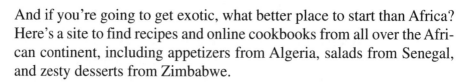

Tired of cheeseburgers, pizza, and Cheetos for dinner? Of course you're not. These foods are staples of every red-blooded, artery-clogged American's diet. Why, giving up junk would be like telling Mom and her apple pie to take a hike. Still, an occasional adventure into exotic dishes never hurts (permanently), if for no other reason than to help you garner new-found respect for anything that comes in a Styrofoam box.

And if you're going to get exotic, what better place to start than Africa? Here's a site to find recipes and online cookbooks from all over the African continent, including appetizers from Algeria, salads from Senegal, and zesty desserts from Zimbabwe.

You may not want to load the images when you access this site unless you've got a lot of time on your hands (there are 65 images on the home page alone), but if you're interested in experimenting with some exotic culinary creations, these African cookbooks are *the* place to begin.

Where

http://www.african.upenn.edu/African_Studies/Cookbook/

Links

Dozens of links to online recipes and cookbooks with an African flair

Boat Drinks for Parrotheads

If you have to ask what a parrothead is, then you're probably not one. But Jimmy Buffett's fans aren't the only ones who appreciate the occasional trip to Margaritaville—it's the trip back that's the painful part of the journey.

So if you can't change your latitude, at least change your attitude by surfing over to Toby "The Cyber-Parrothead" Gibson's Web page for the best spirit concoctions on the Net. You'll find recipes from the basics like the Cubra Libre, Mai Tai, and Margarita to the more creative—like the Martinique Martini, Hop Skip and Go Naked, and Margarita Jell-O. Last call!

Where

http://www.ils.nwu.edu/%7Eapril/buffett/tobyboat.html

Links

Beers, Lagers and Whatever Ales You

Party Drinks

Odds & Ends

Like Toby's disclaimer says, these drinks can give you dain bramage— uh, brain damage—so imbibe with caution.

Do You Have a Reservation?

Tired of the same old thing for dinner? Maybe you need a night on the town. But first you've got to pick the town. From Tuscaloosa, Alabama to Wakefield, Virginia, here's an incredible compilation of restaurant reviews organized by state. Looking for something a little more worldly?

There's also an excellent international guide with listings from over a dozen countries.

There are also links to several other Internet sites devoted to gourmets and gourmands alike. John Troyer pleads insanity for ever having created this list in the first place, but his loss of mental stability is everyone else's gain as he takes you on a culinary cruise across the Web.

Where

http://www.cmpharm.ucsf.edu/~troyer/dish/diningout.html

Links

Comprehensive Sites

US Sites

International Sites

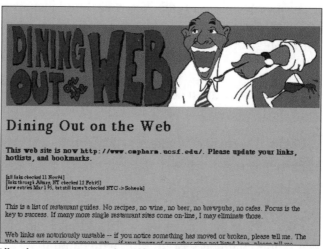

Like the motto says: Enjoy Life, Eat Out More Often

Country Cookin'

If you can't come to the restaurant, let the restaurant come to you. That seems to be the attitude at Country Fare. Tucked away in Midtown Palo Alto, California, Country Fare serves up blue ribbon country-style cooking just like Mom never made. Great for Palo Altians, bad for the rest of us.

But now Country Fare is making some of their recipes available on the Web, along with information on ordering their cookbook, *Country Fare for City Folk*, featuring over 200 easy-to-prepare meals. Try a couple of these recipes and I guarantee you'll keep coming back. Even if you never get there in the first place.

Where

http://www.service.com/cf/book.html

Links

Table of Contents

Find out what's cookin' at Country Fare.

The Dessert Page from Hell

One of the most important, yet often overlooked, food groups is, of course, dessert. No other group has gotten a worse rap. Sure, it might contain a few more calories than all your other meals of the day combined, and nutritionally it's beyond redemption, but dessert isn't food, it's *medicine*.

This site dedicates itself to "the finer things in life," namely that part of the meal reserved for pure indulgence. You'll find great recipes to satisfy the most saccharine of sweet tooths, guaranteed to give you the leverage you need to make your kids obey your every command. After all, no parent ever said, "Eat all you liver and you can have more broccoli," right?

Where

http://www.aus.xanadu.com/GlassWings/food/recipe.html

Links

The Chocolate Biscuits of Doom

Hotcha-cha Nachos

Really Gross Over-Sweet Popcorn Balls

 You're welcome to send me samples of anything you make here. No treat will be considered too small, no package will be refused (unless it comes C.O.D., of course).

I Simply Must Have Your Recipe!

Combine one part technology with one part creativity, then mix in input from thousands of Internauts, and you've got the ingredients for some exciting and delicious recipe ideas. This site has gathered together recipes, electronic cookbooks, and menu planners into one site you're sure to enjoy.

With a definite slant toward the vegetarian crowd, Recipes from the Net includes lots of great Chinese recipes, archives from the Usenet recipe newsgroups, the online magazine *Electronic Gourmet Guide*, and more. Definitely the place to go to whet your appetite.

Where

http://alpha.acast.nova.edu/fun/food.html

Links

Wine Enthusiasts

Things Possibly Involving Dead Animals and Possibly Not

Usenet Cookbook

International Food Information Council

Everyday, new research on food and nutrition is reported, but the sheer volume of data has made it increasingly difficult to stay on top of the latest findings. Inevitably, much of this information goes unreported to the public and those responsible for shaping food policy.

The International Food Information Council home page.

Consequently, while a larger number of consumers today are more aware than ever of the relationship between diet and health, they don't always have the information to make informed decisions about the foods they eat. The International Food Information Council (IFIC) Foundation was created to help communicate information about food safety and the role of nutrition in health to the general public and policy shapers. This non-profit organization has now made accessing this important information much easier by allowing anyone who's interested to access its research via the Web.

Where

http://ificinfo.health.org/

Links

Healthy Eating During Pregnancy

Children's Nutrition

Sorting Out the Facts About Fat

These are the kinds of Web pages that (finally) make you feel as though you're getting a valuable return from your tax dollars.

Safety First

Safety in the kitchen means more than keeping your fingers away from the blades while you perform your steak-knife juggling act for Uncle Al and Aunt Freda. It means washing your hands *before* you start juggling. And *never* put the hot dogs back on the plate after dropping them, unless you're positive nobody saw you. Of course, not everyone shares my common sense, so it's a good thing you can access the Florida Agricultural Information Retrieval System's guide to food safety and handling.

In addition to providing some great tips on food safety for babies and young children, home canning, and information on pesticides, maybe this collection will help me decide the best way to prepare and serve my little culinary treat cum lab experiment.

Where

http://hammock.ifas.ufl.edu/text/he/foodsf.html

Links

Recreational Seafood Safety

Egg Handling Handbook

Botulism: It Only Takes a Taste!

Are You a Winer?

Whether you're a casual oenophile ("Tastes great! Less filling!") or a seasoned connoisseur of fine vintages ("Pompous, yet alluring with a rather Bohemian sort of obsequiousness"), you'll find much to enjoy at The Wine Page. While primarily covering the wines of Washington State, The Wine Page includes links to several other wine sites around the globe.

You'll find an archive of tasting notes, as well as a tour of Washington wineries. You can even join the Virtual Tasting Group, in which you buy a set of pre-determined wines, taste them, and share your opinions.

Where

http://augustus.csscr.washington.edu/personal/bigstar-mosaic/wine.html

Links

Tasting Archive

Tour of Washington Wineries

The Wine Net Newsletter

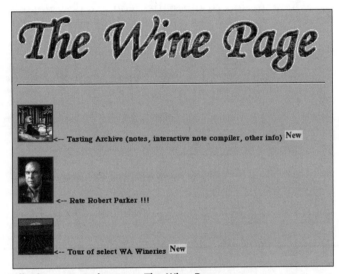

All winers are welcome at The Wine Page.

The Recipe for Success

If you're the kind of person who keeps recipes in a shoebox, it's time somebody brought you kicking and clawing from the Dark Ages into the 21st century. You probably balance your checkbook once a month with a computer, so doesn't it make sense to optimize the hours you spend in the kitchen every day?

Here are a few of the many Windows shareware programs you can download to help ease your domestic burden a little. There are recipe organizers, grocery managers, electronic cookbooks, and, when it all gets to be too much, a professional bartender.

Where

http://www.acs.oakland.edu/oak/SimTel/win3/food.html

Download

bartn21a.zip

cookw110.zip

gc218.zip

 There are lots of other files you can download here. I couldn't try them all, so let me know which are your favorites.

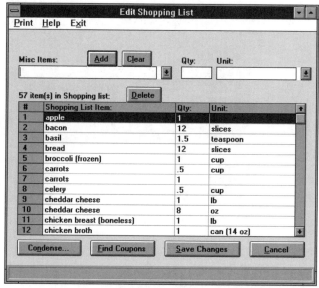

Let The Grocery Consumer lend a cyberhand in the kitchen.

A Drive-Thru On the Information Highway

Here's a great site to help the culinarily challenged learn the difference between a sieve and a salad bowl, a garlic press and a vegetable grater, a...well, you get the idea.

Actually, this Web page includes information on three of the most important life-sustaining elements for writers: food, coffee, and beer. You can see why this is one of my favorite sites.

Where

http://pubweb.ucdavis.edu/Documents/Quotations/web/drivethru.html

Links

Vegetarian

Coffee

Homebrew

Godiva Chocolate

To paraphrase Patrick Henry: "Give me chocolate—especially the caramel-filled ones with marshmallows on top—or give me death!" This site is not for weight-conscious surfers. From Cocoa Clouds to Mocha Madness, these recipes are as tasty as they are fattening (funny how that works).

If you're looking for exotic drink recipes, you won't be disappointed. You'll find some absolutely decadent liqueur recipes that ought to be illegal. And if you don't know the difference between a torte and a tart, there's help to turn you into a true connoisseur, as well as a fascinating chronology of our 4,000-year obsession with anything—or anyone for that matter—dipped in chocolate.

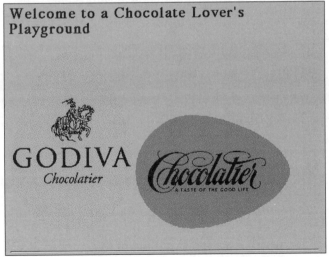

Careless recovering chocoholics can easily fall off the wagon right into this site.

Where

http://www.godiva.com/

Links

Recipes to be Approached with Reckless Abandon

Godiva Liqueur Recipes for the Utterly Indulgent

An Age-Old Obsession

Pay Homage to the Caffeine Gods

Caffeine junkies who can't function without a java jump start in the morning will want to point their browsers to Over the Coffee, a Web page devoted to spreading the Gospel According to Joe.

In addition to providing a great directory of mail-order coffee vendors, links to coffee-related newsgroups, and a fun-to-read coffee reference desk, Over the Coffee has lots of links to other coffee Web pages and resources for coffee professionals. And here's a special bonus: a listing of coffee nicknames (Peruvian love drops?) to add a little variety when you request another bucket of jolt juice.

Where

http://www.infonet.net/showcase/coffee

Links

Specialty Coffee/Espresso Drinks

Coffee Varieties, Blends & Roasts

Glossary Of Coffee Terminology

Songs Mentioning Coffee

Slimy Yet Satisfyin'

Looking for some high protein, low-fat dessert ideas your family will love? Here are some treats you won't be able to keep in the cookie jar. It's not that everyone will want to eat them, it's just that they may get up and walk away on their own.

The Iowa State entomology department has made available their list of culinary creepy crawlies on the Web for all to enjoy (your tuition dollars at work). Each recipe contains some variety of insect or invertebrate—and what a variety! I hear the Banana Worm Bread is to die for, though I know how hard it can be to find good army worms out of season. And the Rootworm Beetle Dip is right for any occasion.

I never really got the chance to test any of these recipes, busy as I am, but they sure sounded yummy. Now when your kids complain that there's nothing to eat, you can show them some of these recipes. Maybe *then* they'll stop complaining about the lime Jell-O.

Where

http://www.public.iastate.edu/~entomology/InsectsAsFood.html

Links

Iowa State's Entomology Image Gallery

The Smithsonian Institution

Biology Image Archive

Surfin' for Suds

The hops and barley crowd will love this site devoted to finding, linking, and disseminating every beer-related site that exists on the Internet—no small task. There's information on beer-of-the-month clubs, supply stores for home brewers, reviews on pubs and breweries around the world, and much more.

Have a question about brewing? Check out Ask the Brewmaster in the Beer Topic pages for answers from the experts. You can also download shareware and freeware for Windows, the Mac, DOS, or Unix.

Where

http://www.mindspring.com/~jlock/wwwbeer.html

Links

Ask the Brewmaster

Regional Beer Guides, Pubs & Brewpubs

Beer-related Software

Commercial Breweries

Beer Dictator Selection

Chugach Porter

88 Chugach "Brown Bear" Porter $2.69
   Kittle Co-op Brewers, Fremont, WA.

Early indications suggest good things are in the works here at this upstart-operation in Fremont, WA. Their spring-release Porter hits the mark with a careful balance of style and flavor. Brewed in a softer style for the warming, spring weather, this Porter fuses healthy doses of black-patent and chocolate malts with a trio of hops (Cascade, Centennial, and Willamette) to create a subtly charming drink. Strong chocolate overtones with hints of toffee and butter emerge on the lingering finish. Sure, some may bemoan the move towards styles emphasizing charm and finesse over pomp and tradition. Then again, many of these same folks are responsible for 200-odd years of uptight European brewing.

One of several homebrew labels worth browsing through at this site.

Recipes Unlimited

This site is your window into possibly the largest collection of recipes available on the Web and the Internet. You'll find literally thousands of recipes—one for each day of the rest of your life if you just *hate* the idea of falling into a routine. Of course, if you love to cook, accessing this recipe archive will probably become a routine if not an addiction.

There are actually several recipe archives you can access from this starting point. A good bet is to click on the first GO button that appears. From here, you can navigate through a list of recipes by category and by dish—from A to Z.

Where

http://nearnet.gnn.com/wic/cook.04.html

Links

You gotta be kidding. I couldn't even *begin* to list them all.

The first GO button actually takes you to the recipe archives of the rec.food.recipes newsgroup. So if you like what you find here, you might want to subscribe to this group.

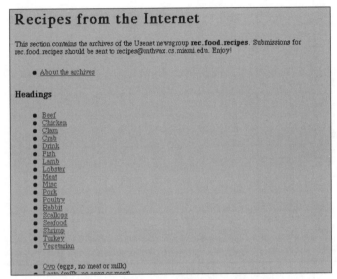

This list shows some of the categories of recipes you can access. For each category, dozens and sometimes hundreds of recipes are available.

Where to Find More Goodies

With so much to see and do on the Web, who's got time to eat? Go make a snack, then come back and try some of these sections for more food and cooking ideas:

- Try the *Health and Nutrition* section for great tips on eating right.
- The *International* section shows you eating and drinking precautions to take when traveling in foreign countries.

FREE $TUFF

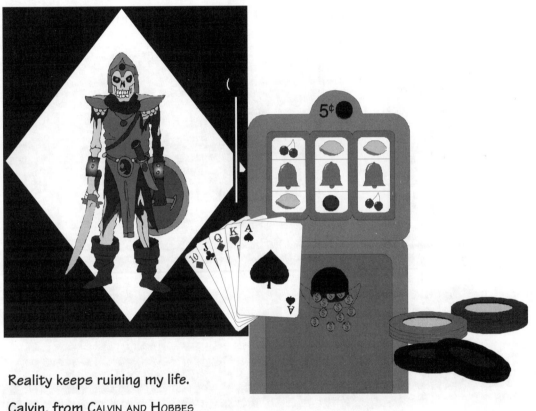

Reality keeps ruining my life.

Calvin, from CALVIN AND HOBBES

Games

It's Just a Game

Graphical gaming across the Net? You'd better believe it! And nobody's doing it better than Outland. And with a free five-hour trial offer, there's no reason not to give this site a try (other than the fact that you might not be a Mac user with a MacTCP-based Internet connection).

Try your hand against other Net users around the world with games like:

- Spaceward Ho!
- Backstab
- Galley
- Reversi
- Go
- Hearts
- Backgammon
- Chess

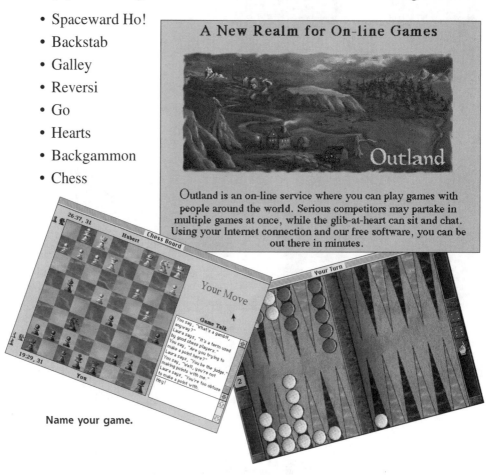

Name your game.

The software needed to get started is free, and you can download it right from Outland's home page. Depending on how serious you take your gaming, you can play multiple games at once, or just watch and chat with other spectators. True hardcore gamers can even save their matches as QuickTime movies.

Where

http://www.outland.com/

Links

The Games

The Pricing

The Software

After your five free hours are up, Outland charges a flat $9.95 per month, which allows you to play as much as you'd like with no hourly fees. Hear that CompuServe, AOL, and Prodigy?

High Rolling on the Web

Who says you have to go all the way to Vegas or Monte Carlo to feel the thrill of losing all your (or your significant other's) hard-earned silver dollars in those bottomless coin eaters affectionately known as slot machines? This site doesn't offer the potential payoff of those towns' one-armed bandits, but neither will you risk the potential losses.

Just a mouse-click away, the Internet Slot Machine lets you try your luck for free. If you still miss the thrill of going against the real thing, just drive by one of the casinos and toss your money out the window. Think of the time you'll save.

Where

http://www.datawave.net/slotmachine/register.html

Links

WebFax

Interesting and/or Useful things at this site

Games for Heretics

It's not just the noncomformists who are going to love this shareware game. Anybody looking for the thrilling pace of Doom coupled with the feel of an online Dungeons and Dragons will be unable to turn off Heretic. Though the gore factor is about what

If you long for the days of Pong or Pac-Man, you'd better skip this site.

you'd expect from id Software (do those guys stay up nights thinking of bizarre, grotesque ways of doing someone in?) you won't be disappointed in this action-filled predecessor to Wolfenstein and Doom.

This shareware version of Heretic contains the first episode, *City of the Damned*, complete with flying gargoyles, golems, and axe-wielding undead warriors (just another day in cyberspace). Those of you who get hooked, which, judging by the sales figures, will be just about everyone, can order even more episodes from id Software for a price.

Where

http://www.crayola.cse.psu.edu/~bielby/id/heretic.main.html

Links

ftp.cdrom.com (to download a copy)

Artifacts

Cheat Codes/Secrets

Weapons

 This game runs in the Gargantuan Download category—about 3 megabytes—so bring a good book to read while you wait, especially if you're using any modem under 28.8 baud. Is it worth it? A lot of people think so.

Luck Be a Lady, Tooniiiiiiight!

Cyber Mavericks can bet it all playing high stakes, cutthroat, winner-take-all blackjack against a virtual dealer. You'll be surprised at how courageous your betting becomes when you're playing with electronic cash. It's a great way to hone your gambling skills before you take that junket to Atlantic City.

The Blackjack Engine works like the real thing. It starts you with $1,000, but after providing you with a quick review of the rules, you're on your own. Card counters will be interested to know that hands are dealt from a stack of six decks, and you're constantly updated on how many decks remain. You can hit, stand, double—then clear out to make room for the next sucker—er, surfer—once you've lost all your virtual money.

Where

http://www.datawave.net/blackjack/bj.html

Links

Whitehouse

Music Through a Fax Machine

Weather

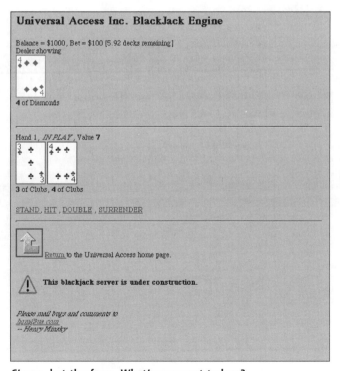

C'mon, bet the farm. What've you got to lose?

Let the Games Begin

Videophiles and game junkies will love the fact that they don't have to unplug to get their fix of game talk. Each month *Game Bytes* magazine, an online trade journal for PC gamers, brings you the latest on IBM/MS-DOS diskette and CD-ROM games, Super Nintendo cartridges, and Sega Genesis cartridge and CD-ROM formats.

In addition to great previews of games yet to be released, you'll get hot tips and screen shots to help you get the most out of the games you already have. There's also news, interviews, and lots of interesting talk about industry rumors.

Where

http://sunsite.unc.edu/GameBytes/

Links

Links to current issues, as well as back issues you can browse.

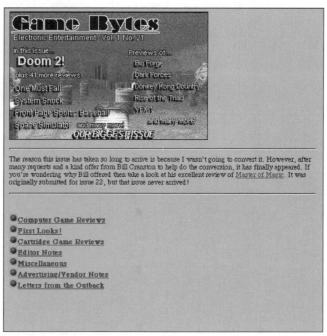

Pick a game, any game.

Crossword Grid Generator

The Sympathy Crossword Grid Editor for Windows is an editor in name only; it does everything but provide the clues. You simply choose the size of the grid, the length and direction of the "lights" (crossword-ese for where the words go), and fill in any particular words you want included in the puzzle. Sympathy quickly fills in the remaining lights from a huge database of words, then numbers the squares. You might have more fun playing with this easy-to-use puzzle creator than you would actually solving a puzzle.

Where

http://www.acs.oakland.edu/oak/SimTel/win3/educate.html

Download

symp10.zip

 Don't bother trying to save your puzzle until you've registered. Only registered software has the Save feature enabled. But this one's too good *not* to purchase.

Creating crosswords doesn't have to leave
you puzzled.

169

A Citupre's Thwro a Soutnadh Dosrw

After you've blown up all of the aliens in the galaxy for the umpteenth time, here are a couple of games that will help get the blood flowing back to your cerebral cortex. DeJumble lets you race the clock as you try to descramble three- and four-letter words. Just click on Start Practice, then click on the jumbled word and type the correct word over it. Hit Tab to get to the next word, and so on. Click on Solve to stop the clock and check your answers. The registered version lets you solve words with as many as six letters.

Winzle is sort of an electronic jigsaw puzzle in which you point and click to move pieces around. If you get stuck, there are plenty of help screens to get you back on track. The registered version provides a converter that lets you create Winzle puzzles from your own bitmaps.

Where

http://www.acs.oakland.edu/oak/SimTel/win3/entertn.html

Download

dejumb11.zip

winzle.zip

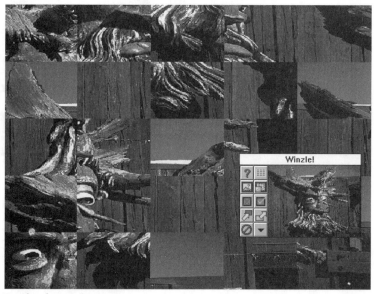

Tge hte itreucp?

170

Games Galore

If you're looking for a goldmine of shareware games to try, you'll hit the mother lode here. This site offers a huge variety and number of games for you to enjoy. And isn't that the *real* reason you bought your computer?

You'll find somewhere in the neighborhood of 200 games, from the classics (solitaire, cribbage, Tetris) to the wild (like squishing bugs on your desktop, making subliminal messages appear on your screen, shooting everything that appears, and so on). If you don't find something here to enjoy, you're probably incapable of having fun anyway.

Where

http://coyote.csusm.edu/cwis/winworld/games.html

Links

No links, just games. Now isn't that nice for a change?

One noticeable flaw with this site: You're not given any indication as to the size of the program you're downloading. Most seem to be relatively small, but you'll never be sure of that, so consider downloading as part of the adventure. Also, some of these programs require you to have a Visual Basic DLL (Dynamic Link Library) file called VBRUN100.DLL, VBRUN200.DLL, or VBRUN300.DLL loaded in your WINDOWS\ SYSTEM directory in order to run them. If you don't already have these, you can download the zipped files from:

http://www.acs.oakland.edu/oak/SimTel/win3/dll.html

Going Doooooown

If you liked Doom, you'll love Descent, or so claim the designers at Parallax Software. In Descent, you play the part of an outside contractor working for the Post Terran Minerals Corporation, a company known for its power, technology, and shameless materialism. Sounds like a couple of my past employers.

I'm sure you've guessed PTMC's evil ways are about to come back to haunt them, and bodies in blue suits are no doubt about to start flying. Next thing you'll know, it'll be your job to save the world—and collect a little overtime in the process. Descent is a heart-pounding, gut-wrenching, edge-of-your-seat experience. Aside from that, it's nothing like the real world.

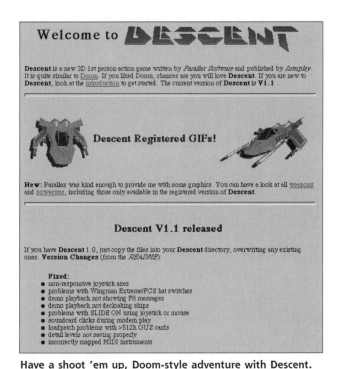

Have a shoot 'em up, Doom-style adventure with Descent.

Where

http://doomgate.cs.buffalo.edu/descent/

Links

janus.library.cmu.edu (to download a copy of Descent)

Another Descent Page

.coNsOle .wORlD's .viDeO .gAMe .daTabASE

Somebody's got to tell these guys that their Caps key sticks. But if you can get past the crazy type without your eyes crossing, you'll find Console World to be a great place to get the latest information on the hottest video games.

You'll get lots of links to images, FAQs, and newsgroups that discuss your favorite games, cheat sheets to give you a little—or a lot of—help when you need it, gaming magazines you can access on the Net, and much more.

Where

http://www.cm.cf.ac.uk/Games/index.html

Links

Doom!
.viDEo .gAme .inFoRMAtiOn
.imAgEs, .aRChiVeS, .maGAziNes .aNd .oTHer .siTes
.vIDeO .gamINg .newSGRoUp .lIsTS .anD .aRChiVES

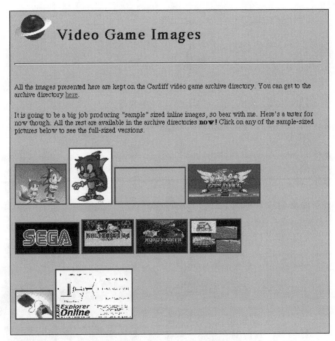

Info, images, and archives are available here for the hottest video games on the market.

Now You're Doomed

Here's the one that has set the standard for 3D action adventure for the home PC. Created by id Software, Doom takes you on a space-age, heart-pounding, highly addictive battle to the death against some of the scariest aliens you'll ever blow to bits.

In Doom, you're a space Marine stationed on Mars. Evil Corporation fiddles where it shouldn't and before you can say "I ain't afraid of no aliens," it's you against the bad guys, and they're taking no prisoners. This Web site points you to the best Web locations for downloading Doom, getting updates, finding other Doom addicts, and much more.

Where

http://doomgate.cs.buffalo.edu/index-html.html

Links

Descent

Heretic

Quake

 This chapter may seem a little heavy on id Software hype, but let's face it—no other company comes close to matching the popularity of id's shareware games. My conscience is clear.

How much doom can you take?

Games

Master of Your Domain

It's not always easy to get in at the GamesDomain home page, but when you do you'll see that it's worth it. This Web site provides links to hundreds of shareware games, magazines, game-related home pages, and much more for Amigas, PCs, and Macs.

In addition, you'll find dozens of FTP links to find even more games, help and hints for when you're stuck, and many gaming FAQs. So, what are you waiting for?

Where

http://wcl-rs.bham.ac.uk/GamesDomain

Links

Way too many to list. Browse and enjoy.

MacFun Stuff Unlimited

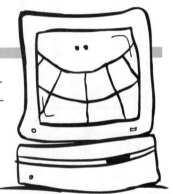

Robert Lentz has been busy recently, constructing links to great Mac software for several categories. Apparently, Robert still has time to have fun, since his Classic Macintosh Games page is loaded with links to Mac games you can download for free.

For each game listed here, Robert provides a brief description along with the required screen resolution and, in some cases, an opinion or two about the game itself. If you're a game player and you've got a Mac, you'll definitely want to add this one to your Hotlist or Bookmark list.

Where

http://www.astro.nwu.edu/lentz/mac/recreation/classic-mac-games.html

Links

Don't get me started. There are too many to list.

Where to Find More Goodies

If you've tried all the game-related sites mentioned in this section, but are still hungry for more, you've got entirely too much time on your hands. But who am I to judge? Try these sections for even more:

- Go to *Science and Technology* to dissect a computer-animated frog—sort of an online version of that classic board game, Operation.
- Look for lots of links to sports-related games in the *Sports, Recreation, and Hobbies* section.
- The *Travel* section includes a geography program you can download.

FREE $TUFF

Reader, suppose you were an idiot.
And suppose you were a member of
Congress. But I repeat myself.

Mark Twain

Government
and Politics

POW/MIA Archive

The Vietnam Conflict invokes a myriad of emotions and memories, but none are so powerful as those relating to the U.S. men and women killed, imprisoned, or still missing in Southeast Asia.

This database, titled "Correlated and Uncorrelated Information Relating to Missing Americans in Southeast Asia," has been established to assist researchers and investigators interested in U.S. Government documents pertaining to Vietnam. Researchers can access information by last names, country names, service branches, keywords, and statements such as "downed over Laos."

Where

http://lcweb2.loc.gov/pow/powquery.html

Links

POW/MIA Home Page

Library of Congress Home Page

Life, Liberty, and the World Wide Web

When Thomas Jefferson wrote nearly 200 years ago that "to seek out the best through the whole Union we must resort to other information," he no doubt had the World Wide Web in mind. And why not? After all, this man was truly ahead of his time.

In the spirit of Thomas Jefferson, THOMAS—a database of legislative information on the Internet—is one of the best things to come out of Washington since the Redskins. You'll find the full text of all versions of House and Senate bills searchable by keywords or bill number, plus background information on how laws are made. You can even download the full text of the Congressional Record.

Where

http://thomas.loc.gov/

Links

C-SPAN Gopher
House of Representatives Constituent E-Mail

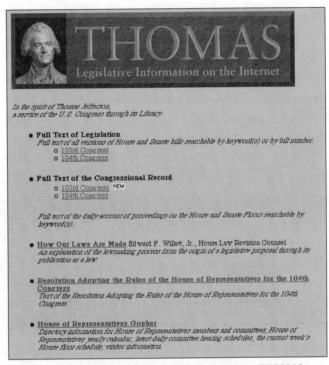

"In the full tide of successful experiment" comes THOMAS.

Future enhancements to THOMAS will include summaries and chronologies of legislation integrated with the full text of bills, so stay tuned.

This Is One Big Library

Though still under construction at press time, the Library of Congress Global Electronic Library is already well on its way to being one of the best resources for government and Web information.

The Global Electronics Library includes information on all branches of the U.S. government as well as links to a huge assortment of government agencies wired to the Internet. There's also lots of information on Internet resources and Web how-to's, links to local and state governments, and maps of individual states.

Where

http://lcweb.loc.gov/global/globalhp.html

Links

USA Search Engines

State and Local Governments

Newspapers, Current Periodicals & Government Documents

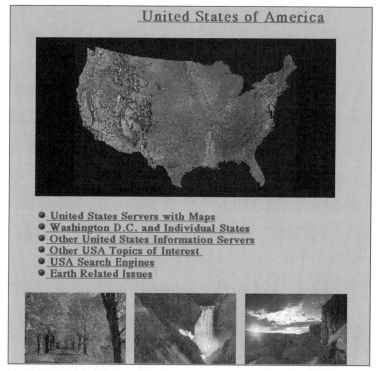

My country 'tis of thee.

Smoking Guns, Grassy Knolls, and Nazi UFOs

Who doesn't love a good conspiracy theory now and then? If you believe that everything from fluoridated water to pre-sliced bread is some

kind of government plot to control the minds of the young and impressionable, this site is for you. If you like to chuckle at the conspiritorial crowd, this site is *definitely* for you. In addition to excerpts from Jonathan Vankin and John Whalen's popular book, *50 Greatest Conspiracies of All Time*, you'll find conspiracy theories galore. Some of the chapters excerpted are:

- The Jonestown Massacre: CIA Mind Control Run Amok?
- Aliens on the Moon
- Those Christ Kids: Descendants of Jesus or Scam Artistes Extraordinaire?

Look! Up in the sky!

Spanning the spectrum from plausible to improbable to downright ludicrous, this site includes links to many other paranoia-filled Web sites, with theories on the truth behind UFOs, the Kennedy assassination, satanic cults, and more. First make sure you're not being followed, then check out this site to find out what the media have been covering up.

Where

http://www.webcom.com:80/~conspire/

Links

Conspiracy Archives

Conspiracy Currents

Sinister Connections

Presidential Libraries

The Presidential Library system began in 1939 when the Franklin D. Roosevelt Library became the first Presidential archival depository. Since then, all succeeding Presidential libraries have been constructed with private funds or funds from non-federal agencies. Now, information about each of these libraries can be accessed using the Internet.

While this site at the National Archives and Records Administration (NARA) is only a clearinghouse, it does provide a fascinating look at the breadth and depth of historic materials contained at the nine Presidential libraries. Included is information on:

- more than 260 million pages of text
- more than one million still photographs
- more than one million feet of motion picture film
- hundreds of hours of disc, audiotape, and videotape recordings
- more than 280,000 museum objects

With that kind of output, how did these guys ever find time to be leaders of the free world?

Where

http://gopher.nara.gov:70/1/inform/library

Links

Nearly everybody's here, from Franklin D. Roosevelt to Ronald Reagan, with only Harry Truman missing the show.

Become a Washington Insider

The Washingtonian, published since 1965, has now entered the '90s with *Washingtonian Online.* In addition to reviews of the best restaurants and shopping around the Beltway, this insider's guide to the nation's capital includes travel tips, jokes (no, I'm not talking about exclusive interviews with Congressional representatives), and need-to-know info for local residents.

Be sure to browse the links to the Library of Congress and other specialized libraries around Washington, DC, as well as the Home Shopping Guide for the best in auctions, outlets, and specialty stores. Being an insider *does* have its privileges.

Where

http://www.infi.net/washmag/

Links

Business, Careers and Investing

Children, Schools and Community Service

Health and Medicine

Mr. Internet goes to Washington.

I Do Solemnly Swear...

Available in a text-only format, as a series of images, or as an illustrated text narration, the Clinton Inaugural Tour takes you on a fascinating journey through Bill Clinton's first official day in office.

Compiled from photographs in the Smithsonian Archives, the Inaugural Tour includes dozens of thumbnail images taken throughout Inauguration Day, all of which you can download. Choose a format, then enjoy.

Where

http://sunsite.unc.edu/doug_m/pages/inaugural-tour.html

Links

Text-Only Format

Series of Images

Illustrated Text Narration

 There are a lot of images here that can take some time to load, especially during peak hours. While the best format is the Illustrated Text Narration, you can also try the Text-Only Format for descriptions of the photos, then click on the ones you'd like to view.

President Clinton does his first number on—er, for—the American people.

Know Any CyberSocialists?

According to its statement of principles, the Socialist Party's goal is to establish a non-racist, classless, feminist democracy that places people's lives under their own control. Sounds good on paper, but it's quite another thing to actually enact it, as the Soviets and others have discovered. Founded in 1901, the Socialist Party USA hopes to bring its message of social change into the 21st century via cyberspace.

Hey, who am I to judge? Whether you believe that socialism is true democracy or think that its members are just another bunch of radical left-wingers, you'll agree that the information here makes fascinating—albeit somewhat biased—reading for anyone interested in the evolution of our two-party system. You'll also find lots of other information about joining the Socialist Party, Socialist journals, Internet discussion groups, and more.

Where

http://sunsite.unc.edu/spc/index.html

Links

The Socialist Party: Who We Are

Socialism as Radical Democracy: The SP Statement of Principles

How To Be A Socialist

A Brief History of the Socialist Party

Socialists Around The World

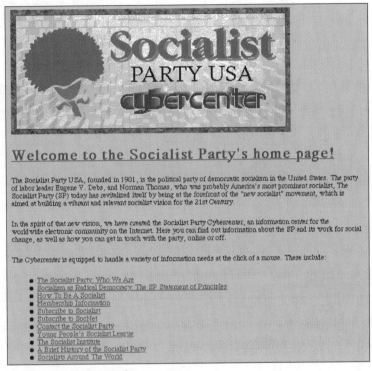

Welcome to the Socialist Party's home page!

The Socialist Party USA, founded in 1901, is the political party of democratic socialism in the United States. The party of labor leader Eugene V. Debs, and Norman Thomas, who was probably America's most prominent socialist, The Socialist Party (SP) today has revitalized itself by being at the forefront of the "new socialist" movement, which is aimed at building a vibrant and relevant socialist vision for the 21st Century.

In the spirit of that new vision, we have created the Socialist Party Cybercenter, an information center for the worldwide electronic community on the Internet. Here you can find out information about the SP and its work for social change, as well as how you can get in touch with the party, online or off.

The Cybercenter is equipped to handle a variety of information needs at the click of a mouse. These include:

- The Socialist Party: Who We Are
- Socialism as Radical Democracy: The SP Statement of Principles
- How To Be A Socialist
- Membership Information
- Subscribe to Socialist
- Subscribe to SocNet
- Contact the Socialist Party
- Young People's Socialist League
- The Socialist Institute
- A Brief History of the Socialist Party
- Socialists Around The World

The Socialist Party USA home page.

Do You Know Where Your Tax Dollars Went?

As one senator said: "A billion here, a billion there . . . Pretty soon you're talking about real money." Where does it all go? FinanceNet can help answer that question. By letting you participate directly in the sharing of ideas about how your tax dollars are spent, FinanceNet is helping to improve fiscal accountability at all levels of government.

Comprised of federal executive agencies and departments, as well as international, state, and local governments, FinanceNet crosses all public/

The FinanceNet home page.

private sector boundaries to provide a huge electronic library of government financial information to those who are footing the bill—*you*. This global effort was designed to help improve the way governments manage the public's resources.

Established by Vice President Gore's National Performance Review and operated by the National Science Foundation, FinanceNet provides access to general government financial management documents, news, announcements, and notices.

Where

http://www.financenet.gov/

Links

World Bank

NASA Goddard SFC

Treasury

WWW General Resources and Starting Points

For complete information on all FinanceNet services, send a blank E-mail message to info@financenet.gov.

Opening the Doors

Throughout the Cold War, nearly all of the nuclear testing carried out by the United States was shrouded in secrecy. Through the Freedom of Information Act, many of the documents pertaining to these tests are now being made available to the general public.

With the promise of even more to come, the Department of Energy has created OPENNET, a bibliographic database consisting of over 250,000 DOE documents. This online index, consisting mostly of previously classified documents, provides a fascinating glimpse into the history of nuclear

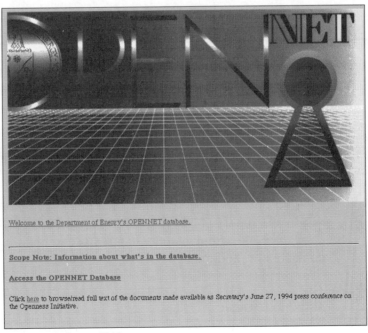

Welcome to the Department of Energy's OPENNET database.

_____

Scope Note: Information about what's in the database.

Access the OPENNET Database

Click here to browse/read full text of the documents made available as Secretary's June 27, 1994 press conference on the Openness Initiative.

Open up and say ahhhh.

testing by the United States, including human radiation experiments, nuclear testing, radiation releases, fallout results, and much more.

While this is only an index, documents can be ordered through E-mail (read the FAQ to find out how), and users will eventually be able to access many of the documents directly.

Where

http://www.doe.gov/html/osti/opennet/opennet1.html

Links

Access the OPENNET Database

Begin Searching the Database Now

Frequently Asked Questions

 Until the Department of Energy starts practicing a little energy conservation itself, you'll end up wasting a lot of it waiting for the graphics here to load. While some of the pages may be large, it's still worth the wait to see what's available here.

A Change in Policy

Did you know that a recent policy change proposal by the FCC could limit 911 emergency access for cellular phone users? Here's a Web site that's attempting to harness the power of the Internet into an online lobbying organization of sorts. Policy.Net keeps Internauts abreast of public policy issues and changes affecting the communications industry, how they might be affected, and what to do about it.

You'll get the facts on different policies and issues related to the FCC, what you can do to make a difference, how to contact key policy makers by E-mail and sample E-mail letters to send them, dates they should be contacted by, and more.

Where

http://policy.net/

Links

CapWeb: A Guide to the U.S. Congress

Policy Issues

Publications

Campaigns

Alerts

Only you—and 25 million other Internauts—can make a difference.

Once Upon a Politically Correct Bedtime Story

Apparently I'm not the only one who bristles at the Political-Correctness craze sweeping the country, and here's proof: *Politically Correct Bedtime Stories*, the best-selling spoof by James Finn Garner. This book takes the madness of political correctness to new lows by putting a PC spin on many of children's literature's most classic stories.

In addition to ordering information, this site provides the full text from at least one story plus audio clips by Garner himself reading excerpts. This one is a lot of fun!

Where

http://www.mcp.com/general/news1/polit.html

Links

Cinderella

Chicken Little

Little Red Riding Hood

The Three Little Pigs

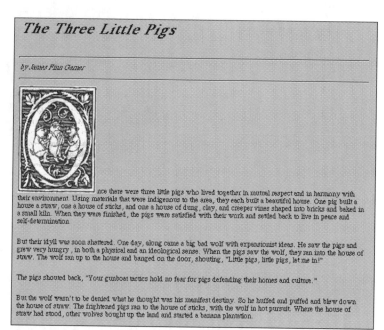

Mother Goose meets George Orwell.

House on the Hill

Do you know who your Congressional representative is? If you're like most Americans, you probably don't. But here's a site that can help you learn more about the people you're paying to represent you and how they're spending your tax dollars.

The U.S. House of Representatives Web site provides public access to legislative information, the text of recent bills, how your representative voted, legislative schedules, and much more. Plus, you'll find dozens of links to other valuable government resources like FedWorld, the Federal Information Center, and the President's Cabinet.

Where

http://www.house.gov/

Links

Who's Who and How Do I Contact Them

The Legislative Process

Schedules

Other Government Information Resources

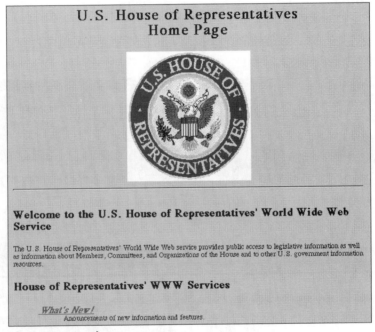

**U.S. House of Representatives
Home Page**

**Welcome to the U.S. House of Representatives' World Wide Web
Service**

The U.S. House of Representatives' World Wide Web service provides public access to legislative information as well
as information about Members, Committees, and Organizations of the House and to other U.S. government information
resources.

House of Representatives' WWW Services

What's New!
Announcements of new information and features.

I hate House work.

I Spy a Web Site

Pssst. The Central Intelligence Agency's Web server is so secret, after
you access it, you have to eat your hard drive. If you should decide to
take a peek, however, you'll find quite a lot of useful information here.

Actually, despite its covert reputation, the CIA offers a Web site that's
wide open to the public. Once you're in, you can access the CIA World
Factbook, about the best online almanac you'll find on the Internet, with
information about hundreds of countries around the world and their geography, people, politics, and more.

You also get *The Factbook on Intelligence*, a great link that provides lots of interesting information on the CIA, including its history, how to apply for a job, and fallacies about the organization itself.

Where

http://www.ic.gov

Links

Key Events in CIA's History

How to Obtain Publications and Maps Available to the Public

A bird's-eye view of CIA headquarters.

Always Look On the Right Side of Life

If you're not already saturated with conservatism, the Right Side of the Web will give you your fill. The Right Side gives you the latest on Rush, Newt, Reagan, and many other things certifiably, um, in right field. If you prefer dirtier fare, there's lots to read and hear about Whitewater, Al Gore, Presidential appointees, and much more.

Where

http://www.clark.net/pub/jeffd/index.html

Links

Newt Gingrich WWW Fan Club
Audio Clip Library

A World of Information

First introduced on the Internet in 1992, FedWorld was implemented to help make it easier for you and me, Joe and Jane Q Public, to access the many mountains of government documents made available each year. Originally linked to about 50 government bulletin boards, FedWorld has grown into an enormous clearinghouse of government information, with links to over 130 federal agencies.

Just how much documentation can one government produce?

In addition to links to government Telnet and FTP sites, FedWorld includes hundreds of links to agencies and documents on nearly any conceivable subject. From aeronautics and business to transportation and urban technology, you'll find something useful at FedWorld.

Where

http://www.fedworld.gov/

Links

Way too many to list. Start browsing to see what's available.

And the Reviews Are In

The majority of Americans believe that the U.S. Government spends too much and gives back too little; definitely not the best way to run a business. But then, if it were a business, there would have been a fire sale a long time ago. With this in mind, the National Performance Review was created to help

Al Gore, behind the wheel at the National Performance Review.

reshape government into a leaner, more cost-effective organization that will cost taxpayers less while delivering more—with your help.

This site includes the "tools" you need to help reshape government. You'll find lots of success stories from local and state governments, weekly progress updates, highlights of Phase II, and much more. Here's to a leaner—not meaner—government.

Where

http://www.npr.gov/

Links

Toolkit

Success Stories

From Red Tape to Results

The Last Frontier

Founded in 1990 to help ensure that "the principles embodied in the Constitution and the Bill of Rights are protected as new communications technologies emerge," the Electronic Freedom Foundation works to shape communications policy as it strives for online democracy for the 21st century. According to its charter, the EFF is a non-profit civil liberties organization working to protect freedom of expression, privacy, and access to online resources and information. In short, it's the EFF's task to make sure government laws and policies do not infringe on the rights of Internauts.

Sort of an online ACLU, the EFF sponsors legal cases in which it feels that the rights of Internauts have been violated. You can find a library of recent relevant court cases here, as well as an extensive library of other helpful EFF documents, alerts, and more.

Where

http://ftp.eff.org/

Links

Action Alerts

Legal Services

Civil Liberties

Free Telephone Hotline

Stop the Presses!

Since 1908, the National Press Club has been one of Washington's most prestigious institutions. With a membership that spans four generations of American and foreign journalists, as well as many of the 20th century's biggest newsmakers, the NPC has a fascinating history. Beginning with Teddy Roosevelt, 15 consecutive presidents have been members (two even announced their candidacies before the NPC), many of whose speeches to the NPC are included here.

Now that this prestigious institution is online, you can check out its transcripts of press conferences, search tools to help journalists get the most out of the Internet, and even download audio files of speeches by such notables as Al Gore, Garrison Keillor, and Margaret Thatcher.

Where

http://town.hall.org/places/npc/

Links

Leading Newsmakers

Research Services

The National Press Club

At around 30 megabytes apiece, these speeches aren't your run-of-the-mill downloads—but these aren't your run-of-the-mill speakers, either.

At Your Service

One thing you can count on with the federal government is that if you've ever signed your name on anything more official than a postcard, you can bet they have a record of it. This 14-page booklet, *Military Service Records in the National Archives*, explains how you can obtain military records on family members from all branches of the service from as far back as the Revolutionary War.

While, not surprisingly, some records are sketchy at best for some of the earlier years—primarily due to the British ransacking Washington in a little skirmish called the War of 1812—more recent files are very extensive. All the information you need to obtain records is explained here. Who knows, maybe you've got a bona fide hero somewhere in your family tree.

Where

http://www.gsa.gov/staff/pa/cic/misc.htm

Download

Military Service Records in the National Archives

A Day in the Life

While it may seem like Washington politics is nothing but a huge media circus, the fact is that only a fraction of the political wheelings and dealings

are ever seen by the public. Most of the grease that lubricates the Washington wheels is applied behind closed doors. This site shows a typical day in the not-so-typical life of President Gerald Ford. Included is a page from the President's daily diary, listing minute-by-minute his meetings and activities, photos from his April 28, 1975 public appearances, links to information about the people he met with, and more.

Just another day as president for Gerald Ford.

Where

http://http2.sils.umich.edu/FordLibrary/DayInTheLife.html

Links

President's Daily Diary

Where to Find More Goodies

Here's a small sampling of other government sites mentioned in this book:

- Those who lean slightly to the left will want to check out *Mother Jones* magazine in the *Books, Magazines, and Literature* section (this is also the section to check out for inaugural addresses of presidents).

- Government resources for Gulf War veterans can be found in the *International* section.

- You'll find a lot of government agencies plugged into the Net, including the National Science Foundation in the *Science and Technology* section.

 # FREE $TUFF

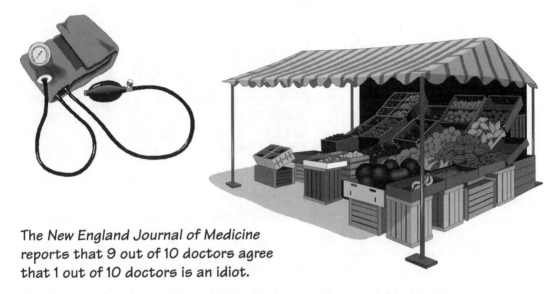

The *New England Journal of Medicine* reports that 9 out of 10 doctors agree that 1 out of 10 doctors is an idiot.

Jay Leno

Health and Nutrition

Drop It Like a Bad Habit

Sometimes it seems that trying to break a habit is more dangerous to your health—or to anyone who gets in your way—than the habit itself. If so, maybe you need to drop by HabitSmart. Created for anyone who suffers from some form of addictive behavior, the HabitSmart Web site

Break the habit.

includes information on how to rid yourself of addictive behavior and drop your bad habits like...well, a bad habit. Whether it's drug abuse, alcoholism, or relentless urges and cravings you're trying to deal with, HabitSmart points you to some help and offers many useful tips.

And if *you're* not the one with the addictive behavior, that doesn't mean you don't suffer. Parents will find lots of useful information for dealing with their children's experimentation with drugs and alcohol and how they can help get their kids off drugs. You'll also find the latest issue of *The Archivist,* a newsletter dealing with recent trends in addiction research, and a self-scoring questionnaire to determine your own level of problematic drinking.

Where

http://www.cts.com:80/~habtsmrt/

Links

Understanding Blood Alcohol Level

Coping with Urges

Smoking Reduction

Drawing On the Latest in Medicine

It's a science. No, it's an art. Whatever you decide, you're sure to agree that the Medical Illustrators' Home Page displays an impressive array of medical illustrations of the human anatomy, as well as surgical procedures from a variety of "artists-in-residence."

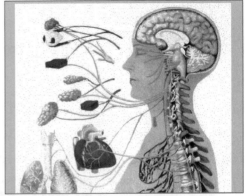

One of the many medical illustrations by artist Susan Gilbert you'll find at the Medical Illustrators' home page.

Fascinating and diverse, these illustrations take you on an awesome voyage through the human body, with illustrations ranging from the inside of the brain down to the circulatory system in the feet. How's that for comprehensive?

You'll also find some terrific links to a variety of medical sites and sounds on the Internet. Just what the doctor ordered!

Where

http://siesta.packet.net/med_illustrator/Welcome.html

Links

Medical Imaging
Veterinary Studies Home Page
Health Resources on the Internet

Here's Something to Smile at

To drill or not to drill? DentalNet may have the answer. The Internet's first online dental health resource, DentalNet allows users to explore new advances in dentistry and learn about dental health options. Users can read about bonding, extractions, crowns, the infamous root canal (I've never actually had the pleasure), and a lot more.

Plus, each month, new dental health tips are provided. A recent feature was titled *Painless Dentistry --Pulp Fiction or Virtual Reality?* Nothing like a dentist with a sense of humor.

Where

http://www.dentalnet.com/dentalnet/

Links

Dental Health Options

Dental Health Tips

Appointments

Rinse and spit.

 For another great dental site—though much more academic in nature—check out Sheffield University's Dental Education Resources on the Web (DERWeb) Project:

http://www.shef.ac.uk/uni/projects/der/derweb.html

Don't Eat the Software

According to one recent study, four of the six leading causes of death—diabetes, heart disease, cancer, and obesity—are related to nutrition. The nutritional software programs from NutriSoft will help you learn more about good nutrition and how you can learn to eat better and learn to be fit—not fat.

One of the programs, NutriSoft Weight Perfect, is based on the Surgeon General's Report on Nutrition and Health's dietary guidelines for weight reduction and prevention of obesity. This excellent program analyzes your food intake to help you reach your ideal weight through a balanced, flexible, and healthful variety of foods. While the software doesn't take the place of a diet program, it's ideal for helping you keep track of the foods you eat and understand better what good nutrition is all about.

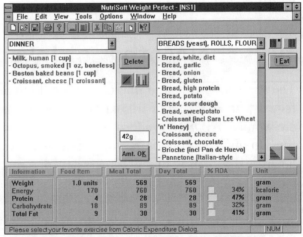

NutriSoft Weight Perfect, one of the many NutriSoft shareware programs.

Here's a listing of NutriSoft shareware you can download and try:

• NutriSoft Diabetic Nutrition for Windows

• High Blood Pressure Nutrition for Windows

• NutriSoft Healthy Heart Nutrition

- NutriSoft Lower Your Cholesterol
- NutriSoft Nutrition for Women
- NutriSoft Pyramid Weight Loss Diet
- NutriSoft Weight Perfect

Where

http://www.acs.oakland.edu/oak/SimTel/win3/food.html

Download

nsdn33.zip

nshbpn32.zip

nshhn35.zip

nslyc32.zip

nsnfw35.zip

nspwld34.zip

nswpw30.zip

Necessity Is the Mother of Invention

The statistics are staggering: Over 15 million people worldwide are infected with HIV, and nearly half of all adult cases being reported today are women. AIDS has indeed reached epidemic proportions. Once confined to small portions of the population, AIDS can strike anyone, whether heterosexual, a practitioner of safe sex, or a practitioner of no sex at all. No one is completely safe.

Now, thanks to a three-year grant from the National Science Foundation, the Clearinghouse for Networked Information Discovery and Retrieval (CNIDR) has set up this free informational site that helps you find information on the latest discoveries and patents in the battle against AIDS. Just enter a keyword or phrase to search for and you're instantly given a list of matches. You can then access the full patent, an abstract, its front page, and images of the patent. You even get a listing of similar patents.

Where

http://patents.cnidr.org/

Links

Access the Patent Databases

National Science Foundation

Smoke Gets in Your Eyes—and Nose and Mouth

Did you know that over a million youths become addicted to cigarettes each year, and that half of them will die from a tobacco-related illness? Not a pretty picture. A war is being waged against the tobacco industry right now, and groups like INFACT are on the front line. Contrary to what you may have heard, INFACT is not against smoking. They *are* against the marketing of cigarettes toward youths who may not have all the facts about the dangers of starting. (Can you say "Joe Camel?")

This site includes tons of information about INFACT's campaign to stop the marketing of tobacco to children and teenagers and how you can help. You'll find lots of facts, a list of companies owned by tobacco corporations (like Kraft, General Foods, and Jello-O), sample letters you can send to the heads of Philip Morris, R.J. Reynolds, and British American Tobacco, and even their toll-free numbers to let them know just how you feel.

Where

http://sunsite.unc.edu/boutell/infact/infact.html

Links

Tobacco Marketing to Young People

Letters For You To Send!

Tobacco Industry Deception Exposed

I've Got Rhythm

Okay, so a lot of people might include it in the same category as Tarot cards and horoscopes, but biorythm study nonetheless has a strong following.

205

Based on the non-scientific theory that humans are governed by rhythmic cycles (intellectual, emotional, and physical) that start on their birthdays, biorhythms supposedly peak and fall during a specific cycle of days. What's more, certain days in each cycle are considered "critical," especially if they coincide with a critical day in another cycle.

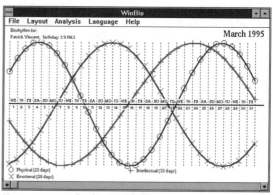

Have you got rhythm or blues?

Getting personal biorhythm analysis is now as close as your nearest Internet connection. Once you've downloaded Winbio 2.0 for Windows, just enter your name and birthdate to get an instant analysis of your biorhythms. Then check your spouse's to determine the safest time to drop any bad news.

Where

http://www.acs.oakland.edu/oak/SimTel/win3/biology.html

Download

winbio20.zip

Oh My Aching Hands

Hours of surfing the Net can lead to more than just falling asleep at the keyboard. Do you ever suffer from:

• Tightness, discomfort, stiffness, or pain in the hands, wrists, fingers, forearms, or elbows?

• Tingling, coldness, or numbness in the hands?

• Clumsiness or loss of strength and coordination in the hands?

You may suffer from Repetitive Strain Injury. As more and more people begin using computers, the number of RSI cases has started to mushroom.

The repetitive movements of typing and using a computer mouse can result in this serious and very painful condition that is far easier to prevent than to cure. Learn all about this potentially debilitating byproduct of the computer revolution and what you can do to prevent becoming one of its statistics.

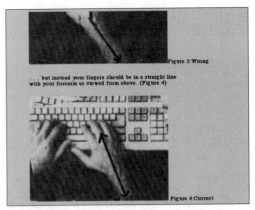

Help on preventing Repetitive Strain Injury.

You'll also find links to other great RSI resources, discussions on books about RSI, and even pictures and movies you can download showing you exercises to help prevent RSI.

Where

http://www.engr.unl.edu/ee/eeshop/rsi.html

Links

Occupational Safety and Health Service

Preventative Posture and Correct Technique

Typing Injury Frequently Asked Questions Archive

A Running Program for Your Running Program

If your idea of an invigorating run is a dash to the bar at the sound of "Last call," you might want to skip this section. But if you can recite personal bests, split times, and motivational quotes by Jim Fixx without breaking stride, you'll want to stick around.

Boston marathoners or even marathoner wannabe's will appreciate RunStat 3.0. This program includes a handy pace calculator and log book, keeps track of your total mileage and times, plots your training progress, and more. You could run a 10K while waiting for it to download (over 1 megabyte in its zipped format), but it'll be worth it at the finish line.

Where

http://www.acs.oakland.edu/oak/SimTel/win3/calc.html

Download

runstat3.zip

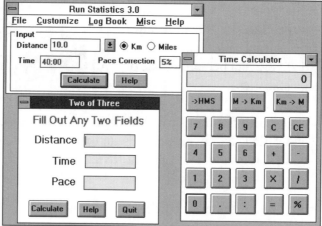

Run—don't walk—to get your copy of RunStat.

 An added bonus to RunStat is that it includes a fully hypertexted version of the Internet's rec.running FAQ with information such as world records, Internet resources for runners, and much more. This program is for PC users only.

Who's Who and Who's Dead

This Web site provides a listing of celebrities who've gone on to play that "Great Command Performance in the Sky." Still fairly new on the Net, this listing of celebrity obituaries only dates back to the end of 1994, though sadly it's growing fast. Besides the basic information (name, date of birth, date of death), you'll get a hyperlink to any other available information on the Net about the celebrity. You can even add information about your favorites, if you choose. Try *that* with the obits in your local paper.

Where

http://catless.ncl.ac.uk/Obituary/

Links

Death Hoaxes

Movie people who were born or died today

Rock 'n Roll Deaths

A Veritable Victual of Virtual Vegginess

This searchable index of more than 1,500 vegetarian recipes is sure to go over well with the carrot and celery crowd. Just enter your query, with any single word or phrase, for an in-depth listing of tasty veggie dishes and desserts. In addition, you'll find some great links to many other sites for the health conscious.

Where

http://www-sc.ucssc.indiana.edu/cgi-bin/recipes/

Links

Recipe Index

Health, Medical, and Nutrition Sites

One Step at a Time

Has your life been affected by someone else's drinking? Al-Anon and Alateen (for younger members of Al-Anon) is a worldwide program for the families and friends of alcoholics. If you're concerned about someone else's drinking, or were raised in an alcoholic home, Al-Anon or Alateen may be able to help you.

This Web site will give you all the information you need to find help through a network of worldwide support groups. There are no dues or fees for membership.

Where

http://solar.rtd.utk.edu/~al-anon/

Links

The 12 Steps

The 12 Traditions

Questionnaire

 If you don't have a Web browser, you can Telnet to solar.rtd.utk.edu and enter **al-anon** (in lowercase) at the login prompt. But then, if you don't have a Web browser, why are you reading this book?

The Facts on Cancer

If you or somebody close to you has been diagnosed with cancer, the fears and anxieties you have are matched only by your questions about treatments and cures. Here's a site that offers lots of information about your diagnosis and treatment, and where to find support services to get further help.

In addition to information on many different types and causes of cancer, you'll find essays detailing personal experiences with cancer, where to find financial support, cancer databases on the Internet, and the different treatments available.

Where

http://asa.ugl.lib.umich.edu/chdocs/cancer/CANCERGUIDE.HTML

Links

Descriptions of Cancer

Possible Causes of Cancer

Specific Types of Cancer

Information for Caregivers and Family Members

Get Off the Emotional Rollercoaster

Everyone goes through rough times. But most people wait until things get completely out of control before finding the help they need to get through them. By then, though, it might be too late. Get the help you need *before* it's too late.

This guide to emotional support resources on the Internet is for people suffering through a loss, chronic illness, or bereavement, as well as their friends and families. You'll find lists of electronic discussion groups, directories to various non-Internet support groups around the country, and real life personal experiences to show you that, no matter what the problem, you're not alone.

Where

http://asa.ugl.lib.umich.edu/chdocs/support/emotion.html

Links

General Emotional Support Resources

Physical Loss Resources

Chronic Illness Resources

Bereavement Resources

A Woman's Place Is on the Net

While the Internet is indeed for everybody, the profile of its millions of members looks more like something you'd find at an exclusive men's club. The Net is hardly a refuge for women. That's why it's good to see sites like this one popping up. This health guide offers loads of information specifically geared toward women. You'll find information on eating disorders, fitness and nutrition, menopause, and much more.

Where

http://asa.ugl.lib.umich.edu/chdocs/womenhealth/womens_health.html

Links

Emotional Health Issues

Physical Health Issues

Sexual Health Issues

Be Productive

If you and your spouse are dealing with the problem of infertility, be sure to check out this site for the latest in high-tech fertility options. In addition to tons of information on women's health issues, this site from the Atlanta Reproductive Health Centre has in-depth coverage of infertility and its many treatments for hopeful mothers—and fathers.

An added bonus: the book *Miracle Babies and Other Happy Endings,* which describes various infertility treatments, is included online. There's even a photo gallery illustrating some of the various problems that result in pelvic pain and infertility, along with some of the surgical treatments.

Where

http://www.mindspring.com/~mperloe/index.html

Links

Miracle Babies and Other Happy Endings

Stress Test

For Husbands Only!

Working for Better Health

To take advantage of one of the largest selections of health-related sites on the Net from a variety of links, there's no better starting point than the National Institutes of Health home page. By uncovering new medical knowledge on all fronts—from the rarest genetic disorder to the common cold—the NIH is working to provide better health for everyone.

The NIH conducts research in its own laboratories, supports the research of universities, medical schools, hospitals, and institutions throughout the world, helps train new researchers, and helps to publicize new biomedical information.

Welcome to the National Institutes of Health (NIH) Home Page, maintained by the Division of Computer Research and Technology (DCRT).

National Institutes of Health (NIH) Gopher
Search NIH Gopher Menus for topics of interest
NIH Gopher Users Guide

The National Institutes of Health home page.

Where

http://www.nih.gov/

Links

Search NIH Gopher Menus

NIH Library

Help for Cancer Patients through Cansearch

Sponsored by the National Coalition for Cancer Survivorship, Cansearch can be used by cancer patients and their families to guide them through the maze of cancer-related resources available on the Internet.

Marshall Kragen, a twelve-year survivor of colon cancer, developed Cansearch to help cancer patients learn more about their illness and show them the plethora of online resources available to them. There's lots of excellent information on bone marrow transplants, breast cancer, lung cancer, and more.

Where

http://www.access.digex.net/~mkragen/cansearch.html

Links

CancerNet

OncoLink

800 Numbers and Information

Day by Day with a Bone Marrow Transplant Patient

Pharm-er's Market

PharmInfoNet delivers the latest pharmaceutical information to pharmacists, physicians, patients, and anyone else interested in pharmacological topics. (Don't you just *love* the medical profession's penchant for big words?) You'll find:

- FAQs about drugs, with answers from pharmaceutical manufacturers and other approved sources

- Links to pharmaceutical manufacturers' home pages, catalogs, and product information

- A rotating exhibit of pharmacy-related art, photographs, and multimedia museum tours

- A moderated archive of drug-related discussion threads from the sci.med.pharmacy newsgroup

Where

http://pharminfo.com

Links

DrugDB

PharmMall

Gallery

Free Audio Files for Better Health

Family Health, a daily series of 2-1/2-minute audio programs, provides practical, easy-to-understand answers to some frequently asked questions about health and health care. Dealing with a wide variety of common health-related subjects, this series of recordings includes information on:

- Athlete's Foot
- Bicycle Helmets
- Cookware
- Fiber
- Morton's Neuroma
- Postpartum Depression
- Your Medicine Cabinet

Each Family Health file is about 1.2 megabytes.

Where

http://www.tcom.ohiou.edu/family-health.html

Download

Dandruff

Dizziness Treatments

Drug Advertising

Heart Attack Risk

Heel Pain

Interferons

The audio files in this collection are in .AU format. If your PC is not set up to play back .AU files, download the DOS conversion program WVANY10.ZIP from:

http://www.acs.oakland.edu/oak/SimTel/win3/sound.html

To convert .AU files to .AIFF for the Mac, download the program SoundMachine from:

http://www.uwtc.washington.edu/Computing/WWW/Macintosh.html

The Cure for Your Insurance Questions

If any organization knows how to leave a paper trail, it's the U.S. government. At least now you can save a tree or two by downloading these medical-related pamphlets and booklets dealing with Medicare.

You'll find information on:

- Health insurance for people with Medicare to help you avoid paying for duplicate benefits
- How to set up a living will to help you receive the medical treatment you want if you become physically or mentally unable to communicate
- What to do if you disagree with a medical charge
- Getting Medicare coverage for second surgical opinions
- How to apply for Medicare

Where

http://www.gsa.gov/staff/pa/cic/fedprogs.htm

Download

Guide to Health Insurance for People With Medicare

Medicare & Advance Directives

Medicare & Your Physician's Bill

Medicare Coverage for Second Surgical Opinions

The Medicare Handbook

Let's Be Careful Out There

Safety is the watchword at this site. You'll find booklets detailing everything from the risks of exposure to magnetic fields generated by common household items and what measurements are safe, to what products have been recalled. You'll also learn how to get information from the FDA on drugs, foods, pesticides, medical devices, radiation safety, pet foods, and more.

For even more information, you can download a copy of the *Consumer's Resource Handbook*. This 123-page book lists an assortment of contacts to help you with consumer problems or complaints, including corporate consumer representatives, private resolution programs, automobile manufacturers, government agencies, and more. You'll even find help on how to write an effective complaint letter.

Where

http://www.gsa.gov/staff/pa/cic/misc.htm

Download

EMF in Your Environment: Magnetic Field Measurements of Everyday Electrical Devices

Staying Healthy and Whole: A Consumer Guide to Product Safety Recalls

Consumer's Resource Handbook

Getting Information from FDA

Just for the Health of It

From silicone breast implants to second-hand smoke, caffeine concerns to chicken pox, estrogen to eyewear, this site will answer many of your medical questions. Nowhere on the Internet will you find such a wide assortment of books, magazines, pamphlets, and brochures dealing with common medical- and health-related topics.

You'll find information on how to make exercise a life-long habit; how to quit smoking; food, drug, and cosmetic regulations; lead poisoning; and much more.

Where

http://www.gsa.gov/staff/pa/cic/health.htm

Download

Personal Health Guide

Why Do You Smoke?

Prescriptions to Help Smokers Quit

Using Over-the-Counter Medications Wisely

217

Alzheimer's Disease

Chicken Pox

Chronic Fatigue Syndrome.

Don't Lose Sight of Glaucoma

Fever Blisters & Canker Sores

Insulin-Dependent Diabetes

Lyme Disease

Let's Talk About Depression

—*and many, many more*

Get a Line on Life

The Lifelines home page is one of the best sources on the Web for general information on nutrition and healthy living. You'll find great links to:

- Clinical studies and research in health, fitness, nutrition, and fat reduction
- Medical and health science sources
- *Lifelines* online newsletter
- Software to enhance your knowledge of nutrition and health

This is a great site for links to a wealth of health and nutrition information.

- A bibliography of books, videos, and audio tapes on personal health and athletic performance.

Where

http://www.rain.org:80/idsolute/lifehome.html

Links

The Lifelines Health Science and Research Library

Nutrition, Health and Medical Connections

The LIFELINES Newsletter

I.D. Solutions

The Best of Lifelines: Health Improvement Resources

Your One-Stop Medical Resource

Einet's Medicine home page is little more than a list of links, but what a massive collection of links it is! Pick any category of health, and you're bound to find a link (maybe more than one) here. This page is as historical as it is progressive. In other words, you'll find additional links to the history of medicine to holistic medicine topics. If you're aching to take charge of your own health, this is the site to visit.

Where

http://www.einet.net/galaxy/Medicine.html

Links

Allergy

Anesthesiology

Cancer

Cardiology

Dermatology

Endocrinology

Family Practice

Forensics

Gastroenterology

Geriatrics

Hematology and Oncology

Imaging and Radiotherapy

Immunology

Infectious Diseases

Internal Medicine

Medical Molecular Biology

Microbiology and Molecular Genetics

I've only made it halfway through the alphabet; there are many other links, but you get the idea.

 Much of the information at these links is consumer oriented, but much of it is geared for medical professionals. So this is a good site for both lay people and medical professionals looking for research information.

Where to Find More Goodies

For more information on staying healthy, try these:

- Check out the *Food and Cooking* section for great examples of what *not* to eat if you're trying to get in shape. You'll find lots of recipes ripe for indulging.

- The *Government and Politics* section contains lots of information on human radiation experiments, nuclear testing, radiation releases, fall-out results, and more from government testing in the 1950s.

FREE $TUFF

What experience and history teach is
this—that people and government never
have learned anything from history, or
acted on principles deduced from it.

G.W.F. Hegel

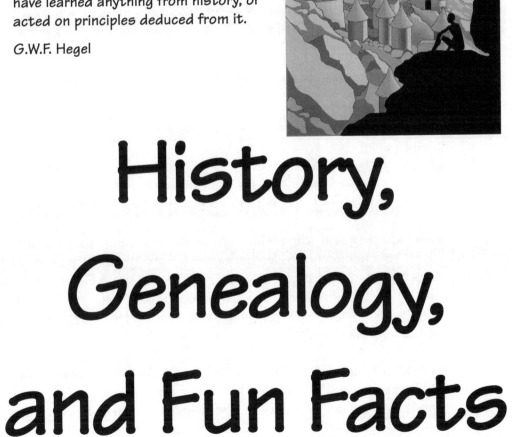

History,
Genealogy,
and Fun Facts

On This Day

What happened on this day in history? Well for the day on which I write this, in 1899 the first woman was put to death by electrocution. Download a copy of On This Day for Windows to get other light-hearted fare you can blurt out at the water cooler. On This Day keeps you abreast of famous births, deaths, victories, defeats, and other historical events of ages past.

—	On This Day for Windows	▼

Go To   Options   Help

<<	March 1995	>>

Sun	Mon	Tue	Wed	Thu	Fri	Sat
			1	2	3	4
5	6	7	8	9	10	11
12	13	14	15	16	17	18
19	20	21	22	23	24	25
26	27	28	29	30	31	

Unregistered Copy

Oh, what a day.

And when you can't get anybody to listen to you anymore—which shouldn't take too long—hit 'em with what it all means in history's big scheme by quoting from Windows in Time, a collection of historical timelines to help you keep track of who was conquering what, where, and when. Your listeners will flock back in droves.

Where

http://www.acs.oakland.edu/oak/SimTel/win3/educate.html

Download

wotd_201.zip

wit.zip

An Art Gallery 20,000 Years in the Making

This site may deal with prehistory, but its Web site is strictly 21st Century. This fascinating collection of the Combe d'Arc cave art recently discovered in France depicts a wide assortment of prehistoric wildlife, including horses, rhinoceros, lions, bison, wild ox, bears, panthers, mammoths, ibex, owls, and so on, along with symbols, handprints, and stencils dating back nearly 20,000 years.

France's Ministry of Culture was quick to make these images available to Internauts, and has promised that even more are soon to follow. Experts have judged the paintings already examined to be at least equal in quality to the world-famous ones at Lascaux, and the newly found larger cave may prove to hold a larger number of paintings as well. More than a rarity, this site is France's latest national treasure.

Where

http://www.culture.fr/gvpda.htm

Links

Research Into Prehistoric Wall Paintings Elsewhere

The Cosquer Cave

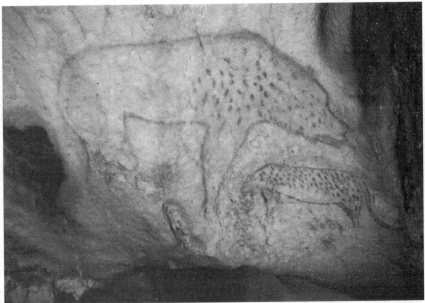

Just one example of the cave paintings discovered at Combe d'Arc.

Dear Hannah...

These letters by Newton Scott to his friend (and later his wife) Hannah offer an intriguing glimpse into the daily hardships, loneliness, and frustrations of a soldier's experiences in the U.S. Civil War. With all the drama of *Gone With The Wind*, this wonderfully documented love story is fascinating reading for history buffs or for anyone who likes a good love story. Who needs *The Bridges of Madison County* when you can have the real thing? There are also links to some great Internet sites, picture archives, and reading lists devoted to the study of America's bloodiest war.

One of Newton Scott's letters from the war.

Where

http://www.ucsc.edu/civil-war-letters/home.html

Links

Civil War information

1862

1863

1864

1865

Get to the Root of Your Family Tree

I've often wanted to trace my family tree, but have never quite worked up the nerve. Maybe I'm the lost heir to the throne of some country I've never heard of—but then again, I'm more likely the sole survivor of a family of corporate raiders who've left me with a fortune in unpaid back taxes. Who's to say? One thing is certain: Genealogy is more than digging up information on a bunch of dead guys. It's a way of learning about yourself and how seemingly unconnected events of the past work to shape your future.

And you don't have to be a member of the Daughters of the American Revolution to trace your heritage back to the Mayflower and beyond.

The Internet offers tremendous resources for anyone tracing his or her family tree. You'll find links to get you started in genealogy, as well as information for the pros. And, hey, let's remember this is the Internet, so nothing's limiting your search to the United States. There are plenty of links to non-U.S. sites, too.

This site also lets you access software archives to make your journey through the past a little easier. There's software for PCs, Macs, even Unix. And since you're wired to the Net, be sure to check out the link to using the Internet for genealogical research.

Where

http://www.xmission.com/~jayhall/

Links

Using the Internet

Ancestor Research Tool

Genealogical Archives and Libraries

Special Genealogical Resources

Do You Remember When?

The Library of Congress seems to be working overtime to put as much of its material on the Internet as possible. One recent addition is the American Memory, an online exhibit of American history and culture. Accompanied by introductory material, users' guides, and bibliographies for further research, the materials here offer serious researchers and casual gawkers alike access to a vast array of historical information.

In addition to photographs and historical documents and manuscripts, this site includes motion pictures and sound recordings of famous events, playable on PCs or Macs. Some of the movies available include turn-of-the-century scenes from New York and President McKinley at the Pan-American Exposition of 1901.

Where

http://rs6.loc.gov/amhome.html

Just two of the thousands of WWII-era photos available for downloading.

Links

Early Films of San Francisco

Photographs

Sound Recordings

Not-So-Ancient History

Do you remember the *Banana Splits*? How about *The Time Tunnel*? And whatever happened to those crunchy little nuggets called Quisp and Quake that we all munched while watching Saturday morning cartoons? Find out the answers to these pressing questions and more by checking out the Nostalgic Wave, a Web site dedicated to reliving the past, no matter how trivial the past might be.

Lifetime charter members of the Banana Splits Club will be happy to know that they can still find Fleagle, Bingo, Drooper, and Snork alive through the magic of syndication on some cable stations, and can even download a copy of the catchy theme song. You used to drive your parents crazy with this stuff, now the Web provides a great way to drive your kids crazy, too.

Where

http://www.hype.com/nostalgia/home.htm

Links

Hype! International

Major Matt Mason, Profile of an American Action Figure

Seeing Double

Here's a fun-to-view collection of photos from turn-of-the-century Yosemite that offers a look back at the pristine beauty of this national park. Plus, you get the bonus of seeing these pictures in 3-D. Thanks to Patch American High School in Stuttgart, Germany, this 19th century version of virtual reality lets you view, print, and download numerous stereogram photographs, which you can view if you have a stereogram viewer sitting around. If you don't have a stereogram, you can still view each photo by holding it close to your nose, looking past it, and then gradually moving the photo away from you until the 3-D image appears. You'll probably look a little foolish doing this and everybody will no doubt be staring at you. But, then, people probably looked at you the same way when they saw you buying this book, so you should be used to it by now.

There are also stereograms taken of San Francisco shortly after the 1906 Great Earthquake and of World War I. In addition, be sure to visit the Patch Home page for many interesting, albeit non-history-related, links.

Where

http://192.253.114.31/Projects/stereograms/Stereoscopic_Photographs/ Stereoscopic_Photographs.html

Links

Forth Bridge, Scotland

World War I

The Great 1906 California Earthquake

Other Assorted Images

 While this site comes close to winning the dubious honor of longest URL, give it a try anyway; it's worth it.

A Stitch in Time...

Arguably, no other man did more to shape the United States than Benjamin Franklin. But how much do you really know about this 18th-century statesman? Scientist, inventor, businessman, philosopher—Benjamin Franklin was truly America's first Renaissance man.

This special exhibit at the Franklin Institute Science Museum gives you a peek at the man behind the myth. You can trace Franklin's family tree and learn about his illegitimate son who sided with England during the Revolutionary War, read his last will and testament, and read a timeline of his long and fascinating life.

Where

http://sln.fi.edu/franklin/rotten.html

Links

Franklin Institute Science Museum

Family Tree

Resource Materials

Enrichment Activities

There's much more to this site than information on the life of Ben Franklin. Be sure to follow the links to the Franklin Institute and browse through one of the best museums on the Web. Also, teachers will want to look at the Resource Materials and Enrichment Activities links for some great ideas for the classroom.

Monsters Among Us

What began as a purely utilitarian device designed to direct rainwater away from the walls of buildings evolved into one of the most bizarre yet breathtaking displays of architecture ever created: gargoyles.

While gargoyles are certainly weird and more than a little disturbing, their history and how they came to be erected on some of the most beautiful churches and other buildings around the world is a fascinating story.

Gargoyles Then and Now

Greeting Message (Audio)

Just What Is A Gargoyle?

This site devoted to these stone beasts will fill you in on their origins, history, and symbolism—all strange but true.

Where

http://ils.unc.edu/garg/garghp4.html

Links

Origins

Symbolism

The Cathedral of Notre Dame

The Winchester Cathedral

The Cathedral at Canterbury

Faces that even a mother might have a little trouble loving.

Science and American History

While the Internet has long been the ideal tool for gaining instant access to the latest scientific information as it becomes available from anywhere in the world, it—along with the World Wide Web—is now being used to read about the latest scientific discoveries—minus 160 years.

You can now access hypertexted versions of *Penny Magazine, Appletons' Cyclopaedia of Applied Mechanics*, and *Scientific American* dating from as far back as 1835, complete with text and pictures. You'll find information

229

about the latest in modern office accessories like the "hoist" (translated: the elevator), and even learn about the rapid advances in modern transportation that make it possible for railroad cars to "fly" at speeds in excess of 30 miles per hour. Hold onto your hat!

While this project is still in its infancy, the Webmasters here promise there is more to come. Hey, you've waited this long to view this stuff online, what's a few more weeks?

Where

http://www.history.rochester.edu/index.htm

Links

Scientific American On Line

Appletons' Cyclopaedia of Applied Mechanics

Penny Magazine

History of Science

Titled *The Art of Renaissance Science, Galileo and Perspective*, this site combines history, art, and science into a dazzling exhibit of Galileo's life and achievements. Beginning with Galileo's early experiments and his increasing reliance on mathematics to disprove many of the accepted theories of his day, this exhibit traces Galileo's life through the Inquisition, his arrest for heresy, and the secret publishing of his greatest work, *Discourses on the Two New Sciences*, which has been called the cornerstone of modern physics.

Where

http://www.cuny.edu/multimedia/arsnew/arstoc.html

Links

The Early Years

Heavenly Bodies

The Inquisition

Do You Have a Record?

Your taxes pay for the storage of all those records at the National Archives; you at least ought to be able to get a peek at them. Well you can, at least some of them. And here are some free booklets that will show you how.

Using Records in the National Archives for Genealogical Research, a 25-page booklet, will show you how to obtain census records, naturalization and passport applications, and other government records containing facts on your family history. Plus, *Where to Write for Vital Records* and *Your Right to Federal Records* will show you how to obtain certified copies of birth, death, marriage, and divorce certificates, as well as how to use the Freedom of Information Act and Privacy Act to obtain other records from the federal government.

Where

http://www.gsa.gov/staff/pa/cic/misc.htm

Download

Using Records in the National Archives for Genealogical Research

Where to Write for Vital Records

Your Right to Federal Records

Where to Find More Goodies

History is repeated throughout this book, including:

- The Egyptian artifacts exhibit in the *Arts* section.
- The Clinton inauguration is captured on the Web in the *Government and Politics* section. It may not be *ancient* history, but it's history nonetheless.
- For the history of civilization—at least as far as Canada's goes—go to the *International* section.
- The history of movies—especially the silent era—is covered in the *Movies and Videotapes* section.
- Go waaaay back in time and visit the Museum of Natural History mentioned in the *Nature and the Environment* section.

FREE $TUFF

The hardest thing in the world to
understand is the income tax.

Albert Einstein

Household
and Family
Finances

Home Sweet Home

If you're ready to buy your dream property, but you're still not sure where you want to live, make the Global Real Estate Guide your first stop. This site includes tens of thousands of homes and businesses for sale or rent around the world. While not all the links were up and running at the time I browsed through here, this site still holds a lot of promise, and it's great for retirees of all ages. Before long, you'll be able to access information on properties in the Dominican Republic, Pacific Rim, and even South Africa.

If you're looking for something a little closer to home, just key in a ZIP code or the name of a city to find thousands of listings throughout the U.S. and Canada. Happy house hunting!

Where

http://www.gems.com/realestate/

Links

Property Directory

Other Real Estate Resources

One of the 30,000+ properties for sale at the Global Real Estate Guide.

Get Your Portfolio Back in the Black

Wouldn't it be nice to have your own personal investment manager to guide you through the tricky waters of financial investing? Well this is cyberspace, remember, where all your wishes come true.

The Personal Finance Center (PFC) lets you pick the brain of top investment strategists like Frank Armstrong, certified financial planner, chartered life underwriter, founder and principal of Managed Account Services, Inc. of Miami, Florida, and all-around good sport for taking so much time to answer all the questions posed by investment newbies on the Net.

Users posted questions to Frank about their personal finances, then PFC posted Frank's replies. He even provided free help in planning or evaluating Internauts' investment portfolios. While this round of questioning is closed now, you can still access the answers, and PFC promises to hold more of these Q and A's in the future. In the meantime, you can still access the information from previous discussions for help in:

- Saving for college
- Finding good financial books
- Investing for retirement

And much, much more.

Where

http://gnn.com/meta/finance/feat/armstrong/index.html

Links

Finance Center
GNN Home
First PFC Q&A

Free Mortgage Analysis

Naive as I am when it comes to matters of the pocketbook, I nevertheless have a difficult time passing up anything labeled "free." Needless to say,

235

this site caught my eye. The Mortgage Strategies Web page offers a free mortgage analysis that might help you save money and lower the term of your mortgage by converting to a bi-weekly mortgage payment schedule.

While some of the text here reads like a get-rich scheme, the fact is bi-weekly payments can save you thousands of interest dollars over the life of your loan, and it costs nothing to give it a try. With bi-weeklies, you'll:

- Save thousands in interest
- Shorten the term of your mortgage
- Build your equity as much as 300 percent faster
- Increase your net worth and help you become debt-free 10 to 15 years sooner

Where

http://www.ais.net/netmall/mortgage

Links

The Magic of a Bi-Weekly

Disturbing Facts Revealed About Your Mortgage

FREE Analysis Order Form

How Much Does That $10,000 Car Really Cost?

If you're looking for bells and whistles in a Web site, you'll have to look somewhere else. But if you're looking for a handy, convenient way to quickly figure your auto loan payments, you've come to the right place.

Just enter the price of your car, the down payment, interest rate, and number of years of the loan to get your monthly payment. Surprise! That car just might cost you a bit more than you thought.

Where

http://pond.cso.uiuc.edu/cgi-bin/loan.pl

Links

Click on Car Lot for lots of links to stuff for sale on the Net.

Mark Your Calendar

As my family and extended family continue to grow, it's become practically impossible to remember every birthday, anniversary, special event, and not-so-special event. And by the time I *do* get it all figured out, the year is over and I've got to start again. My wall calendar looks as jumbled as my day planner and becomes just as useless.

But with a program like Family Calendar for Windows, I can throw the lame excuses out with the scraps of paper I've been using to keep track of all the dates I have to remember. This shareware program lets you store all your important family dates, including birthdays, anniversaries, deaths, divorces, and other special events. You can even use it to print a handy shopping list for presents. Now you'll have to come up with some other lame excuse for forgetting your anniversary.

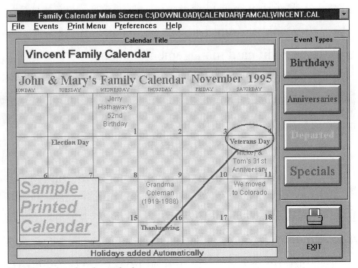

Family Calendar for Windows.

Where

http://www.acs.oakland.edu/oak/SimTel/win3/calendar.html

Download

famcal11.zip

Financing for the Numerically Challenged

I'm as enthused about keeping track of my family's finances as I am about cleaning up after the dog in the backyard. But put off either for too long and I'd be in some serious...well, you get the picture. The Internet can't help me much with the latter, but when it comes to smoothing out my finances, there's no shortage of software for helping to manage my money.

While some of these programs may lack the bells and whistles of the ones you'll find at the shopping mall, they don't cost anything to try, and the registered versions cost much less than the competition. Besides, I haven't yet needed to display or print a record of my savings account as a 3D pie chart. Here's a sampling of the programs you can find here:

• Mortgage analyzer
• Retirement planner
• Bank account tracker
• Credit card management database
• Cash flow analyzer
• Portfolio manager
• Home budget manager
• Financial modeling tool

I couldn't possibly try them all, but the ones I did experiment with were easy to use. Some—if you can believe it—were even fun. See for yourself. Now about the dog....

Where

http://www.acs.oakland.edu/oak/SimTel/win3/finance.html

Download

mking11.zip

retirea.zip

am_bb12.zip

ccplus12.zip

cshfl3_3.zip

fundmn71.zip

hbw20.zip

tmval3_2.zip

	Home Budget - SAMPLE.TRN - [Account Book]					

File Transaction Account Setup Edit View Window Help

(Bank Account) **Bank**

Start Bal: 500.00 Budget: 0.00 Rec Bal: n/a

Debit: 16159.95 Credit: 16630.30 End Bal: 970.35

Date	Item	Account	Num	Debit	Credit	R	Balance
01-Jan-94	Morgage Payment (A)	Morgage		800.00	0.00		-350.00
01-Jan-94	Paycheck	Day Job - Inc		0.00	1000.00		700.00
01-Jan-94	Xfer from Bank to Checking	CheckBook		700.00	0.00		0.00
01-Jan-94	with-draw for Spending	Misc Spendi		200.00	0.00		-200.00
15-Jan-94	Paycheck	Day Job - Inc		0.00	800.00		600.00
20-Jan-94	Paycheck	Alternate Jot		0.00	100.00		700.00
01-Feb-94	Morgage Payment (A)	Morgage		800.00	0.00		-100.00
01-Feb-94	Paycheck	Day Job - Inc		0.00	1000.00		900.00
01-Feb-94	with-draw for spending	Misc Spendi		300.00	0.00		600.00
01-Feb-94	Visa Bill	Visa		433.30	433.30		600.00
02-Feb-94	Xfer from Bank to checking	CheckBook		600.00	0.00		0.00
15-Feb-94	Paycheck	Day Job - Inc		0.00	800.00		800.00
20-Feb-94	Paycheck	Alternate Jot		0.00	400.00		1200.00
01-Mar-94	Morgage Payment (A)	Morgage		800.00	0.00		400.00
01-Mar-94	Paycheck	Day Job - Inc		0.00	1000.00		1400.00
01-Mar-94	With-draw for spending	Misc Spendi		300.00	0.00		1100.00
01-Mar-94	Visa Bill	Visa		257.00	257.00		1100.00
03-Mar-94	Xfer from Bank to checking	CheckBook		650.00	0.00		450.00
15-Mar-94	Paycheck	Day Job - Inc		0.00	800.00		1250.00

53 Transactions.

Home Budget for Windows, one of several shareware programs to help you make sense of your family finances.

A Fair to Remember

Buying a new house is the largest purchase most people will ever make. With so much money changing hands, you'll want to make sure you make the right choices. The Homebuyer's Fair makes finding your dream home just a little easier. Start by filling out the online order form to get a free subscription to one of the many new-home guides for over 20 cities around the country, complete with photos, features, prices, and easy-to-read maps. Some of the guides can even be viewed online.

Once you've found the right home, you'll want to know if you can afford it. Go to the online qualification calculator to determine how much you need to beg, borrow, or steal to get in the door. If you've got the first-time-buyer jitters, this site includes a listing of free publications to help you get up to speed and explains how you can order them. Not quite ready to buy? There's also an apartment locator service for cities across the U.S.

Where

http://www.homefair.com/

Links

New Homes Plus

Homebuyer's Information

Rent or Buy?

Before You Kick the Tires

Buying a used car doesn't have to be like taking a trip to the fruit stand. These free booklets will help you distinguish between a peach and a lemon. You'll learn what to look for—and look out for—when buying a used car, how to lower your insurance costs, which cars are most economical, and much more.

And not all the costs of owning a car are immediately apparent. Find out some of the hidden costs of owning and operating your auto, *before* you get stuck with the bills.

Where

http://www.gsa.gov/staff/pa/cic/cars.htm

Download

The 1995 Fuel Economy Guide

Nine Ways to Lower Your Auto Insurance

Cost of Owning & Operating Automobiles, Vans, and Light Trucks

New Car Buying Guide

I Hate Housework

If you're thinking of hiring that live-in maid, think again, and then get a copy of this free booklet from the Consumer Information Center. *Hiring Someone to Work in Your Home* is four pages of helpful tips to keep you from breaking any of the federal laws set up to protect your in-home employees. There's helpful tax and payroll advice, descriptions of which services are exempt (no, you don't have to withhold taxes for your in-home baby-sitter), and steps to take when hiring an employee.

Where

http://www.gsa.gov/staff/pa/cic/employ.htm

Download

Hiring Someone to Work in Your Home

Shop Till You Drop

Smart shopping means more than clipping coupons for the supermarket or finding a bargain on the clearance rack. Here's a menagerie of booklets free to download from the U.S. government that will help savvy shoppers get their money's worth, regardless of what they're shopping for. Some examples:

Funerals: A Consumer Guide describes what costs and services a funeral provider is required to give you when you inquire in person or by phone.

Protecting Your Privacy shows you how to check your credit files and medical records, handle phone marketers, and have your name removed from mailing lists.

A Consumer's Directory of Postal Services and Products describes the costs and benefits of priority and express mail, explains how to make claims for lost or damaged mail, and much more.

Where

http://www.gsa.gov/staff/pa/cic/misc.htm

Download

Funerals: A Consumer Guide

Protecting Your Privacy

A Consumer's Directory of Postal Services and Products

Consumer's Resource Handbook

4 Br, 2 Ba, 1,001 Headaches

So you've made it through the nightmare and headache of buying your own house. If you think your pain and suffering are over, you'd better wake up and smell the paint peeling. Now is when the fun really starts: termites, busted pipes, leaky roofs—and that's the good part. The real potentials for disaster are the things you have no control over: mudslides, earthquakes, floods, water shortages, and neighbors who work on their cars at 2 a.m.—and that's just in L.A.

To the rescue comes the U.S. government. Hey, they stick it to you through property taxes, so giving a little something back is the least they could do. Here's where to get many free booklets that can help you step through the new homeowner minefield without making a misstep. You'll find answers to questions about flood insurance and repairing a flooded home, how to keep birds from destroying your plants and damaging your home's exterior, tips for controlling pests, how to test your water for pesticides, and much more.

Where

http://www.gsa.gov/staff/pa/cic/housing.htm

Download

Answers to Questions About the National Flood Insurance Program

Backyard Bird Problems

Citizen's Guide to Pesticides

Home Buyer's and Seller's Guide to Radon

The Inside Story: A Guide to Indoor Air Quality

And many, many more.

Save It for a Rainy Day

A savings account has long been and still is one of the smartest investments you can make for your family's future. Here's a site that will help answer many of your family's savings, investing, and financial planning questions. There's information on:

• How to compare different banking accounts

• How to protect your credit after a divorce

- The difference between deposits and investments
- How to avoid being taken by an investment swindler
- How to make informed investment decisions
- How to plan for financial independence
- Answers to 29 frequently asked questions about private pension plans

These are but a drop in the financial bucket. There's plenty more for you to browse through and download.

Where

http://www.gsa.gov/staff/pa/cic/money.htm

Download

Investors' Bill of Rights
Your Guaranteed Pension
Invest Wisely
IRS Guide to Free Tax Services
Federal Credit Unions

Get Out of Debt Free

No, this isn't a card you draw in Monopoly, but it *is* a great Web resource for anyone who's struggling to make ends meet and is fighting a losing battle. The fact is, very few people know what to do in a financial emergency, and end up suffering for their ignorance.

Debt Counselors of America is a non-profit organization that can help you manage your debts and teach you how to take control of your finances again. In most cases, there are no charges for their services. So avoid the "quick fixes" like consolidation loans and bankruptcy, which can make things worse in the long run. Contact Debt Counselors for the help you need to get back on the road to being debt-free.

Where

http://www.ip.net/shops/GET_OUT_OF_DEBT/

Links

Debt Consolidation

Common Questions & Answers

Mortgage Sweet Mortgage

This program will help you decide just how much that house is going to cost you month to month. Enter the principal loan balance, interest rate, and length of the loan to find out what your monthly payments will be. You'll get a complete listing of the payment schedule—right down to your final payment.

Find out how much home of your own you can own.

Where

http://ibc.wustl.edu/mort.html

Links

GNN Home Finance and Real Estate Page

Income Tax Calculator

Death and Flat Taxes

The idea of paying a flat tax is nothing new in Washington, but Hugh Chou is the first person I've heard of who has made crunching the numbers as simple as logging on to the Web. Based on Senator Dick Armey's Flat Tax Proposal of 17 percent, Hugh wrote this program to help you see just what it might ultimately mean to your pocketbook.

Hugh even includes a link to the Treasury Department and another program to calculate your current taxes for the sake of comparison. Even my accountant doesn't work this hard—but then, maybe I need a new accountant.

Where

http://ibc.wustl.edu/~hugh/armey.cgi

Links

U.S. Department of the Treasury

Are All Your Eggs in One Nest?

Playing the stock market is a tricky business—so tricky it makes playing the wheel in Vegas seem like an exact science. You'll want to hedge your bets as much as possible by getting all the help you can *before* taking the financial plunge into the icy waters of investing.

Geared more toward the high-income crowd, the Nest Egg Web page is still a valuable resource for all us poor slobs stuck on the other side of the financial tracks. You'll find lots of interesting investment news and ideas by clicking on the current issue of *Nest Egg Magazine*, or by browsing the back issues to learn about the ones that got away.

Where

http://nestegg.iddis.com/

No rotten eggs in this nest, just good financial advice.

Links

Nest egg Index

Performance Leaders

Resource Center

Nestdiver

Money for Nothin'

When the issue is money, Money Issues Online is the site for you. You'll find lots of great advice to help you with your personal finances, as well as links to dozens of other related Web sites and financial software for you to download.

Some of the shareware, public domain, and demo software that you can download includes:

- EZ-Quicken
- MetaStock Professional
- Captool
- Folioman

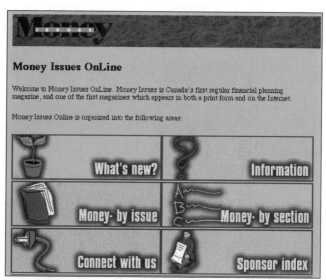

It's only money.

Where

http://www.cyberplex.com/CyberPlex/MoneyIssues/MoneyIssues.html

Links

Money By Issue

Money By Section

Events

Program Download

Coupon Connection

While not exactly free, this site does offer enough coupons at a cheap price to pay for this book 10 times over (so go out and buy nine more copies for your friends).

The Coupon Connection lets consumers order manufacturers' coupons for national name-brand groceries and products available in nearly any grocery store in the United States, Canada, and many other cities around the world. Just $19.95 buys you $200.00 worth of name-brand coupons that you select from a huge list of products. Not a bad return on your investment. The coupons will be delivered to you in about two weeks. Then, it's off to the store to start saving money.

Where

http://www.pic.net/uniloc/coupon

Links

Basics on Coupons

Sample Product Listing

Order Form / Contact Information

What's Your NETworth?

I mentioned this site earlier in the *Business* section, but I wanted to include it here too, to make sure you don't miss it because it's a worthy service for individuals as well as businesses. NETworth is a free mutual

247

funds resource site offered by Galt Technologies, Inc., and it's one of the best resources anywhere for do-it-yourself mutual fund investors. The service provides information on more than 5,000 mutual funds, including prospectuses, performance figures, and pricing (all the "P" stuff). Current mutual fund stock information is provided online; it's on a 15-minute delay to satisfy SEC regulations.

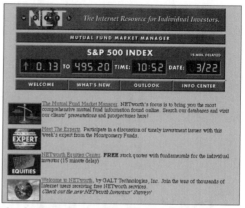

The feeling's mutual at NETworth online.

To access NETworth, all you have to do is register (again, registration and use of the site is free). Registration is as simple as supplying your name, address, phone number, and a personal password. The process takes only a minute or two and there's no delay between registering and getting online.

Where

http://networth.galt.com/

Links

Once you've registered, you'll have access to these and many other links:

The Mutual Fund Market Manager

Meet the Experts

NETworth Equities Center

NETworth Market Outlook

Internet Information Center

Where to Find More Goodies

For more family links, look for genealogy information in *History*, information on adopting children from other countries in *International Affairs*, and how to turn your back yard into an aviary in *Nature and the Environment*.

FREE $TUFF

They all laughed at Columbus.
They all laughed at Einstein.
Unfortunately, they also all
laughed at Bozo the Clown.

William H. Jefferys

Humor

FREE $TUFF from the World Wide Web

Comics on the Web

If it's a comic strip and it's on the Internet, you can bet this site has a link to it. Christian Cosas has compiled an enormous list of strips, sequential art, one-panel cartoons, and editorial cartoons from around the world. Whether you prefer the classics, like Krazy Kat, or something a tad more modern—for instance, Netboy or Internet Man—if it exists in cyberspace, you can bet Christian has it here.

Where

http://www.phlab.missouri.edu/HOMES/c617145_www/comix.html

Links

Calvin and Hobbes

Doonsebury

The Far Side

Fox Trot

Dozens of others

Did You Hear the One About...?

I was a little suspicious about this site when I first browsed through it. Its self-billing as "America's First Web Site" sent me immediately into one of my eyeball-rolling "yeah, right" moods. But my cynicism took a nose dive when I found myself getting caught up in this cyberzine's cover story about burrowing whales wreaking havoc along the coast of California. How did *USA Today* miss this story? Hey, I'm as  gullible as the next sucker, so what the heck, I read on. Now I'll believe anything these guys throw at me.

Melvin, a *National Enquirer*-like cyber-tabloid offers fare as farfetched as its hardcopy cousins and is just as readable. Besides, you have to admire their straightforwardness. *Melvin* is advertised as "News for Dumb People." The *Enquirer* should be so honest....

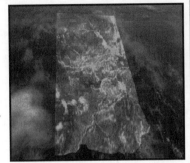

Puerto Rico Secedes from Union

53rd State pursues separate national identity

Members of the U.S. Armed Forces are on high alert today, cleaning weapons, scouting targets and planning for a war that most had hoped never would come. Their target: Puerto Rico, tropical island paradise and traitor to the principles of Unionhood for over twenty years.

Puerto Rico's treachery was uncovered late

According to freshman Senator Hank Speer of South Dakota, evidence of Puerto Rico's treachery continues to mount. Since quietly withdrawing their Senators and Representatives from Congress in 1967, Puerto Rico has abandoned capitalism, violated provisions of the Constitution and even adopted a secret national tongue they call "Spanish." Furthermore, Speer

What? Puerto Rico's turning on the good ol' US of A?!

Where

http://www.melvin.com/

Links

Man On The Street

Today's Horoscope

Laugh, and the Whole Web Laughs with You

LaughWEB is a huge collection of jokes, quips, bumper stickers, insults, even computer humor. Whether it's politics or parodies, education or entertainment, or a dozen other topics—there's plenty to find amusing at LaughWEB. Though this site certainly has its share of groaners, there are definitely enough gems here to tickle even the most reluctant funnybone.

Where

http://www.misty.com/laughweb

Links

Canonical Lists

Insults

In The News

Life Archive

Movie Scripts

Political Humor

You might find some of the material here offensive—but then, humor isn't always pretty. So look for the warning labels if you want to steer clear of the cruder fare:

L=Strong Language

R=Risque

E=Ethnic

S=Sexist (although not always against women)

+=Religious

*=Gross and Disgusting

Magical Mystery Web

Here's a site devoted to the humor, magic, and bizarrities of prestidigitators Penn and Teller. Winners of two Emmy Awards and best-selling authors of *Cruel Tricks for Dear Friends* and *How to Play with Your Food*, these guys know how to entertain. Check out the links to the Penn and Teller alt.fan newsgroup; download interviews from *Wired* magazine, the *Boston Globe*, and other hardcopy pubs; and find out about some of their upcoming appearances and projects. Also, find out why Penn Jillette has been called "the most wired magician on this planet."

Penn and Teller (or make that Teller and Penn).

This site also includes loads of links to other humor- and magic-related sites. An added bonus: Witness the Internet's first card trick. You'll be truly amazed, you'll laugh, you'll cry—just don't send them any money.

Where

http://krusty.eecs.umich.edu/people/nielsen/penn-n-teller.html

Links

Skeptical Inquiries

Movie Database

David Letterman

Fortune Cookie

When you're in the mood for burgers, you can still get your fortune without having to sit through a Chinese meal. This site serves up a random (or maybe it's not...) fortune each time you access it. If you don't like what you get, no problem. Keep logging on until you find something that makes you say, "Hey, I've always thought that was true about me!" How's that for being master of your own fate?

Where

http://uhunix.uhcc.hawaii.edu:8080/cgi-bin/fortune

Links

No links in the physical sense, but the possibilities are endless if you believe in this kind of thing.

Don't forget to tack the words "in bed" to the end of your fortune for an interesting spin on the typical yarns. This is an immature, juvenile practice to be sure, and one that I frankly would *never* participate in.

LeJoin LeClub

Groucho Marx once said that he'd never join a club that would have him as a member. You may want to put that maxim aside, however, and sign up for a charter membership to LeClub International, *the* Comedy Club on the Internet. If you enjoy the lighter side of computing, you'll fit right in with LeClub's other members. And membership has its privileges, like the LeClub International mailing list, delivered like clockwork to your E-mailbox. Okay, make that every so often. Uh, when they get around to it. Hmmm...if you're lucky. As you can see, I'm still waiting for mine, but I *was* able to access the archives and liked what I saw.

You'll find links to The Mother of All Humor Archives, including "30 Signs that Technology Has Taken Over Your Life," The World Birthday Web, Schlake's Humor Archives (where you can find out what Freud would have said about Seuss), and lots more. You can even view QuickTime comedy skits (for Mac users or for Windows users who have QuickTime for Windows).

Join some of the other hackers, editors, philosophers, professors, skydivers, musicians, Internauts, and Internutcases that make this site a regular stop for a good laugh or an amusing discussion.

Where

http://yucc.yorku.ca/home/leclub/

Links

Internet Wiretap (Humor Collection)

Jay's Comedy Club

Rutgers Quartz Text Archive

David Letterman

LeClub on LeWeb has lelots of lelaughs.

Dave's Top Ten Lists

Straight from the home office in Sioux City, Iowa, with only a slight detour through New York—or maybe it's Los Angeles—comes David Letterman's Top Ten Lists. This site is still fairly new but contains many of Dave's lists—starting in early 1995—and the list of lists is growing every day.

Read Dave's Top Ten spins on:

- Ways to annoy Judge Ito
- Things Dan Rather would never say on the CBS Evening News
- Dallas Cowboy excuses
- Signs you're not the sexiest man alive
- Household uses for your copy of *Free Stuff from the World Wide Web* (hah! hah! Just kidding!)

Where

http://weber.u.washington.edu/~drdoctor/davet.html

Links

Lots of links to lots of lists.

Hacks from MIT

You may call them practical jokes, but at MIT they're called hacks. And these aren't the garden variety raspberry-Jell-O-in-the-fountain kind of college stunts you might have pulled or seen pulled at other campuses. At MIT, they've turned the practical joke into an art form that becomes more elaborate each year. Think you've seen 'em all before? How about a campus police car on top of the school dome, complete with lights, a fake cop, and donuts?

Visit this site and find out how students welcomed their new dean by making his office disappear. After browsing around here, you ought to be able to come up with a few of your own hacks. Try 'em on your friends, your family, your boss—they'll *love* it!

This police cruiser has a bird's-eye view of the MIT campus.

Where

http://fishwrap.mit.edu/Hacks/misc/gallery_menu.html

Links

Best of...

Chronological Listing of Hacks

Hacks by Location

Hacks by Topic

Tell Me a Story

No matter what kind of sense of humor you've got, if you have one at all then you're sure to find something to laugh about at the Humorous Stories Web page. There are jokes, quotes, news articles, and lots of lists that poke fun at everything from computer newbies to rap music to *The Twelve Days of Christmas*.

Dave Barry fans will like the large collection of his columns available here in which he espouses on everything from legalizing gambling to the safety of flying. Hey, I'm not making this up.

Where

http://www.ugcs.caltech.edu/~werdna/humor.html

Links

Stupid Band Names

Dates from Hell

Devils Dictionary

FYI

Warning! One person's joke may be another person's fighting words. While this site's loaded with good, clean humor, you'll definitely find a few off-color jokes as well. If you don't like to face the possibility of being offended, crawl back into bed, pull the covers over your head, and stay away from this site.

I don't kill flies, but I like to mess with their minds. I hold them above globes. They freak out and yell "Whooa, I'm way too high."
—Bruce Baum

I like to sing to the songs on the radio in my car. When you go into a tunnel, it's hard to come out on the right note. Actually, the news is more difficult.

I like to go to concerts that are related, like Talking Heads with Simple Minds. I also rent videos together too. Last week I rented "Bambi" and "The Deerhunter."
—Mark Pitta

Hotels are tired of getting ripped off. I checked into a hotel and they had towels from *my* house.

I play golf even though I hate it. I'm not done with a game yet. I hate those windmills.
—Mark Guido

An excerpt from Comedy Day Celebration Jokes at the Humorous Stories web site.

Bork! Bork! Bork!

If you have to ask what the Swedish Chef page is all about, then you must not have been a Muppet fan as a kid. This site is for diehard Chefheads who like to discuss the Swedish Chef, want to download pictures of him, and who don't mind a migraine or two trying to

Feesit zee Cheff, et zee Svedeesh Cheff Veb pege-a.

translate mock Swedish into some semblance of English. You'll find lots of pictures and sound files you can download, too.

There's also a form you can use to "encheferize" English into pseudo Swedish or download a copy of the program and use it on all your ASCII text files. What fun! Noo, vhere-a deed I leefe-a my buttle-a ooff Ixcedereen?

Where

http://www.stir.ac.uk/~sac06/chef/chef.html

Links

Visit the Chef

Pictures and Sounds of the Chef

I Want the Chef for My System

 You might have heard that their also used to be a "Jive Editor" on the Net. Yep—*used* to be. Similar to the Swedish Chef, the Jive Editor took your E-mailed prose and translated into Jive—that is, until some politically correct yahoos deemed it "racist" and removed it. Frankly, if Barbara Billingsly could speak Jive in *Airplane*, then we should all have that same privilege. Oh well, maybe the Jive Editor will surface again elsewhere on the Net.

Kings of Comedy

The battle of the late-night talk shows continues, though most of the contenders have fallen, KO'd by the two reigning kings: Jay and Dave.

Here's a site that lets Mosaic for X users hear and see the monologues of *The Tonight Show's* Jay Leno and *Late Show's* David Letterman. Listen to these two do their show openers, joke for joke, mano y mano. Who's the real king of the late-night airwaves? You decide. On the other hand, I don't have Mosaic for X, so I'm going to bed.

Where

http://www.tns.lcs.mit.edu/cgi-bin/vs/vsjoke

Links

Jay Leno

David Letterman

 To run this demonstration, you need to be running Mosaic for X version 2.0 or higher, have a color screen that is eight planes deep, and have a reasonably fast IP connection to the MIT Laboratory for Computer Science. You can hear audio, too, if you have AudioFile installed on your computer. Jeez, these guys are really going for the big audience. Anyway, see this site for more details.

File It Under Humor

The Humor Archives Web site is a laugh-a-minute library of humor for all tastes (good and bad). Get the latest blonde jokes (yes, they're still going strong), Barney bashing, computer smileys, Norm quotes from *Cheers*, and much more.

Where

http://144.118.52.153/Contents/HumorArch.html

Links

Dozens of links to jokes, stories, songs, lists, and lots of other Web sites. Here are some of the best:

How the Gingrich Stole Congress

A Politically Correct Dictionary

Norm

Real Foreign Signs

Elvis Versus Jesus

CyberWreck on the Information Highway

From the rec.humor newsgroup to your computer comes the Wrecked Humor Web site. No subject's off limits here, including Al Gore, lawyers, and Microsoft (okay, so these are all easy targets). You'll also find lots of links to other humor sites scattered around the Net.

Where

http://www.cs.odu.edu/~cashman/humor.html

Links

Songs and Parodies and the like

Rec.Humor FAQ

Proof that Barney the Dinosaur Is Actually Satan

Poking fun at the Prez and Vice Prez at Wrecked Humor.

Where to Find More Goodies

For those of you with an insatiable funny bone, try these sections:

- *Law* (yes, *Law*) for links to three different sites devoted to lawyer jokes (they wouldn't all fit into one).
- *Television* for links to your favorite comedies.

FREE $TUFF

It's a small world, but I wouldn't want to paint it.

Steven Wright

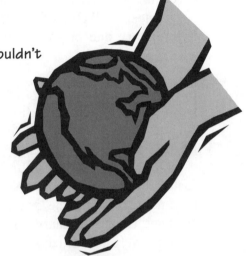

International

Affairs

(The Real Web)

Sheko:li (Greetings), Web Walkers

Located in the heart of New York State, the Oneida Indian Nation has prospered while managing to retain its traditional system of government. Now the Oneida have created this Web site to share their history and culture with cyberspace.

You'll find links to treaties between Native American nations and the U.S. available via the Internet, monthly museum exhibits from the Shako:Wi Cultural Center of the Oneida Indian Nation, audio samples of the Oneida language, a tour of its nation, and many other items of interest, including little-known historical facts that have been passed down orally through generations.

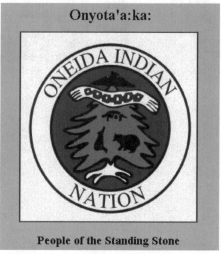

Onyota'a:ka:

People of the Standing Stone

A link to America's past through the Oneida Indian home page.

Where

http://nysernet.org/oneida/

Links

Little Known Historical Facts

Treaties Project

The Shako:Wi Project

The Language Project

Education

Directory of East Asian Electronic Information

Anyone interested in East Asia or Asian studies will find these Web pages from the Committee on East Asian Libraries to be extremely useful. You'll find pointers to specific resources, such as the largest Internet site for Chinese software. With links to information on Japan, China, Taiwan, Hong Kong, Macau, South Korea, North Korea, and the Asia/Pacific Basin, there's a wide variety of information available here. Here's just a small sample of links you'll find for each country:

- Art
- Business
- Dictionaries
- Education
- Language
- Law
- Military
- Music
- Sports

One of Japan's greatest monuments, Hiroshima Castle.

Where

http://darkwing.uoregon.edu/~felsing/ceal/welcome.html

Links

East Asian Internet Resources

Library Resources

General Internet Resources

Displaying the East Asian Vernacular Text

Wanted: Parents

This site was created in the hope that an Internet photolisting would increase public awareness about the needs of adoptive families. The Precious in HIS Sight Internet Adoption Photolisting includes photos and bios of orphaned and abandoned children from around the world, available for international adoption.

This site's Webmaster, Annette Thompson, is not affiliated with any adoption agency. She's a computer network administrator who describes herself

Andrey, Slava, Worku, Lubaba, and Sada are just some
of the many children waiting for adoption from the
Internet Adoption Photolisting.

simply as "a person who loves children and wants to help them find
homes." It shows.

Annette has also included links to lots of great adoption information
available on the Net, especially international adoption. Be sure to check
out her special feature from a recent trip made to Ethiopia, which includes photos, video clips, and audios of hopeful orphans. But before
you access this site, be warned: It will tug your heart strings.

Where

http://www.gems.com/adoption/

Links

Adoption Information Elsewhere on the Internet

Precious in HIS Sight

Search for Children

Canadian Museum of Civilization

The Canadian Museum of Civilization is more than a museum; it's a
walk back in time as you explore the history and culture of Canada.
Starting with a fascinating exhibit of the Norse landings around 1000 AD,
the exhibits take you on a fascinating journey through a 17th century

whaling village, an archeological expedition, a native village, and much more. There's also a great collection from the Children's Museum. What a great way to explore the folk culture, civil history, and military history of our Neighbor to the North.

Where

http://www.cmcc.muse.digital.ca

Links

Lower Level

Main Level

Mezzanine Level

Children's projects from the Canadian Museum of Civilization.

Is This the Party to Whom I Am Speaking?

You know the phone number, maybe you even know the city, but what was the area code again? No problem, just pull up this Web page and enter the information you *do* know to find out the information you don't. Simply enter the city, state, or area code and let this searchable database do the rest. It'll help you find the area code for any city around the world or all the area codes for a specific state or province. You can even get phone rates and country codes. Start dialing!

Where

http://www.xmission.com/~americom/aclookup.html

Links

AmeriCom Long Distance

International Business Opportunity

Operation Gulf War Veteran's Page

If you served in the Gulf War, you'll find this site to be an invaluable tool for finding resources and information for veterans. If you didn't serve, this site will humanize the faces of the thousands of men and women you've read about who served their country in Operation Desert Storm.

Compiled from the Veterans Administration, the Gulf War mailing list, and other Internet resources like the National Library of Medicine, the Gulf War Veteran Resource Page is an important repository for topics related to the Gulf War and its veterans.

Work and play during Operation "Send Saddam Packing."

There are links to the VA Home Page, the Long Beach VA Medical Center Web Server, The House of Representatives Home Page, and The Vietnam Veterans Home Page. More links are being added regularly, so check here often for the most up-to-date info for veterans.

Where

http://www.wwa.com/~szabo/gulf.html

Links

An Introduction to Gulf War Veteran Concerns

The Controversy - A Political Maelstrom

Environmental and Chemical Factors

Resources for Gulf War Veterans

Activism - What to Do?

Veteran Support for Other Eras

Gulf War Veteran Resource Pages Photo Gallery

Newsletters of Several Gulf War Veteran Organizations

Be sure to check out the gallery of personal photos of Gulf War vets, as well as the page devoted to the Desert Voices Project, which made it possible for Gulf War soldiers to communicate with loved ones back home.

The Taj Mahal of Web Sites

India Online has managed to link Web pages from around the world to provide a great source of information on India and the surrounding area, including Nepal and Sri Lanka. Look for information on travel, food, culture, news, telecommunication, international trade, and much more.

This comprehensive guide includes lots of travel tips, as well as lists of things to do, places to visit, and how to get there, along with lots of pictures of local sites. There's also plenty of information on the various cultures, food, news, and trade. And for those who prefer to experience as little adventure as necessary during their vacations, there are bulletins advising you what areas to stay clear of to avoid any civil unrest.

Where

http://IndiaOnline.com

Links

Travel

Food

India Travel Guide

Nepal Guide

Sri Lanka Guide

Mt. Everest peeks through the clouds of Nepal at 28,108 feet.

Do Not Enter

In some parts of the U.S., getting across the border is as easy as knowing who won the 1949 World Series. It's not that easy in other countries. This 20-page booklet shows you the requirements for getting your feet firmly planted in the soil of many foreign countries. You'll learn what kind of identification is required even if you don't need a passport, as well as what countries require immunization certificates, what you don't want listed on your visa when traveling to certain areas, which countries require proof of funds (presumably in case you need to buy your way out), and much more. There's even a list of embassy and consulate addresses where visas may be obtained along with any special requirements. Oh yeah, I almost forgot: 1949 was the year of the Yankees.

```
BANGLADESH -- Passport, visa, and onward/return ticket
required. Tourist/business visa requires 2 application forms, 2
photos. Business visa also requires company letter. For longer
stays and more information consult Embassy of the People's
Republic of Bangladesh, 2201 Wisconsin Ave., N.W., Washington,
D.C. 20007 (202/342-8373).

BARBADOS -- U.S. citizens traveling directly from the U.S. to
Barbados may enter for up to 3 months stay with proof of U.S.
citizenship, photo ID and onward/return ticket. Passport
required for longer visits and other types of travel. Business
visas $25, single-entry and $30 multiple-entry (may require
work permit). Departure tax of $25 is paid at airport. Check
information with Embassy of Barbados, 2144 Wyoming Ave., N.W.,
Washington, D.C. 20008 (202/939-9200) or Consulate General in
New York (212/867-8435).

BELARUS -- Passport and visa required. Visa requires 1
application form and 1 photo. The visa processing fee is $30
for 7 working days, $60 for next day, and $100 for same day
processing. (No charge for official travelers.) Transit visa is
required when travelling through Belarus ($20). For additional
information contact Embassy of Belarus, Suite 619, 1511 K
Street, N.W., Washington, D.C. 20005-1403 (202/638-2954).
```

A sample from Foreign Entry Requirements, downloaded from the Consumer Information Center.

Where

http://www.gsa.gov/staff/pa/cic/trav&hob.htm

Download

Foreign Entry Requirements

Give 2.54 Centimeters, They'll Take 1.6 Kilometers

At last there's help for those of us who never quite caught on to the metrification frenzy of the 1970s. This handy booklet includes an easy-to-read FAQ explaining what the metric system is all about and why it's so *darn* important that we learn it. There are loads of equivalency charts for basic measurements, as well as conversions for liquid and dry measurements, oven temperatures, weather units, and more. Still not a convert? There's even a chocolate-chip cookie recipe written entirely in metric measurements. If you want 'em, you gotta think metric to make 'em. Talk about hitting below the belt!

```
"Metric Chocolate Chip Cookies"

     Recipe reprinted from "Living With Metrics" courtesy of
Reader's Digest Association, Inc., Pleasantville, New York

550 mL     unsifted flour
  5 mL     baking soda
  5 mL     salt
250 mL     butter or margarine, softened
175 mL     granulated sugar
175 mL     firmly packed brown sugar
  5 mL     vanilla extract
    2      egg
    2      168 gram packages semisweet
           chocolate chips
250 mL     chopped nuts

[Graphic Omitted]

     Preheat the oven to 190 eC. In small bowl, combine flour,
baking soda, and salt; set aside. In large bowl, combine
```

Metricookies, downloaded from Metric Measures Up.

Where

http://www.gsa.gov/staff/pa/cic/misc.htm

Download

Metric Measures Up

100 Percent All Natural

Becoming a U.S. citizen is a little more complicated than knowing who the Father of Our Country is (George somebody) or how two reed and rite English, though not by much. And there are restrictions (murderers, habitual drunkards, and polygamists need not apply). But for most people who dream of becoming American citizens, it's an attainable goal. This 46-page booklet will show you how to make your citizenship dreams come true. If you're already a citizen, you can always give the booklet to somebody who isn't.

Naturalization Requirements and General Information explains the main requirements for naturalization, the special exemptions, and what you must do to become a naturalized citizen of the United States. There's also a brief discussion on how to obtain a copy of a naturalization or citizenship paper, how to file a declaration of intention, how to obtain a Certificate of Citizenship, and how to legalize an alien's residence in the United States so that he or she can apply for naturalization.

Where

http://www.gsa.gov/staff/pa/cic/misc.htm

Download

Naturalization Requirements and General Information

It's a Long Way to Tipper—er, Norway

The Norwegian Travel Information Network is a virtual world of valuable and interesting tidbits for anyone interested in visiting or learning more about the cities, sites, and sounds of Norway. This virtual guidebook of Oslo, Bergen, Halden, and other major cities of Sweden's cousin will show you the best restaurants, hotels, towns, and sightseeing hot spots, including the famous glaciers, fjords, midnight sun, and northern lights. Get a taste of the Arctic

All your Norwegian travel questions are answered at the Norwegian Travel Information Network.

from the comfort of your own computer terminal by checking out NTIN.

Where

http://www.oslonett.no/NTIN/NTIN.html

Links

Different Resources within NTIN

Clickable Map of Norway

A Virtual World of Cities

City slickers will think they've died and been sent to some kind of virtual nirvana when they log on to City.Net, arguably the most comprehensive online international guide to communities around the world.

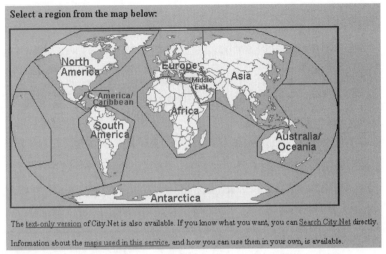

Select a region from the map below:

The text-only version of City.Net is also available. If you know what you want, you can Search City.Net directly.

Information about the maps used in this service, and how you can use them in your own, is available.

Click on the map to get information on a jillion cities (give or take) around the world, like Timisoara, Romania.

You'll find easy access to timely information on travel, entertainment, and local business, plus government and community services for thousands of cities in over 100 countries, territories, and commonwealths around the world. There are maps, tour guides, weather forecasts, interesting facts, boring facts, fun things to do, landmarks, news, local times, useful phone numbers, not-so-useful phone numbers, historical info, currency exchange rates... somebody stop me!

Where

http://wings.buffalo.edu/world/vt2/

Links

Search City.Net

Standard Time Zones of the World

Mapping Out a Good Time

After you get through viewing this map, you'll probably think the United Kingdom is one big university. From Scotland to England, you'll find links here to dozens of schools and their surrounding communities throughout the United Kingdom. In addition to information on the different degree programs and courses offered at each university, you'll find tourist and travel information, local hot spots, and lists of links to other Web sites throughout Europe. Not a bad study aid, especially if you're majoring in fun.

Where

http://scitsc.wlv.ac.uk/ukinfo/uk.map.html

Links

UK Tourist Map

Other Places

Plus, links to universities throughout the United Kingdom.

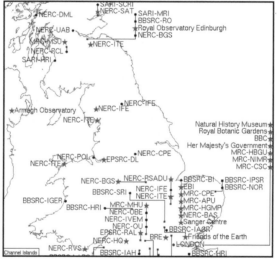

Click a star, any star, to browse information on dozens of universities throughout the UK.

Euro Central

Centered in the crossroads of Western Europe, Belgium offers a diverse multicultural experience that will impress even the most hard-to-please cybertraveler. One thing that stands out is the architecture, with seemingly every church and town hall declared a monumental work of art dating back to the Middle Ages.

Come see for yourself at this site, where, in addition to general travel information, you'll find interesting facts on the geography, politics, and economy, as well as travel information, including weather forecasts, guided tours, and—most important—lots of links to information on Belgian beers.

Where

http://www.iihe.ac.be/hep/pp/evrard/BelgCul.html

Links

Travel Information for Belgium

Weather Forecast

Belgium Page

Belgian expatriates will want to check out the Belgians Abroad Home Pages for Web sites that include information for and by Belgians living outside of their homeland.

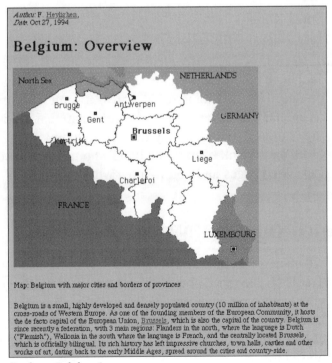

Author: F. Heylighen,
Date: Oct 27, 1994

Belgium: Overview

Map: Belgium with major cities and borders of provinces

Belgium is a small, highly developed and densely populated country (10 million of inhabitants) at the cross-roads of Western Europe. As one of the founding members of the European Community, it hosts the de facto capital of the European Union, Brussels, which is also the capital of the country. Belgium is since recently a federation, with 3 main regions: Flanders in the north, where the language is Dutch ("Flemish"), Wallonia in the south where the language is French, and the centrally located Brussels, which is officially bilingual. Its rich history has left impressive churches, town halls, castles and other works of art, dating back to the early Middle Ages, spread around the cities and country-side.

Bonjour, Belgique!

Country Studies

This series of books published by the Library of Congress is the beginning of what is to be a long series of in-depth studies on foreign cultures and societies. Each book deals with a different foreign country, offering a unique perspective on its history, as well as its political, economic, social, and national security systems and institutions. If you live in or are planning to visit Egypt, Israel, Japan, the Philippines, or any of the other countries included here, these books are must-reads.

Where

http://lcweb.loc.gov/homepage/country.html

Links

Ethiopia

Indonesia

Singapore

Somalia

South Korea

Yugoslavia

 Judging by the sheer volume and quality of Web pages and Internet sites produced by the Library of Congress, I sometimes think they must have an annual budget larger than the gross national product of many emerging nations. (Actually, they do.) In my opinion, it's money well spent. Click on the link back to the LOC's home page to see some other great LOC Web pages and you'll know what I mean.

A Groundhog's View of the World

All aboard for Austria, Hong Kong, Sweden, and all points in between. The URL for this Subway Navigator would be a great one to keep on your laptop computer, especially if you're a traveling stranger in a strange land. Nothing is more frustrating or scary than needing directions in a city in which you don't speak the language. Smiling and nodding only go so far.

This service will help you find the best route from one metro station to another, in dozens of cities around the globe. You can get subway maps and routes in:

- Vienna
- Calgary
- Santiago de Chile
- Helsinki
- Paris
- Frankfurt
- Athens
- Budapest
- Calcutta
- Milan
- Tokyo
- New York

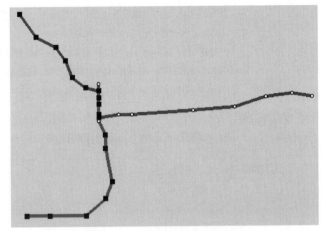

You can get there from here, at least according to the Calgary Subway System.

and 36 other cities in 20 countries around the world. And the list keeps growing.

Select the city you want, then click on your departure and destination stations for information on the best route, schedules, approximate travel time, and more. If you're not sure of the names of the stations, you can also get a list to choose from.

Where

http://metro.jussieu.fr:10001/bin/cities/english

Links

Subway lines galore. Just start clicking; you never know where you'll end up.

Asia Online

The famed Silk Road that ran from China to Europe a thousand years ago may be closed, but traffic detours onto the Information Highway, resurfaced and built for speed just in time for the 21st century. And the mode of transportation has been upgraded from horses and carts to bytes and bits.

The Digital Silk Road includes listings of Asian business and information services, online exhibitions, news, and convention schedules. There's even an online shopping mall and travel guide. Sure, it may lack some of the romance and adventure of the original Silk Road, but, then, you'll make the trip a lot faster now.

Where

http://silkroute.com/silkroute/

Links

TravelASIA

Asia News

AccessASIA

World Communities

The Internet is turning the world into one big global community, but one in which you don't have to join a block watch or worry about your neighbor's sprinklers soaking your car. How's that for progress? EINet Galaxy World is one site that's shrinking things down to size by making information about hundreds of cities and dozens of countries available to you at the click of a mouse.

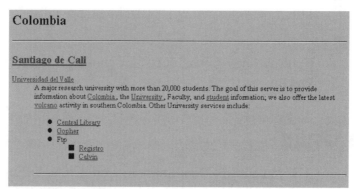

Columbia is just one of the many countries you'll find listed at EINet Galaxy World.

Whether you're interested in world history, international government, traveling, or even the weather, you'll find dozens and dozens of links at this site to satisfy your information lust. The Galaxy is a guide to worldwide information on international organizations, important documents, world travel information, International Web sites, and much more.

Where

http://www.einet.net/galaxy/Community/World-Communities.html

Links

Chernobyl and Its Consequences

World Constitutions

World Flags

World Politics Magazine

UNICEF

United Nations

Comprehensive List of Web Sites

Gluttons for thoroughness will have a field day browsing this comprehensive-as-they-come database of Web sites. Select a country and fire away for pages of URLs. Did I say pages? I meant *pages* and pages. The only major downside is that you won't find any descriptions of each site's contents, but click away and see what's in store. That's what hyperlinks are for.

Where

http://www.netgen.com/cgi/comprehensive

Links

Links and links *ad infinitum* (well, almost)

Where to Find More Goodies

This book is made up of the best of the Web from around the world. Some sites with a truly international flair include:

• International art exhibits in the *Art* section, including an online Russian exhibit and works by African artists.

- A peek into Greek mythology and Japanese haiku in the *Books, Magazines, and Literature* section.
- Internet resources for globetrotters who travel with their laptop computers in *Computers and Software.*
- International restaurant guides in the *Food and Cooking* section.
- Games you can play against people around the world in the *Games* section.
- *Music* for what's hot in the international music scene.
- *Nature and the Environment* for international resources and groups working to save the Earth's environment.

FREE $TUFF

The secret of dealing successfully
with a child is not to be its parent.

Mell Lazarus

Kid Stuff

World Wide Web Jr.

While the Web may contain enormous amounts of information, only a small part of it is useful, intelligible, and interesting to school-children. And, let's face it, most of the search utilities are less than friendly for the younger kids. Result: frustration.

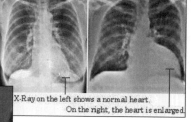

X-Ray on the left shows a normal heart. On the right, the heart is enlarged.

Live long, prosper, and get a checkup at least once a year.

But here's an idea that's helping: a subset of the Web targeted at the kindergarten through 12th grade crowd. Simple to navigate and containing lots of useful and fun information for this select audience, Kid's Web is proving to be an invaluable resource to help educators, well, educate.

Each subject section contains a list of links to information targeted at schoolkids, including:

- A tour of a virtual heart
- The history of medicine
- Pointers to hundreds of bands and music sites
- Science fiction resource guide
- Digitized movies
- World maps
- Comics
- Games

And the list goes on. There are also links to external lists of material on each subject, which more advanced students can browse for further information.

Where

http://www.npac.syr.edu/textbook/kidsweb/

Links

Tons of links to keep junior surfers surfing for hours.

Virtual Pooh and Tigger, Too

Although this one is a relative newcomer to the Web, the Pooh Corner page has the feel of an old classic. This site is dedicated to the discussion of A.A.Milne's Winnie the Pooh, as well as all his friends in the Hundred Acre Wood.

Check out the Pooh FAQ for lots of interesting information about this lovable bear of very little brain, or join the mailing list for fun discussions on Pooh, Tigger, Heffalumps, Woozles, Backsons, and Jagulars. You can also find lots of information on Pooh collectibles, or just download some of the many images available.

Where

http://www.lehigh.edu/jll4/public/www-data/pooh.html

Links

The ALL NEW & official Pooh FAQ

Poohrapheralia

The Children's Literature Page

Christopher Robin, Pooh, and the rest of the gang explore the Hundred Acre Wood.

Free Kittens to Good Homes

Kids, your parents won't be able to turn you down when you ask them if you can keep this cyberkitty. This fun Windows utility displays a kitten that chases after your mouse, yawns, and falls asleep. Feeding your cyberkitty is a piece of cake, er, tuna, to say nothing of changing the kitty litter.

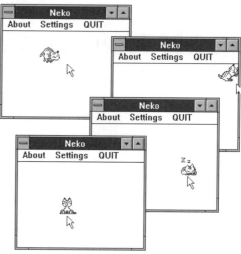

This online mouser is free to good homes.

And if your computer doesn't have enough bugs already, there's also a program here that will fill your screen with ants scurrying across your monitor, hiding behind windows, and darting out after you've forgotten they were there to scare the heck out of you. Maybe the next version will let you squash 'em.

Where

http://www.acs.oakland.edu/oak/SimTel/win3/animate.html

Download

ants.zip

neko.zip

Magic 8-Ball

The Brady Bunch, Twister, pet rocks.... Who says the '70s gave us nothing of value? Everybody had a favorite, and The Magic 8-Ball certainly wasn't mine. But it must have been somebody's because it's come back to haunt us all as some kind of cyberspace reincarnate spewing prodigious revelations to anyone daring enough to ask it for predictions.

If you're too young to remember the Magic 8-Ball, here's your chance to get acquainted. Simply ask it a question, then click the button and await your response. You'll be astounded, amazed, and relieved that you didn't actually have to pay for this thing the way the rest of us did when we were kids.

Where

http://www.resort.com/~banshee/Misc/8ball/index.html

Links

No real links in the physical sense, but from a metaphysical standpoint, the links are endless.

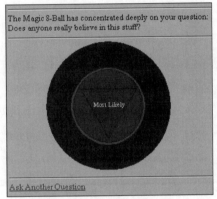

I never would have believed it if I hadn't seen it with my own browser.

It's FalconStar to the Rescue

You won't be able to resist this story line: Earth's natural resources are kaput. All its energy is provided by three massive power stations orbiting the planet and guarded by three superheroes who hold the fate of all mankind. If they let down their guard, the rest of us are global toast. Holy sunspots, Batman!

Follow superheroes FalconStar (WAP!), FireShrike (POW!), and SunHawk (BAM!) as they fight to save the planet in this masterfully drawn E-comic published by ElectroniComics, exclusively for Web surfers like you. Check back often for the latest installment in this adventure series.

Where

http://www.infi.net/falconstar/

Links

Click on the FalconStar icon to get to the comic. The actual links change for each installment.

It's FalconStar, Websurfing superhero extraordinaire, to the rescue.

I Just Can't Wait to Be Mass-Merchandised

Anyone out there ever hear of a little flick, made by some fledgling company named Disney, called *The Lion King*? I didn't think so. But if you know anybody who has, point them to this site for photos, movie footage, behind-the-scenes production info, and credits for everyone involved, right down to the animated guy whose job was to clean up after all the animals. Yuck!

While you're there, be sure you surf over to the Lion King Theatre for links to lots of other great Disney stuff, including an online coloring book you can download to your favorite paint program or print out and color by hand. (Do kids still do that?) Welcome to cyberspace, Disney!

Where

http://bvp.wdp.com/BVPM/PressRoom/LionKing/LionKing.html

Links

The Lion King Theatre

Promotional Stills

Movies

Press Kit

Coloring Book

The Oscar-winning LION KING.

It's Internet Barbie

Barbie, every little girl's fantasy doll—and a few little boys', has joined the Web. Feminists will no doubt cringe at the thought of this Barbie Web page, but little girls who don't know any better will love this site. She may be 30-something now, but she's as popular as ever, and new generations of girls continue to be mesmerized by Mattel's biggest seller.

You'll find lots of links to Barbie-related Web pages, as well as collector information, Barbie bios, and information on Barbie spinoffs, like Shopping

Spree Barbie, Silver Sweetheart Barbie, Little Debbie Barbie, Holiday Barbie, and on and on. Hey, shouldn't Ken get equal time?

Where

http://silver.ucs.indiana.edu/~jwarf/barbie.html

Links

Zoli's fabulous Plastic Princess Page

The South Bay Barbie Doll Collectors Club

Friends of Barbie

Barbie, the doll that has taught generations of girls the meaning of the word "accessorize."

Let Go of My LEGO

I know of at least one college where you can take Frisbee as a P.E. course, but when I heard you could actually earn college credits toward an engineering degree by playing with LEGOS, *that* made me pause. That is, until I saw what these guys were building.

At MIT, they take their LEGOS *very* seriously. You may not be able to major in it yet (though I imagine that day will come eventually), but the LEGOS robotics course at MIT gets students to incorporate LEGOS into

their designs of sophisticated, futuristic machines that walk, talk, roll, probe, violate traffic laws, and more.

Although there's not much leg room, this robot looks like it'll do about zero to 60 in eight seconds flat.

You'll also find lots of links that have a more recreational feel to them, including project ideas, LEGO games, and pictures of home-built constructions.

Where

http://legowww.homepages.com/

Links

LEGO Robots

Our LEGO Travel Destination

The LEGO Builders Club

Games with LEGO

Projects, Ideas, and Information

A LEGO Theme Song

History

KidWare

This site has tons of shareware programs for kids, including interactive story programs, math tutors, word scramble games, and lots of other programs that tout themselves as "educational." But what they mostly are is fun. Download a few to see what I mean.

Teach your children all about the bears and the bees.

Check out *The Bear and the Bee*, a fourteen-panel illustrated story about a bee who seeks the hand of a bear in marriage. Recommended for children under nine, this book includes pictures that you click on to display the names of the different objects. This one was kid-tested at my house, and was a big success.

Where

http://www.acs.oakland.edu/oak/SimTel/win3/educate.html

Download

bear_bee.zip

cbmath15.zip

color12.zip

scrazy30.zip

Operation Glass Slipper

The Cinderella Project is a text and image archive containing a dozen English versions of the classic European fairy tale *Cinderella*. This archive includes the most common of the nearly 700 versions of the story in which:

1. Boy meets girl.
2. Boy loses girl.
3. Girl loses shoe.
4. Boy finds shoe.
5. Boy finds girl.
6. Boy and girl live happily ever after.

In addition to the text from different versions of *Cinderella*, you'll find actual photos of the pages from rare 18th- and 19th-century books, including beautifully drawn pictures of this cinders-to-riches story.

A page from just one of the many versions of the classic fairy tale CINDERELLA for you to download here.

Where

http://www.usm.edu/usmhburg/lib_arts/english/cinderella/cinderella.html

Links

Archives Inventory

Images Only

de Grummond Children's Literature Research Collection

Dear Pen Pal

Communicating with a pen pal has been a fun and popular way for kids of all ages to learn about different people and cultures around the world since the invention of the written word. And that long history is continuing on the Web.

Now you can make friends across the globe and learn a few things you won't find in the geography or sociology books. And it's not just other countries you'll be learning about. Having a pen pal makes you think about your own culture, too, as you find out how the people in different parts of the world feel about your country. You'll be surprised—and you won't even know you're learning.

Where

http://www.mbnet.mb.ca/~lampi/penpal.html

Links

Snailmail Penpal Lists

Email Penpal Lists

Learn about the World

Link Up with Other Kids

KIDLINK is a grassroots project striving to get as many children as possible between the ages of 10 and 15 talking to each other in a massive global dialog, and it appears to be working. Since its start in 1990, KIDLINK has had over 30,000 children participate from 67 countries on all continents. Okay, maybe not Antarctica.

Have a kid-to-kid talk at KIDLINK.

Any time of day or night, you'll find kids around the world chatting with each other online on subjects as diverse as current events, politics, books, music, and anything else kids talk about (like girls talking about boys, and boys talking about sports).

These dialogs allow kids to compare their personal views with other kids who have their own unique perspectives on the world and where it's headed. Browse around this site to learn more about KIDLINK and how you can get involved.

Where

http://kids.ccit.duq.edu:70/0/kidlink-general.html

Links

Introduction

KIDCAFE

KIDFORUM

The KIDS-nn Newsletters

Pint-Size Prose

Ah, youth. *CyberKids*, an online magazine for and by kids, offers a kid's view of the world. Published four times a year, each issue is full of interesting articles, fascinating fiction, and powerful prose—all from kids as young as 10 years old. You'll also find lots of games, puzzles, jokes, and other fun stuff for kids.

Where

http://www.woodwind.com/mtlake/CyberKids/CyberKids.html

Links

CyberKids Interactive

CyberKids Launchpad

An online magazine full of online fun.

Color My World

Kids love to color. Anything. In fact, they'd probably color your computer if you turned your back on them long enough. To discourage them from doing anything quite so drastic, point them first to this online coloring book. Bigger kids may think they're a little too old for this site, but get them to try it and they'll soon be fighting with their younger siblings to take their turn.

Online coloring equals online fun.

While the pictures are the same for both links, the Expert Coloring Book allows you to paint multiple areas of an image before updating—great for slower connections. When you're done, you can even save your work to disk as a GIF file. Happy coloring!

Where

http://robot0.ge.uiuc.edu/~carlosp/color/

Links

Simple Coloring Book

Expert Coloring Book

 The pictures used at this site were taken from Coloring Book 3.0 for the Mac. If you're using a Mac, download a copy and try it out by clicking on the *Click Here* link at the top of this Web page.

Zounds! Sounds Abound

Talking computers are okay as long as you don't start talking back. But you'll have a hard time refraining once you've played around at this site for any length of time. The files here let you replace your computer's beeps and whistles with a huge assortment of audios. You can download sound clips from your favorite movies, TV shows, cartoons, and bands, as well as bird calls, whales, and classical music. And that's just for starters.

If you're looking for the sound of silence, you won't find it here. Browse around for more great sounds and links to audio-related sites on the Web. This page has samples of hundreds of sounds for you to download and then drive everyone within hearing distance absolutely batty.

Where

http://www.eecs.nwu.edu/~jmyers/other-sounds.html

Links

Too many to even begin listing. Come see (or, rather, hear) for yourself.

NASA for Kids

3...2...1...*blast off* for fun at this NASA Web site designed exclusively for kids. You'll find historical info about the Apollo missions, including movies, photos, and audio clips. Plus, there are press releases, press kits, and other memorabilia to check out.

It's not all old news, though. You can also get the latest information and launch schedules, find out how to attend a launch, learn about upcoming events, and learn about the history of this fascinating space agency. Also, be sure to browse the library's extensive photo, movie, and audio archive.

Where

http://www.nasa.gov/hqpao/hqpao_home.html

Links

Library
Newsroom
Events
This Is NASA

Children's Literature Web Guide

You won't believe the number of children's books available on the Internet that are free for the taking. Then again, if you're a seasoned Web surfer, nothing should surprise you. Kids or kids-at-heart will love this collection of links to all types of Web sites devoted to children's literature.

This site contains so much information that it's best to just access it and start browsing. In addition to numerous children's books in electronic format—by such notables as C.S. Lewis, Lewis Carroll, Charles Dickens, and L. Frank Baum—you'll find a huge trove of information about the authors, as well as interesting stories behind the stories.

Where

http://www.ucalgary.ca/~dkbrown/index.html

Links

Public Domain Electronic Children's Books

Various Fairy Tales and Fables

Concertina - Books on the Internet

Mark Twain Resources on the World Wide Web

These links barely scratch the surface of what's in store for you at this site. If reading is your passion, you'll want to include this site on your hot list or bookmark list of Web pages.

Internet Accessible Machines

Just what can you hook up to the Internet? The list is as staggering as it is hilarious. This site contains a comprehensive compendium of links to some of the most bizarre uses for the Internet that you can imagine—and then some.

There are links to refrigerators, hot tubs, coffee pots, vending machines, CD players, and even an ant farm. Both kids *and* adults with a sense of humor will enjoy these links. The material at all of these links (at least at this writing) are suitable for viewing by children.

Where

http://www.cs.cmu.edu:8001/afs/cs.cmu.edu/user/bsy/www/iam.html

Links

You have no idea, but be prepared for a trip through some major Web weirdom.

Where to Find More Goodies

When you finally give up the controls and let your kids do some surfing, make sure to point them to some of these sites:

- Lots of children's literature can be found in the *Books, Magazines, and Literature* section.

- Lots of fun programs for kids using Windows are mentioned in the *Computer and Software* section, including a program that lets you change your cursor into a slice of pizza, an eyeball, and more—and even lets you create your own, er, creations.

- Go to the *Television* section for links to information on upcoming PBS shows for kids.

FREE $TUFF

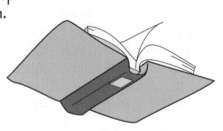

Man invented language to satisfy his deep need to complain.

Lily Tomlin

Language and Literary Pursuits

Multi-Language Learning for Mac Users

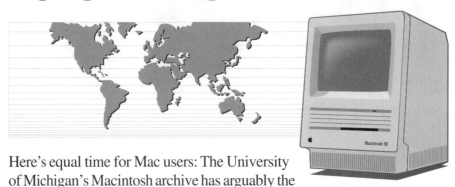

Here's equal time for Mac users: The University of Michigan's Macintosh archive has arguably the best collection of language-learning software for the Mac. You'll find more than 20 freeware and shareware Mac programs available for downloading— Spanish, French, German, Hebrew, Japanese, Greek, Kanji, Mohawk, and other languages are represented here. Take a look at the index (PC users might want to skip reading this site before their eyes glaze over):

SIZE   DATE ARCHIVED   COMPRESSION FORMAT(S)

/mac/misc/foreignlang/alphabetpro1.1.sit.hqx
443   12/17/94   BinHex4.0, StuffIt3.07

Use phonics to teach the alphabet, with pronunciation that you record yourself. Not necessarily limited to English. Requires Sound Manager, microphone.

/mac/misc/foreignlang/apracticarespanol.cpt.hqx
72   1/24/93   BinHex4.0, Compact1.50

Learn Spanish grammar. Requires HyperCard.

/mac/misc/foreignlang/aprendemosespanol1.0011.sit.hqx
238   4/24/93   BinHex4.0, StuffIt3.07

About one thousand Spanish words with English translations. Requires HyperCard 2.0.

/mac/misc/foreignlang/flashworks1.07.cpt.hqx
452   11/12/94   BinHex4.0, Compact1.50

Flash card program for learning foreign languages. Comes with databases for German, Spanish, French, Greek (including PostScript font), and Hebrew (including bitmap font).

/mac/misc/foreignlang/gomtalk1.21.cpt.hqx
92   2/23/92   BinHex4.0, Compact1.50

Resources (cdev, inits, ResEdit templates) that allow users of KanjiTalk (the Japanese operating system) to install System 7.0 on their machines. The manual is in Japanese, too.

/mac/misc/foreignlang/hebrewpad1.92.sit.hqx
24   8/30/93   BinHex4.0, StuffIt3.07

Type short pieces of text from right to left. Useful for Hebrew, Arabic, and some other language fonts. Especially designed for use with the Shalom fonts stored on mac.archive as /mac/system.extensions/font/type1/shalom*

/mac/misc/foreignlang/irishaccessories3.4.sit.hqx
440   3/7/95   BinHex4.0, StuffIt3.07

Irish Accessories is a seamless set of accessories that effectively transform your Macintosh into an Irish keyboard, with appropriate fonts, currency, date, fadas, and so on.

/mac/misc/foreignlang/japaneseprelector1.2.cpt.hqx
891   11/28/93   BinHex4.0, Compact1.50

Study system for students of Japanese, specifically designed to improve the effectiveness of learning vocabulary and Kanji. Also serves as a dictionary, aids students in correct grammar, and assists teachers in arranging and controlling course content.

/mac/misc/foreignlang/kenontsine.cpt.hqx
372   2/5/92   BinHex4.0, Compact1.50

An introduction to the Mohawk language. Click on various parts of David's head and he'll say them to you in English and his native tongue.

/mac/misc/foreignlang/leger1.01.sit.hqx
1909   1/6/95   BinHex4.0, StuffIt3.07

Leger is a text editor for large files integrated with a hypertext English/German dictionary. It can utilize the Apple PlainTalk* extension.

/mac/misc/foreignlang/macinhebrew.cpt.hqx
144   5/22/86   BinHex4.0, Compact1.50

Hebrew word processing DA and font.

/mac/misc/foreignlang/macjdic1.30.sit.hqx

202   8/6/94   BinHex4.0, StuffIt3.07

A lookup program for Jim Breen's Japanese-English and Kanji dictionaries available at monu6.cc.monash.edu.au. Requires KanjiTalk, or System 7.1 with the appropriate Japanese modules.

/mac/misc/foreignlang/mackc0.93.sit.hqx

36   12/5/90   BinHex4.0, StuffIt1.51

Converts Japanese Kanji codes to/from Shift-JIS, JIS, and EUC formats. Also can use Mac, DOS, or Unix-formatted text. If you can't read Japanese, it's probably not very useful. V. 0.93.

/mac/misc/foreignlang/openbook1.01.cpt.hqx

2902   11/28/93   BinHex4.0, Compact1.50

Input your own word list, practice recognition of Kanji, pronunciation, and other language skills. Displays Kanji on any Mac, but needs Japanese system software for input of new Kanji. For students of Japanese.

/mac/misc/foreignlang/prolegomena.cpt.hqx

64   3/23/95   BinHex4.0, Compact1.50

A classic Modern Greek text (the introduction to the 1859 first edition (of Dionysios Solomos'). Word 5.1a format, in Ismini (Greek), Symbol, Times family, and Garamond family (Latin) fonts.

/mac/misc/foreignlang/quranandtranscorrects.cpt.hqx

5   10/9/93   BinHex4.0, Compact1.50

Corrections to typographical errors in /mac/misc/foreignlang/ quranandtranslations.cpt.hqx.

/mac/misc/foreignlang/quranandtranslations.cpt.hqx

1766   4/17/93   BinHex4.0, Compact1.50

Arabic text and translations (M. Pickthal, Y Ali) of the Koran from the Islamic Computing Center, London. Converted to Macintosh format, so that the Arabic can be read along with the translation (under System 7.x, with Arabic resources).

/mac/misc/foreignlang/spanishteacher.cpt.hqx

38   5/29/92   BinHex4.0, Compact1.50

Tests your Spanish skills by asking you to translate words.

/mac/misc/foreignlang/thaitutor1.1a.sit.hqx
   695   2/27/94   *BinHex4.0, StuffIt3.07*

    Learn the Thai numbering system, and how to pronounce it.

/mac/misc/foreignlang/thaitutor2.2.sit.hqx
1352   *2/27/94*   *BinHex4.0, StuffIt3.07*

    Learn the Thai alphabet, and how to pronounce it.

/mac/misc/foreignlang/vocabularry1.0.cpt.hqx
   28   *10/16/92*   *BinHex4.0, Compact1.50*

    Flashcard-style learning utility for foreign words. Features search and comparisons.

Where

http://www.umich.edu:80/group/itd/archive/Public/html/mac/misc/foreignlang/

Download

Use the index I've provided to select programs that interest you.

Languages of the World, Unite!

This site is called the Human-Languages Page, which I suppose differentiates it from animal, vegetable, and mineral languages. Anyway, this is probably the largest collection of foreign language information on the Web. You'll find links to old standbys like French, Spanish, and German, but you'll also find links to information on languages as obscure or specialized as Esperanto, Lojban, Maori, and more—even Klingon.

You'll find links to online dictionaries and language tutorials, international periodicals (including online newspapers), and language-research information. This site is great for just about anybody who's interested in other languages—from first-time travelers to experienced linguists and language educators. This site has been nominated for a 1995 Global News Navigator Best of the Net award, and deservedly so.

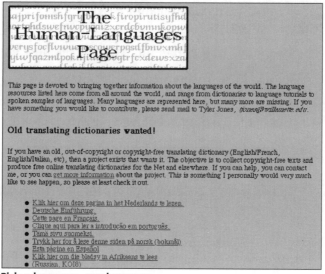

This page is devoted to bringing together information about the languages of the world. The language resources listed here come from all around the world, and range from dictionaries to language tutorials to spoken samples of languages. Many languages are represented here, but many more are missing. If you have something you would like to contribute, please send mail to Tyler Jones, *tjones@willamette.edu*.

Old translating dictionaries wanted!

If you have an old, out-of-copyright or copyright-free translating dictionary (English/French, English/Italian, etc), then a project exists that wants it. The objective is to collect copyright-free texts and produce free online translating dictionaries for the Net and elsewhere. If you can help, you can contact me, or you can get more information about the project. This is something I personally would very much like to see happen, so please at least check it out.

- Klik hier om deze pagina in het Nederlands te lezen.
- Deutsche Einführung.
- Cette page en Français.
- Clique aqui para ler a introdução em português.
- Tämä sivu suomeksi.
- Trykk her for å lese denne siden på norsk (bokmål)
- Esta página en Español
- Klik hier om die bladsy in Afrikaans te lees
- (Russian, KOI8)

Pick a language, any language.

Where

http://www.willamette.edu/~tjones/Language-Page.html

Links

Too numerous to list.

You can also display this page in German, Dutch, French, Spanish, Russian, and several other languages.

I Think I'm Turning Japanese

Here's a program that—believe it or not—makes learning Japanese fun, without making you feel that your tongue has been stepped on by a sumo wrestler. Nihongo Sensei is a Windows program that displays a word in Japanese characters and uses your sound card to say the word simultaneously. In addition to printing quizzes along with your scores and keeping statistics on your progress, Nihongo Sensei lets you input vocabulary words to study. You can even mark especially tricky words you want to concentrate on for repeated practice.

Some of the categories to study are:

- Colors
- At a Hotel
- Greetings
- Relatives

While it would probably take less time to take a slow boat to Tokyo than to download these four programs, the wait will be worth it.

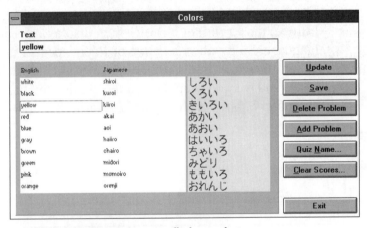

Somebody E-mail me when you find out what
Nihongo Sensei means. I'll be waiting....

Where

http://www.acs.oakland.edu/oak/SimTel/win3/educate.html

Download

japan12a.zip

japan12b.zip

japan12c.zip

japan12d.zip

All four programs are needed to run this package. Download each into a separate directory (like JAPANA, JAPANB, and so on), then unzip each file. Go to the first directory and click on INSTALL.EXE to start the installation. When prompted to insert a new disk, just change the path name to the next directory (JAPANB) and continue the installation.

Here are a couple of other language programs you can download at this site:

mb12.zip   Multi-language learning environment

phaedr1.zip   Latin fables, with vocabulary and notes

European Links for the Language-Savvy

Since this site has been dubbed the European Page, maybe I should have included it in the *International Affairs* chapter. But that's a tough call. The truth is, this page is a map of links to country pages throughout Europe, most (but not all) of which display information in their native language. So if you're a native or fluent speaker in some European language other than English (although even Great Britain is well represented here), and want to keep tabs on the culture and happenings of a particular country, this is a great place to start.

Where

http://s700.uminho.pt/europa.html

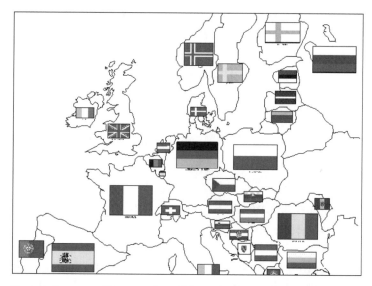

Start at the map of Europe, then click on the country whose home page
you want to visit. From there, you'll usually be provided with an
additional opportunity to visit a host of sites from the host country.

Links

Just click on any country's map, and you'll be transported to its home page.

You'll also find links to foreign language courses as well as online newspapers and publications from around the world.

You're Speaking My Language

If the topic of conversation is languages on the Internet, The Foreign Languages on the World Wide Web page has to enter into the discussion. This comprehensive site is a close runner-up to the Human-Languages Page in terms of depth, and offers its own unique slant on language information.

Look here for links to language tutorials, foreign-language literature, travel information, and online tours of museums from around the world. France is especially well represented here.

This one's highly recommended for travelers and anybody who's curious about other languages and cultures. The author of this page, Steve Thorne,

Your all-in-one source for information, learning aids, travel info, maps, and all things having to do with foreign languages and cultures.

is very discriminating, so only the best foreign language and cultural links are included here—but that still includes several dozen links.

Where

http://www.itp.berkeley.edu/~thorne/HumanResources.html

Links

Too numerous to list—just pick a country or language and go surfing.

The Online Writery

The Online Writery provides a venue for fledgling writers (read, college students) to access information about writing and to post their own literary gems. The folks at this site allow submissions from any genre, but they're also pretty serious, so if you post your works here, be prepared for some serious, honest, and informed criticism.

This site also includes links to other writing-oriented resources on the Web, including the Purdue Online Writing Lab, and to Internet guides and help files from various sites around the Web that might be of interest to writers.

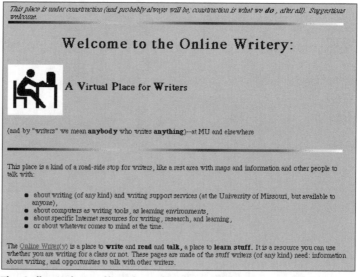

The Online Writery offers tips, criticism, and ideas for serious writers.

Where

http://www.missouri.edu/~wleric/writery.html

Links

The Gallery

Purdue Online Writing Lab

Literature, Unlimited

Literature and Writing Resources on the Web is *the* site to check out for anybody who loves great literature—from educators and literature students to writers to readers.

This site doesn't play favorites. You'll find links to diverse literature and resources from Shakespeare to Twain, and Coleridge to the Beat Poets—including online texts, online literary journals, information on research projects and readers and writers resources, and critical texts. If you love to read or write, you'll feel like a bookworm in a candy apple when you visit here. If you want to know who to thank for this site, remember the name David Elderbrock.

Where

http://www.itp.berkeley.edu/~david/LitITP.html

Links

The English Server

The Complete (and Searchable) Works of William Shakespeare

Storyspace Homepage

RhetNet: A Cyberjournal for Rhetoric and Writing

Bad Subjects: Political Education for Everyday Life

Postmodern Culture

The CMU On-Line Books Page

Journals On-Line

Humanities Focus Group

Can I Quote You on That?

If you're a writer or a speaker, and you occasionally need quips and quotes to spice up your presentation, check here for a large collection of humorous quotations. Currently, there are eight volumes of random quotations, along with links to several other collections of quotations. If I had to make a complaint about this site, it would be the lack of attribution for many of the quotations. Aside from that, this is a truly useful and entertaining collection. My favorite?

Seen on a tombstone: I *told* you I was sick.

Where

http://meta.stanford.edu/quotes.html

Links

Volume 1

Volume 2

Volume 3

Volume 4

Volume 5

Volume 6

Volume 7

Volume 8

[Recently Collected]

Weird

And many more

Tu Parle Francais?

Jacques Leon, a native of France and current resident of Montreal, Canada, has generously made this interactive Web site available to those who want to learn French in the privacy of their homes, but want a more interactive approach than courses found in books or on tape.

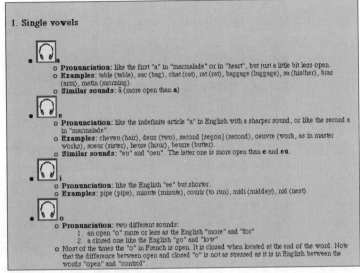

Eet eez a grrreat langueege, Frrench, no?

A nice feature of this site is the liberal use of sound file links that you can click on to hear how the lessons should sound. Currently, the sound files are in WAV format only, so you'll either need to be running Windows 3.1 with the MPLAYER sound extension or you'll need to have a sound conversion utility that can convert WAV files to a sound format that works on your computer. For Mac users, Sound Apple can handle this job.

There are currently six lessons for the beginner, but Jacques is adding other lessons pretty rapidly.

Where

http://www.teleglobe.ca/~leo/intro.html

Links

Just click on the lesson that you want.

MacFun with Languages

Bullfrog is a game engine for the Macintosh, and is now native for the Power Mac. If you have the Bullfrog core application (available from this site), you can also download the various game modules that work

Learning Latin was never this fun when I was in school. In fact, it wasn't fun at all.

with Bullfrog, including educational games for learning Latin, Greek, French, and Spanish at the high school and college level.

The Bullfrog Foundation game engine is freeware, but the individual game modules are time-limited demos until you pay the appropriate shareware fee. In any case, all of the software you need to use Bullfrog is available here.

Where

http://www-leland.stanford.edu/~lefig/index.html

Links

Science Education Software

Download

raves and gripes

reviews

And Don't Forget the Kids...

There might not be anything good on T.V. for kids, but you can't make that same claim about the Web. Whether you're a kid, a kid at heart, a parent, a teacher, or a storyteller, this site gives you all the information you need to find out about great children's books, many of which are available online. All age groups are represented.

You'll also find numerous links to sites that publish stories, poems, and other writings by children, along with announcements about nominees and winners of various children's book award contests from around the world.

Where

http://www.ucalgary.ca/~dkbrown/index.html

Links

Publishers Weekly Children's Bestsellers List

U.S. Regional Bestseller List

American Library Association Notable Books

Best Books for Young Adults - 1995

Quick Pics1995 - Books for Young Adult Reluctant Readers

Read-Along Stories

And so many more it seems a shame to only mention these.

Where to Find More Goodies

Many of the foreign Web sites mentioned in this book are also mirrored in their native languages. If you're interested in other languages, try some of these:

- Once you've mastered a foreign language (or two), check out some of the links in the *Books, Magazines, and Literature* section to download foreign books written in their native languages.

- Foreign language projects at Academy One are mentioned in the *Education and Teaching Tools* section.

- Find out how to speak the language of the Oneida Indians in the *International* section.

FREE $TUFF

We have a criminal jury system which is superior to any in the world, and its efficiency is marred by the difficulty of finding twelve men everyday who don't know anything and can't read.

Mark Twain

Law

Legally Speaking

The Legal Information Institute at Cornell Law School is a one-stop shopping bonanza for law-related Internet documents. Since its establishment in 1992, the LII has continually strived to find new ways of distributing legal documents electronically. Now, in addition to its regular task of distributing hypertext course supplements to Cornell's lawyers-in-training, the dissemination of legal information via the Internet has become one of its mainstays.

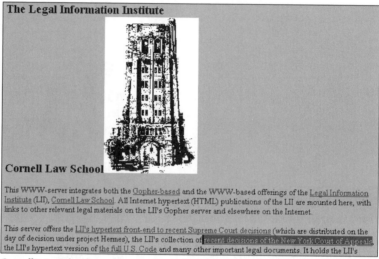

The Legal Information Institute

Cornell Law School

This WWW-server integrates both the Gopher-based and the WWW-based offerings of the Legal Information Institute (LII), Cornell Law School. All Internet hypertext (HTML) publications of the LII are mounted here, with links to other relevant legal materials on the LII's Gopher server and elsewhere on the Internet.

This server offers the LII's hypertext front-end to recent Supreme Court decisions (which are distributed on the day of decision under project Hermes), the LII's collection of recent decisions of the New York Court of Appeals, the LII's hypertext version of the full U.S. Code and many other important legal documents. It holds the LII's

Cornell's Legal Information Institute (as opposed to its illegal one).

You'll find links to a plethora of law-related sites and texts, including:

- *Cornell Law Review*
- Recent Decisions of the New York Court of Appeals
- U.S. Code
- *Financial Executive Journal*

Where

http://www.law.cornell.edu/

Links

Items of Special Current Interest

Additional WWW Sources (Law and Other)

LII's Hypertext Front-End to Recent Supreme Court Decisions

O.J.'s Trial and Tribulations

To me, sitting on the jury for the O.J. Simpson murder trial would be only slightly more appealing than having my fingernails pulled out with a rusty pair of vice grips. But one thing's for certain—as far as the several "Trials of the Century" we've had this year alone, this one has been a doozy.

Cut through the media hype and sound bites and access this Web page for all the daily transcripts of the Simpson trial, as well as attorney motions, rulings by Lance Ito, and other valuable court records. Did he or didn't he?

Where

http://www.islandnet.com/~walraven/simpson.html

Links

OJ's Statement to the LAPD

January Transcripts

February Transcripts

March Transcripts

Know Your Rights

Anyone who's ever watched *Cops* knows you have the right to remain silent and that anything you say can and will be used to boost their ratings, but after that things get a little fuzzy. The Citizen's Guide to Internet Resources on the Rights of Americans can help clear things up. You'll find a huge assortment of Web resources at this site that explain the rights of Americans under federal law.

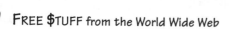

Here is just a smattering of the tons of online legal information and resources you'll find here:

- The Freedom of Information Act
- The Privacy Act of 1974
- General Information on the Constitution
- The Rights of Women

Where

http://asa.ugl.lib.umich.edu/chdocs/rights/Citizen.html

Links

Rights Under the Constitution and Bill of Rights

Rights Under Select Federal Statutes

Rights of Americans by Status or Group

Rights Arising Under Various Federal Programs

General Legal Resources

I Am Woman

Whether the topic is violence, race discrimination, the military, disabilities, or countless work-related scenarios, these complicated issues all have added importance for women.

Here's the best cybersite to find the most current and relevant resources for women's legal and public policy information on the Net. In addition to some great Web links, you'll find Gopher and FTP sites, as well as mailing lists and newsgroups. There are also lots of links to government agencies, non-profit organizations, academic institutions, and for-profit organizations. This guide can help you find information related to women's and feminists' legal, public policy, and political issues available on the Net.

Where

http://asa.ugl.lib.umich.edu/chdocs/womenpolicy/womenlawpolicy.html

Links

Health Care/Reproductive Issues

Lesbians/Bisexual/Queer Women

Mothers and Children

Violence Against Women/Sexual Harassment

Women and Development

Women in the Military

Women of Color

Women with Disabilities

Work Issues

Miss—make that
Ms.—Justice.

Happiness Is a Warm Gun and a Cold Deer

I've never quite grasped the sport of blowing animals to pieces in the wild when there's a Burger King drive-thru just down the block. But if you're of the breed that will defend to the death your right to liquify squirrels with your AK-47 Urban Assault Weapon, I'm sure as heck not going to argue with you. I may be a writer, but I'm not stupid.

Life, liberty, and the pursuit
of 12-point bucks.

Access this Web site to find out more about your rights as a gun owner from the National Rifle Association. You'll find articles and up-to-the-minute alerts on issues affecting NRA members, as well as information on conservation, legislation, hunting, recruiting programs, and women's issues.

Where

http://www.nra.org

Links

Electronic Version of the 1995 Firearms Fact Card

NRA Phone Numbers

Information on the 1995 NRA Annual Meeting

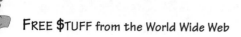

Firearms Laws

Institute for Legislative Action

Another great site for shoot 'em up enthusiasts is the home page for the Citizens Committee for the Right to Keep and Bear Arms at:

http://www.CCRKBA.org:80/ccrkba.org/

Animal Rights Resource Site

If you view animals as merely natural resources to eat or exploit, you certainly aren't alone. While most people probably wouldn't phrase it quite so bluntly, the fact is that most of us give very little thought to how our leather shoes got from there to here or whether that lamb chop used to be somebody's pet Lambchop.

See no evil, hear no evil, speak no evil.

The Animal Rights Resource Site provides plenty of eye-opening information to make you stop and think about the rights of animals as living creatures, including:

• A list of the most endangered animals

• Greyhound racing

• Socrates on animals

• A visit to a slaughterhouse

These are just a few of the many topics you'll find covered here.

Where

http://www.envirolink.org/arrs/index.html

Links

News

Essays, Guides, Journals, and Leaflets

Picture Gallery

Law

Action Alerts and Projects

Internet Resources for Vegetarians

Personally, I'm not much of a meat-eater, except for the occasional hot dog or pepperoni pizza—neither of which, technically, falls into the "meat" category. But this site is bound to make anybody who's ever worn leather (that didn't come from a wild cow that died of old age) feel pangs of guilt. And be warned: This site contains links to some very graphic pictures of tortured animals, ones used for experiments and product testing, and animals raised for food.

If It Pleases the Court

The Supremes (but don't confuse them with the Motown trio).

Article III of the U.S. Constitution established the Supreme Court as the highest court in the land. While its nine justices hold the awesome responsibility of making legal decisions that can affect the rest of the U.S. citizenry for generations, how much do you really know about this judicial tribunal? Here's a site that gives you a variety of information about the Supreme Court.

Click on the Context link to get information about the establishment of the Supreme Court. Also, if you click on the Gallery of Justices, you'll find a group photo of the current court. Clicking on images of the different justices will bring up each of their biographies.

Where

http://www.law.cornell.edu/supct/

Links

Historic Decisions

Key Word Search

Context

Dewey, Cheetham, and Howe

As partners in one of the largest firms in Washington, D.C., Arent, Fox, Kintner, Plotkin, and Kahn are experts in representing governments, international companies and organizations, and trade associations in litigation and arbitration. I'm sure they're well paid for it, too, and next time I'm in charge of running a small country, I'll be sure to call. In the meantime, I'll stick to Call-A-Lawyer to help me collect for my pain and suffering. (Just how much *is* pain and suffering worth these days?)

But wait, these guys also publish an extensive list of free newsletters you can request online, including:

- *Business Bullets*—Real estate, general business, and tax information
- *Employment News*—Labor and employment law issues
- *Environmental Law & Toxic Liability*—Environmental law or liability relating to toxic substances or hazardous materials
- *Government Contracts*—Government contracts developments

This is just a small sampling of what's available. Access this site to find out more. Also, to be put on their mailing list for one or more of these newsletters, send E-mail to:

cbg%arent_fox@mcimail.com

Where

http://www.arentfox.com/home.html

Links

Newsletters

There's No Business Like Law Business

Reinhart, Boerner, Van Deuren, Norris & Rieselbach is one of the many law firms hanging its shingle in cyberspace in recent months. And from what I've seen at this site, it's one of the best—especially for Internauts looking for lots of law-related links and information. Rather than just filling up its Web pages with self-promotional diatribe like many businesses that have established themselves on the Internet, this firm has loads of valuable links to business- and law-related Net pages.

You'll find free stock quotes and daily financial highlights, links to the House of Representatives, FedWorld, and the U.S. Patent and Copyright offices, and lots more. You can also get a free subscription to *The Reinhart Report*, a bimonthly newsletter featuring news, tips, and other important information.

Where

http://www.rbvdnr.com

Links

Intellectual Property

Health Care

Labor and Employment

Employee Benefits

Environmental

Real Estate

Commonly Asked Questions About Estate Planning

The Reinhart, Boerner Newsletter

Is Your Software Protected?

Legal Care for Your Software, still the industry's definitive book on software protection law 10 years after first being published, is now completely revised and on the Web. You'll get practical advice on getting the most for your efforts, as well as learning how to protect your code from software pirates. There are even sample contracts and forms you can use.

Keep your programs safe from pirates, competitors, and freeloaders.

Written by Daniel Remer and Robert Dunaway, this step-by-step guide is a must-have for any code jockeys looking to score big in software publishing. With plenty of common sense advice, *Legal Care for Your Software* is arguably the best guide for unraveling and deciphering the legalese that's a part of protecting your software.

According to the home page, *Legal Care for Your Software* will show you:

- When and how to use trade secret, copyright, patent, and trademark protection for your software
- How to negotiate, write, and agree to contracts that protect both parties and ensure a strong working relationship
- The types of contracts common to software publishing, including work-made-for-hire and royalty agreements
- How to limit your liability when the program is published—protecting not only your program but yourself
- Common sense advice on how to avoid legal hassles before they occur
- How to obtain copyright protection in other countries

Where

http://www.island.com/LegalCare/welcome.html

Links

Expanded Table of Contents

Chapters 1 through 13

They've Got Your Number

When the Social Security Administration began keeping records in 1935, it was faced with the overwhelming task of keeping track of the earnings of every worker enrolled in the new program in order to tally the benefits that would eventually be paid. The answer: the Social Security number, which created the overwhelming task of keeping track of every workers number. Aah, bureaucracy.

While many people use more than one name over a lifetime, Social Security numbers are unique identifiers for every Tom, Dick, and Mary in the workforce. And these days, your Social Security number is used for a much broader range than just paying taxes. In ever increasing numbers, government agencies, schools, and businesses rely on Social Security numbers to keep people straight in their computer systems.

These free booklets explain:

- Why we have Social Security numbers
- When and how to get one
- How to protect its privacy
- Retirement, disability, and survivor's benefits
- What women should know about retirement benefits, disability, widowhood, or divorce

You'll also get facts on:

- The original purpose of the Social Security number
- What the numbers mean
- Types of Social Security cards
- Applying for a new or replacement card

Where

http://www.gsa.gov/staff/pa/cic/fedprogs.htm

Download

Your Social Security Number

Understanding Social Security

A Woman's Guide to Social Security

Breaking Down the Barriers of Discrimination

In addition to the animosity and prejudice generated by the discrimination of the disabled in employment, transportation, and public accommodations, the economical costs are staggering. By sweeping away these barriers, the Americans with Disabilities Act enables all of us to benefit from the skills and talents of the disabled—both economically and socially.

Much the same way the Civil Rights Act prohibits discrimination on the basis of race, color, sex, national origin, age, and religion, the Americans with Disabilities Act gives civil rights protection to the disabled. It guarantees equal opportunity for individuals with disabilities in public accommodations, employment, transportation, state and local government services, and telecommunications.

This free booklet shows you:

• Which employers are covered
• How the ADA applies to state and local governments
• Telephone numbers for ADA information

Where

http://www.gsa.gov/staff/pa/cic/misc.htm

Download

The Americans with Disabilities Act: Questions and Answers

Protection Racket

Here are seven booklets to teach you how to protect your home, car, neighborhood—even yourself—from con artists, thugs, burglars, and cute little kids selling cookies door to door. You'll get lots of valuable advice on how to:

• Spot a con artist
• Protect your neighborhood
• Protect you and your car
• Conduct a security survey
• Report suspicious activities

Where

http://www.gsa.gov/staff/pa/cic/misc.htm

Download

How to Protect Yourself

How Appealing

The Emory University School of Law has made cases heard by the U.S. Eleventh Circuit Court of Appeals available on the Internet. Now anyone linked to the Web can access the full-text versions of Eleventh Circuit Court cases almost immediately after the decisions are handed down.

Starting with November 1994, cases are hyperlinked and can be searched via keywords, date, or title. You can even download the cases in Rich Text Format (RTF). Next stop, the Supreme Court.

Where

http://www.law.emory.edu/11circuit/index.html

Links

Alphabetical Listing
Listing by Month of Decision
Search by Keyword

Prosecutors Will Be Violated

My editor suggested to me that a chapter on law just wouldn't be complete without one reference to the lawyer jokes that seemingly abound on the Web. The more I thought about including one, though, the more I thought maybe it wasn't such a good idea.

Instead, I included three.

I won't give away any of the punch lines, but you'll find lots of references here to snakes, sharks, vampires, leeches, and skid marks on the highway. Juvenile? Without a doubt. Absurd? Certainly, but so is charging $120 an hour for a consultation.

Where

http://deputy.law.utexas.edu/jokes1.htm

http://deputy.law.utexas.edu/jokes2.htm

http://rever.nmsu.edu/~ras/lawyer.htm

Links

Lawyers and Sharks: Separated at Birth?

State of Washington Department of Fish and Game Lawyer Hunting Regulations

Humor Web Page

Humor Gopher Archive

Land of the Lost

Where to Find More Goodies

If you're interested in the law or just interested in staying one step ahead of it, be sure to browse these other sections:

- *Business and Career* for information on business regulations.
- *Education and Teaching Tools* to learn about colleges and universities around the world that offer law degrees.
- *Household and Family Finance* shows you the legal pitfalls of hiring someone to work in your home. I know a few potential presidential appointees who could've used this one.

FREE $TUFF

We now present the conclusion of *The Never-Ending Story*.

From a cable TV broadcast of the movie

Movies and Videotapes

Movie Cataloger

If your video collection is starting to rival the neighborhood rental store in sheer volume, you need to get organized. Here's a shareware program that's great for film buffs, reviewers, students, video rental stores, or anyone else who has piles of videos in shoeboxes and old grocery bags.

Movie Catalog for Windows organizes your collection by title, director, stars, composer, genre, rating, catalog number, and many other categories. You can even store reviews, the amount you paid for a tape, and the date and location where you purchased it. Whew. Whatever happened to alphabetical order?

Where

http://www.acs.oakland.edu/oak/SimTel/win3/entertn.html

Download

am_mc13.zip

The Movie Maven Goes Online

When he's not writing for the *Seattle Press*, talking with callers on his local radio show, or grumbling about Robert DeNiro's Oscar win over Peter O'Toole,

CINEMAVEN ONLINE

HOME OF THE MOVIE MAVEN • DOUG THOMAS

movie reviewer Doug Thomas can be found wired to the Web at CineMavin Online. Doug's site features reviews on movies you should go see now, films to wait on until the video is released, and turkeys to avoid until Thanksgiving.

You'll find Doug's Oscar picks, the top video sleepers from 1994, and a forum for Internauts called *Voices from the cheap seats*, where you can add your own reviews. Now, who brought the popcorn?

Where

http://useattle.uspan.com/mavin.html

TANK GIRL, one of the offbeat movies reviewed at CineMaven Online.

Links

Voices from the Cheap Seats

The Vault

At the Rental Counter: 1994's Top Video Sleepers

If I Had an Oscar Ballot

That's Entertainment

Move fans, stargazers, groupies, and anyone interested in reading about what's hot in Hollywood will love browsing through this online version of *Entertainment Weekly*. In addition to sneak peeks, reviews, and interviews, you'll get the latest dirt from Tinseltown.

And let's not forget fashion. Just what is it with those outfits you see at the Oscars? Did somebody tell these people they actually look good? *Entertainment Weekly* will fill you in on who's wearing what where. The searchable database alone makes this a great Web site to visit. You can search back issues of:

- *Entertainment Weekly*
- *Money*
- *People*
- *Southern Living*
- *Sports Illustrated*

- *Sunset*
- *Time*
- *Time-Life Music*
- *Time-Warner Electronic Publishing*
- *Vibe*
- *Virtual Garden*

Where

http://www.pathfinder.com/ew/Welcome.html

Links

Cover Story

Reviews

Database

Back Issues

Talk About Your Niche Marketing

How's this for a narrow audience: Here's a site called Japanese Animation Fans of Western Australia. Geez, why stop there? Why not really specialize this puppy and make it Japanese Animation Fans of Western Australia Who Are Left-Handed, Drive American-Built Motorcycles, and

One example of the animation art you can download from JAFWA.

Own Pets with Red-Dye Hair Weaves? These guys seem intent on limiting the scope of their page to a pretty darn tiny market. Still, of the 20 million Internet users around the world, there must be *somebody* interested in this or there wouldn't be a Web page devoted to it, and it's my job to make sure the other 19,999,995 of you know about it.

This group's goal is to spread the word that there are forms of animation different from the common American cartoons or animated movies, and invites us all to their screenings on Saturday afternoons (though I suspect if we all show up they'll have to find a bigger place to meet). Still, there are plenty of examples of Japanese animation to download here, as well as lots of information on newsgroups, FTP sites, and other Web pages.

Where

http://iinet.com.au/~gmb/jafwa.html

Links

Japanese Animation Fans of Western Australia

Local Anime And Manga Archive

General Anime And Manga

Coming to a Theatre Near You!

The Internet Movie Database—also known as Cardiff's Movie Database Browser since it originates from Cardiff University of Wales (though that's already more than you need to know)—is playing to a full house of Internauts. This site sweeps the honors for best Web site for movie reviews, news, and trivia. If it has to do with films, you'll find it at Cardiff.

You can search for your favorite movies by title, genre, country of origin, actors, or even characters' quotes—and that's just the beginning. You better load up your popcorn popper before you check this site—you might spend so much time browsing here that you'll never make it back to the theater.

Where

http://www.msstate.edu/Movies/

Links

Vote for Movies

Quick Quiz

Top 100 films

Bottom 100 Films

Famous Marriages

Here are the quotes containing _I'll be back_

1. Matrix in Commando (1985) said
   I'll be back, Bennett!

2. Princess Leia Organa in Empire Strikes Back, The (1980) said
   I'll be back.

3. Jack Slater in Last Action Hero (1993) said
   I'll be back! Ha! You didn't know I was gonna say that, did you?

4. Dutch in Predator (1987) said
   I'll be back!

5. Ben Richards in Running Man, The (1987) said
   Killian! I'll be back!

6. The Terminator in Terminator 2: Judgment Day (1991) said
   Stay here, **I'll be back!**

7. The Terminator in Terminator, The (1984) said
   I'll be back!

8. Douglas Quaid in Total Recall (1990) said

Nobody says it quite like Arnie.

 If your link runs a little slow, here are a few mirror sites around the world that might help:

Cardiff University of Wales in the UK
  http://www.cm.cf.ac.uk/Movies

Griffith University in Australia
  http://ballet.cit.gu.edu.au/Movies

Technische Universitat Munchen in Germany
  http://www.leo.org/Movies

Sony Computer Science Lab in Japan
  http://www.csl.sony.co.jp/Movies

Bond, JAMES Bond

Combine action, suspense, humor, and high-tech gadgetry and you've got the basic formula for every Bond thriller since 1962. And with a combined box-office gross of over $1 billion, the formula seems to be working.

I'm 007, on the Net.
INTER Net.

Browse the James Bond home page for links to all the films, information about the actors (who's *your* favorite?), and links to other 007-related Net sites. You'll also find lots of background on Ian Fleming, creator of Britain's greatest secret agent with a license to kill.

Bond always finished off the bad guy, got the girl (or was that got the bad guy and finished off the girl?), and still manages to maintain perfect hair. Who wouldn't envy this guy?

Where

http://www.dur.ac.uk/~dcs3pjb/jb/jbhome.html

Links

The Actors

The Movies

Other Information Sources

Tried and True-Blue Movie Clichés

Apparently, screenwriters think their audiences have the collective I.Q. of a can of spam, and here's the proof. This site, compiled by movie buff Giancarlo Cairella, lists hundreds of the most often repeated and hilarious clichés ever printed on celluloid. You won't be able to watch a flick again without spotting or hearing at least a few of these worn out gimmicks.

My favorites:

- If a character uses martial arts rather than a weapon, his opponents will always face him one-to-one. Spare bad guys may dance around the fight taunting our hero, but none will engage until his predecessor has been disposed of.

- You can eat as much as you want in a film and you'll never EVER have to go to the bathroom.
- Stripping to the waist makes the hero invulnerable.
- The hero's best friend/partner will usually be killed by the bad guys three days before retirement.
- A hero will show no pain even during the most terrific beating, yet he will wince if a women attempts to clean a facial wound.
- When a phone line is broken or someone hangs up unexpectedly, communication channels can be restored by frantically beating the cradle and saying "Hello? Hello?".

And there are lots more.

Where

http://www.well.com/www/vertigo/cliches.html

Links

Bombs
Bodily Functions
Monsters
Villians
Music

Movie Soundtracks R Us

You may not realize how important a film's background music is to creating the proper mood for a scene, but just think about that eerie Da Dum, Da Dum, DA DUM prelude in *Jaws* where you know that limbs are about to start flying, and you'll see what I mean. Or how about Bolero from *10*? Hey, imagine if we switched those soundtracks—now *that* would be interesting.

Penning a movie score is probably one of the least appreciated but most difficult roles in the making of a film. But if you just consider how important that background music is to the way an audience reacts to a film, you'll probably agree that the musical soundtrack deserves more credit.

Here's a site that gives credit to the musical geniuses that deserve it. You'll find information on who's behind the making of the music for many of your favorite movies, other films to their credits, and biographies of the composers.

Where

http://www.sony.com/Music/ArtistInfo/ArtistInfo_Soundtracks

Links

City Slickers II

Forrest Gump - Original Score

Sleepless In Seattle

True Lies

Wolf

> Having never scored a film and knowing nothing about the process, (Alan) Silvestri picked up a copy of Earl Hagan's book How To Score A Film and read it cover to cover the night before his meeting with the film's producers. "I literally tried everything in the book on this film. I had cues on top of cues, all kinds of things. I thought 'oh gee, this is what you do,'" said Silvestri.

Alan Silvestri, the man behind the music in Forrest Gump and one of the foremost film composers in Hollywood today, recalling his first break 40 films ago with the soundtrack to THE DOBERMAN GANG.

Dammit, Janet!

Take a Broadway flop, turn it into a B-movie, don't spend too much on advertising, and stick it in as few theaters as possible while you try to forget the whole debacle, and you've got all the makings of a hit—at least that was the formula for "success" for the most successful cult movie of all time.

For nearly two decades, *The Rocky Horror Picture Show* has played continuously Friday and Saturday nights at the stroke of midnight in over 200 theaters. With a cumulative gross approaching $100 million, I'm suprised we don't see this formula being used a little more often. Not bad for a million-dollar budget and eight weeks of filming.

Do the time warp at the Rocky Horror home page.

Horror-heads (I just made that up) will love digging through this treasure trove of *Rocky* trivia, FAQs, scripts, sounds, and pictures (look for Susan Sarandon as Janet). You can even download lyrics and theater lists to find out if it's playing in a midnight theater somewhere near you (it probably is).

Where

http://weber.u.washington.edu/~ehammers/rocky.html

Links

Introduction

Information

Images

Sounds

Can Someone Turn It Up?

It's been just shy of 100 years in passing, yet silent movies still carry a charm not found in "talkies." Maybe it's the sheer simplicity of the plots—boy meets girl, boy loses girl to villian, boy rolls eyes several times at camera, then boy saves girl in nick of time. Girl rolls eyes several times and says "My hero." Villian rolls eyes several times and shouts "Curses!" Hmm. Maybe the plots haven't really changed that much. Only these days it's Brad Pitt—not Rudolph Valentino—who has the ladies fainting in the aisles. (Did ladies ever really faint in the aisles?)

This Web page gives you lots of information on the films and legends of Hollywood's silent era, including Charlie Chaplin, Buster Keaton, Lilian Gish, and other stars. You'll also find pictures, scripts, and audio clips (Hah! Just wanted to see if you were paying attention!) you can download.

Where

http://www.cs.monash.edu.au/~pringle/silent/

Links

Stars of the Silent Era

The Great Train Robbery

American Memory Collection (Early Motion Pictures 1897-1916)

Buster Keaton, Lillian Gish, and Charlie Chaplin are just a few of the screen legends you'll find at the Silent Movies Web page.

Hype! Movie Reviews

Hype! And movies! Talk about redundant! Find out what all the hype is about at the Hype! Movies Web page! Read reviews of Hollywood's latest smash hits and dead duds! Each movie is rated on a scale of 0 to

Question:
What is your FAVOURITE line in the Star Wars Trilogy?

⊕ 'Uh...had a slight weapons malfuntion. But, uh, everything's perfectly all right now. We're fine. We're all fine here...now...thank you. How are you?' -Han Solo (ANH) (235)

⊕ 'Try not, do or do not, there is no try' Yoda ESB (116)

⊕ 'You do not know the POWER of the DARK SIDE...' -Darth Vader (ESB) (67)

⊕ 'Awwww...But I wanted to go to Tosche Station to pick up some powerconverters.' - Luke Skywalker ANH (41)

⊕ 'Laugh it up, fuzzball !' (ESB) (40)

⊕ I've got a bad feeling about this (ANH)-(ESB)-(ROTJ) (39)

⊕ I love you! - I know... (Solo to Leia on Bespin, ESB) (37)

⊕ 'The Force is with you young Skywalker.....But you are not a Jedi yet.' Darth Vader, ESB (31)

⊕ 'Apology accepted, Captain Needa...' -Vader (30)

Vote for your favorite quote from the STAR WARS trilogy.

10! If you don't agree, this interactive site lets you rate the films yourself! The exclamation points are provided at no extra charge!

You'll also find information about film festivals from around the world, contests like the recent Oscar predictions, movie polls, and more. And if you get burned out on the movie stuff, check out the Hype! home page for lots of other great links.

Where

http://www.hype.com/movies/home.htm

Links

Movie Review World

Film Festivals

Filmmakers Forum

Hype! Home Page

Hurray for Hollyweb

Hollyweb is the place to go for industry news, what's being filmed currently, and which films are leading the pack in box office grosses for the week. You can also download a list of the 50 all-time top money-makers. You'll even find film and video reviews, and lots of links to other film sites.

Where

http://www.ingress.com/users/spease/hw/hollyweb.html

Links

Studio Briefing

Production Slate

Box Office

Interstate

```
THE NET [Thriller]
A computer systems analyst finds herself caught up in a world of danger
and intrigue after tapping into an off-limits computer system.
CAST: Sandra Bullock, Jeremy Northam, Dennis Miller, Diane Baker,
Wendy Gazelle;
DIRECTOR: Irwin Winkler; WRITERS: John Brancato, Michael Ferris;
PRODUCERS: Irwin Winkler, Rob Cowan;
UNIT PROD. MANAGER: Brian Frankish; PROD. COORDINATOR: Lois Walker;
CASTING: Mindy Marin; PUBLICITY: Bob Hoffman;
PRODUCTION COMPANY: Winkler Films;
U.S. DISTRIB.: Sony Pictures;
LOCATIONS: Los Angeles, CA, San Francisco, CA, Washington D.C.;
START: January 23, 1995
```

It came from beyond cyberspace. The Net, just one of the many movies in pre-production you can read about in Electronic Hollywood, an online magazine about the film industry downloaded from Hollyweb.

And the Oscar Goes to...

Handed out since 1927 by the Academy of Motion Picture Arts and Sciences, the Academy Award is unquestionably the industry's most prestigious honor. And not insignificantly, the awarding of a gold-plated Oscar translates into millions of additional dollars at the box office for any movie. Even Oscar-nominated films that don't actually win still typically get a box-office boost.

This site contains information about all the nominees and winners for the past eight decades, including links to biographies of your favorite stars, lists of other movies they've had roles in (even the obscure ones), and a terrific cross-reference of facts and trivia.

Where

http://www.cm.cf.ac.uk/Movies/Oscars.html

Links

Links to 67 years of the best movies, directors, stars, and more.

Where to Find More Goodies

The Web is a movie buff's dream in living color. Look for some of these sites coming from a Web site near you:

- You'll find lots of *Lion King* GIFs and fun facts—even an online coloring book—in the *Kid Stuff* section.
- If you liked Jurassic Park, try a taste of the real thing in the *Nature and the Environment* section.
- Check out *Television* for links to information about some of your favorite shows before they made it to the big screen, like *The Flintstones*, *The Addams Family*, and *The Brady Bunch*.

FREE $TUFF

If Milli Vanilli are alone in the forest and fall, does someone else make a sound?

Anonymous

Music

Music from the Underground

The Internet Underground Music Archive, a pioneer in the free distribution of music on the Internet, offers a wide array of music to Internauts looking for samples of the hottest up-and-coming bands from around the world. So

Crank up the volume, then check out the Internet Underground Music Archive.

what if you've never heard of Raw Produce, 3D House of Beef, or Neptune Telescope (then again, maybe you have), if you're looking for fresh, hot musical talent that goes beyond the commercial stuff flooding the airwaves, point your browser here.

Whether your musical tastes fall into rock, heavy metal, grunge, reggae, hip hop, rap, or alternative—or whether you have no musical taste at all—there's something for you at IUMA. You can download audio and video clips of dozens of alternative bands to overload your senses.

In addition, you can download the latest issue of *Strobe* magazine, find information about different record labels like Sweden's MNW Records Group, and even get live shots from concerts, including QuickTime video/audio and MPEG audio clips of the shows (the recent Martin Luther King, Jr. Tribute show featuring Stevie Wonder and the Belushi Blues Birthday featuring the Blues Brothers, Steve Vai, and Clint Black is one example).

Where

http://sunsite.unc.edu/ianc/index.html

Links

Random Artist/Band Page

What's New

Check Out the Bands

This site has a tendency to run as slow as a 45 rpm record played at 33-1/3, but it's worth it in the long run.

A Hunka Hunka Burnin' Cyber-Elvis

The King is dead (in real space), but long live the King in cyberspace—unless his lawyers have something to say about it. This site has occasionally been shut down by the Elvis Police in search of copyright violations, but at last check it was up, running, and better than ever.

Sure Elvis is enshrined on the Web, but you're not truly immortal until your image is put on a set of salt and pepper shakers.

Check out this multimedia tribute to Elvis Presley, including a tour of Graceland (that's his mansion for anyone born after the Carter Administration), clips of his tunes, and photos of Elvis in all his glory.

You'll also find Elvis software programs for PCs and Macs, the Amazing Adventures of Space Elvis, memorabilia info galore, and lots of weird links to all-things Elvis on the Net. Elvis, revolutionary rock and roller that he was, has found a fitting home in cyberspace to continue the revolution.

Where

http://sunsite.unc.edu/elvis/elvishom.html

Links

Elvis Applications for Windows and Macintosh

Links to Weird and Wonderful Multimedia Elvis Stuff on the Internet

The Graceland Tour

The Doghaus Collection

CD Software

There are about as many CD software packages and utilities to choose from on the Internet as there are CDs in the stores. Here's a small (and I do mean *small*) sampling of CD software to choose from:

- Super CD-ROM player and database 16 & 32 bit
- Mini-CD Audio CD player for Windows
- CD Player for Windows
- TLG Workplace; View/Search TLG CD
- Win CD Audio Player/Database for Windows

Drive these around the block, kick the tires, and find the one(s) you like best.

Where

http://www.acs.oakland.edu/oak/SimTel/win3/cdrom.html

Download

abcd20.zip

minicd13.zip

musiccd.zip

tlgwp301.zip

wincdp33.zip

Catalog It!

If you're like me, your collection of music CDs and cassettes are piled into a shoe box somewhere near the stereo—about as orderly as a trailer park after a tornado. The result: Your favorite few stay near the top, while the lesser-played get forgotten at the bottom of the heap. Hey, you paid good money for that *Saturday Night Fever* soundtrack; maybe it deserves a little more respect. Okay, maybe not.

Anyway, you'll find it easy to keep track of your music library with Music Catalog for Windows. This program catalogs your music collection alphabetically, by artist, type of music, and more. It won't help you find your lost CDs, but at least you'll know what's missing.

Where

http://www.acs.oakland.edu/oak/SimTel/win3/entertn.html

Download

am_muc13.zip

Be Grateful They're Not Dead

From their bluegrass beginnings in San Francisco's music scene three decades ago to their chart-topping rock recordings in the '90s, the Grateful Dead have remained one of the few bands that outlast the Energizer Bunny.

Jerry Garcia, singing your blues away.

Check out this site for a comprehensive look at the Dead, and find out about other Web sites and software just for "Net-Heads," including:

- WinDead and WinTaper
- Dead icons for the Macintosh
- The Dancing Bear Screen Saver
- Graphics
- Deadbase VIII

Where

http://www.cs.cmu.edu/~mleone/dead.html

Links

Tour Dates and Rumors

Graphics

Song Lyrics

Sounds

Youth Music Resources

If it's true that nothing takes the fun out of enjoying a good book more than making it required reading, it's equally true that nothing makes listening and learning about music more of a drag than being tested on it. Hopefully, the Honors 123 course for students studying music/culture at Drake University won't have that effect. Judging by its Web page, these folks are definitely on the right track.

Janet Jackson, Nirvana, and The Beastie Boys. How's that for variety?

Created by students at Drake, the Youth Music/Youth Culture page offers one of the best varieties of links on the Net to performers, online music magazines, academic sites for music, listings organized by type of music, song lyrics, audio clips, and Usenet newsgroups. Grade: A+.

Where

http://www.drake.edu/univannounce/thomas/honors123.html

Links

Nirvana Web Archive

Music Resources on the Internet

Ultimate Band List

Lyrics Resource List

Resource List of Digitized Songs

Take Five—Better Yet, Take the 50s

In case you weren't there, the 1950s were the decade when jazz turned from be-bop hip to too cool. It was also a period when middle-class white college students (they made Dave Brubeck's *Take Five* a top-forty hit) finally discovered an art form that African Americans had known about for more than 30 years. Hey, better late than never.

This site features photos, discographies, magazine articles, and books from and about jazz's heyday in the 50s. Especially interesting is Ray Avery's famous collection of photos of such cool cats as Dave Brubeck, Paul Desmond, Chet Baker, Gerry Mulligan and many other jazz artists of the period. If you haven't yet discovered this great era in American music, it's still not too late—even if you're already out of college.

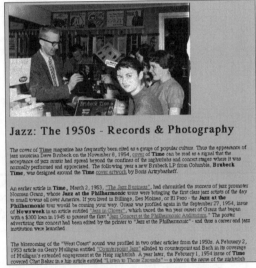

Jazz: The 1950s - Records & Photography

Believe it or not, buzz cuts, horned-rimmed glasses, and ponytails were all in—when jazz was cool in the 50s.

Where

http://bookweb.cwis.uci.edu:8042/Jazz/JPRA2.html

Links

Jazz Record Covers

West Coast Jazz

Tour--The Jazz Photography of Ray Avery

And many others

Print Me a Label

Here's a freeware program that lets you print your own labels for your compact discs. With the CD Jewel Box label printer for Windows, you pick the fonts, styles, and sizes of text to be printed, and the program does the rest. You can even print on the inside and spine.

Where

http://www.acs.oakland.edu/oak/SimTel/win3/cdrom.html

Download

cdlab203.zip

Creativity counts when you make your own CD labels.

To run this program, you must have a Visual Basic DLL (Dynamic Link Library) file called VBRUN300.DLL loaded in your WINDOWS\SYSTEM directory. If you don't already have this run-time library, you can download the zipped file from:

http://www.acs.oakland.edu/oak/SimTel/win3/dll.html.

Music Nettwerking

The dust has finally settled at Nettwerk Productions, and after a complete facelift, this site is better than ever.

Awesome album art from the alternative band Itch.

Nettwerk Productions, home to alternative artists such as Sarah McLachlan, Delerium, Ginger, Single Gun Theory, and a host of other bands, has completely overhauled its Web site with a new interface, including lots more graphics and music information.

You'll find:

- Audio samples (some unreleased)
- Videos
- Bios
- Discographies
- Behind-the-scenes photos
- Tour updates
- Mail order information

Where

http://www.wimsey.com/nettwerk/

Links

Sarah Newsletter

News/Tours

Artists

The Long and Winding Information Highway

John, Paul, George, and Ringo—together again in cyberspace. Get all the facts on the Fab Four's music and history. You'll find lyrics, essays by the fortunate few who have met the Beatles, album info, and even a tour of their hometown.

No, it's not Mt. Rushmore.

Also, remember the "Paul is dead" rumors?
Be sure to check out the link to the Beatles newsgroup that "proves" Paul was actually the only surviving Beatle. (Be sure your tongue is planted firmly in cheek.)

Where

http://www.eecis.udel.edu:80/~markowsk/beatles/

Links

Discographies

Mini Tour of Liverpool

John's Whimsical "History" of the Beatles

John Lennon's ABC's

For more Beatles info, try http://bazaar.com/Beatles. Though it was temporarily down when I tried it last, it's still a great site and includes lots of previously unreleased Beatles music from the BBC archives. The page should be back up by the time you read this (keep your fingers crossed).

Welcome to Woodstock—Again

Twenty-five years after the main event, comes Woodstock '94—and the Whole Earth 'Lectronic Link brought it all to the Internet. In addition to

An event 25 years in the making.

concert information and maps of the area, the WELL has created individual Web pages for concertgoers to share their experiences with those less-fortunate Internauts who were unable (or unwilling) to attend.

Over 300 participants posted their impressions of and stories about the landmark event; they appear here unedited, including pictures, sounds, and text. Read through a few to get a unique perspective on the concert and the fans that attended, unfiltered through the traditional media.

Where

http://www.well.com/woodstock/woodflash.html

Links

The Digital Scrapbook

Live Onsite Conference

Woodstock '94 Site Map

Some of the text in the Digital Scrapbook contains language you might find offensive. Such is the price of letting real people share their real impressions directly with the rest of the real world.

World Wide Web of Music

Billed as the Web's largest interactive list of music links, the Ultimate Band List links you to the home pages of hundreds of bands and music sites on the Internet. Browse through the listings by artist, genre (like pop, rock, or new age), or resource (like Web pages, mailing lists, or newsgroups) to find what you're looking for. Can't find it? I guess it's possible, though barely. This site even lets you add the latest links for your favorite bands.

The Boss, just one of the hundreds of megastars, along with not-so-mega-stars, you'll find linked to the Ultimate Band List.

Where

http://american.recordings.com/wwwofmusic/ubl.html

Links

Links to hundreds of music-related Web pages.

Music Scene International

See it! Hear it! Buy it! So proclaims the Music Scene International Web site. Get information about the latest recordings of some of alternative rock's hottest bands, then download images and samples of their music. Do you like it? Purchase the music online.

Where

http://www.musicscene.com

Links

Artists

Location

Genre

Labels

Help for Rock and Roll Addicts

Rock journalism leaps into cyberspace with *Addicted to Noise*, a monthly online rock magazine that provides a blend of features, audio samples, and graphics of rock's hottest sounds. Unlike many of its print counterparts that have recently gone online, *Addicted to Noise* is 100-percent Web born and bred.

Look for the latest album reviews and artist profiles while you listen to sample music and interview clips. Want to see what you've missed? Browse through the back issues to get up to speed.

Cover Story: ADDICTED TO NOISE is on the Web.

Where

http://www.addict.com/ATN/

Links

The links change with each issue.

Sing, Sing a Song

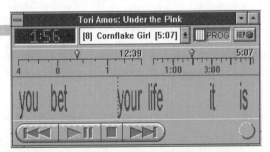

Karaoke on the Web? Sort of. While karaoke machines are springing up in bars all over the world, closet singers like me need more than a few 16-ouncers of courage before we'll stand in front of a crowd and belt out *Unchained Melody*.

Follow the bouncing ball and, before you know it, you'll be doing two shows a night in Vegas with Wayne, Frank, and da boys.

As usual, help has arrived through the Internet. Vocal CD is a shareware program for your computer's CD player that lets you enter the lyrics to your favorite songs and have them scroll across your screen in time to the music. Now would-be crooners can load their CDs and sing to their heart's content in the privacy of their own room. The help screens even show you links on the Internet where you can download lyrics. Now if they would only tell you where to find perfect pitch....

Where

http://www.acs.oakland.edu/oak/SimTel/win3/cdrom.html

Download

vocl147c.zip

Death by Electric Guitar

For rock fans with a morbid streak running through their veins, this Web page offers information on "untimely demises, morbid preoccupations, and premature forecasts of doom in pop music." I'm not entirely sure what all of that means, but suffice it to say this site offers electronic info on the deaths of rock legends.

Excerpted from the book *The Death of Rock and Roll*, this site includes "Famous Dates In Rock 'n' Roll Death," lots of info on drug overdoses, Elvis, John Lennon, Sid Vicious, and, many others. Long live rock.

Where

http://weber.u.washington.edu/~jlks/pike/DeathRR.html

Links

The Big Elvis

Famous Dates In Rock 'n' Roll Death

Beatles Bugouts

Samples

Like a Rolling Stone

The Official Rolling Stones Web Site is one of the best hangouts for rockers on the Web. And if you've got some strange fetish for images of tongues, you're definitely in the right place.

The Rolling Stones meet cyberspace, and neither will be the same again.

You'll find audio samples from the Rolling Stones' *Voodoo Lounge* CD, pictures of the band, and lots of Stones memorabilia. Find out about the band's latest projects, including films and recordings, then download the interviews with Keith, Mick, and the boys.

Where

http://www.stones.com/

Links

The Spoils of Our War to Bring You Live Rolling Stones

Our Picture Collection — Tongues, Albums, Photos

Hear Sound Samples from the Voodoo Lounge CD

Interviews with the Stones on the making of Voodoo Lounge

The Pure Text Offerings of the Rolling Stones

Help us Write Rolling Stones Fiction

Where to Find More Goodies

Surfing the Web's a lot more fun when you're in good company: Bizet or Liszt for me, and of course the Boss. Regardless of your musical tastes, the Web's got you covered. Here are a few other sections to check out:

• Find out how to get excerpts from *Guitar Player* magazine in the *Books, Magazines, and Literature* section.

355

- *Food and Cooking* includes a list of Parrothead boat drinks just for Jimmy Buffett fans. No fair peeking if the only Buffet tune you know is *Margaritaville*.

- The *Kid Stuff* section isn't necessarily just for kids. Download sound bites from your favorite bands and turn your computer into a virtual jukebox.

- If you're into movie soundtracks, try the *Movies and Videotapes* section for information on the people behind your favorites.

FREE $TUFF

It is inexcusable for scientists to torture animals; let them make their experiments on journalists and politicians.

Henrik Ibsen

Nature
and the
Environment

How Does Your Garden Grow?

The Garden Patch Web site is an up and comer on the Internet, offering a growing list of Net resources for those with a penchant for mulch under their nails, aching backs, and ladybugs.

You can almost touch the flowers on these azaleas from the Missouri Botanical Garden, just one of the many links to the Garden Patch.

Whether you're blessed with a green thumb or don't know the difference between a rhododendren and a rototiller, you'll find others who share your interest (or problem) here. There are lots of gardening tips, gardening resources on the Internet, and more. You can even enter a monthly guess-the-mystery-plant contest.

While you're there, be sure to check out the Garden Exchange, where you can post requests for seeds, plants, or information from other gardeners, as well as offer items to trade. This is the place to go for getting your hands on those hard-to-find plants the local nursery never has in stock.

Where

http://mirror.wwa.com/mirror/garden/patch.htm

Links

The Garden Exchange

The Garden Spider's Web

Garden Tips from Sesbania Tripeti

What's Shakin'?

When the devastating Kobe earthquake struck Japan on January 17, 1995, the Internet community was quick to respond. Damage reports from the 7.2 quake as well as the ensuing aftershocks, fires, and landslides were available almost immediately, and quickly spread across the Internet. While the Japanese government was criticized severely for failing to respond quickly or adequately to the crisis, Internauts who worked around the clock to keep the world abreast of the damage were universally praised.

Fires and structural damage to the area hardest hit by the Kobe quake.

Here's a site that provides fascinating information on the quake and its aftermath in both English and Japanese—including aerial photos of the fault line and damage—and links to dozens of other quake-related Web pages. You'll also find pointers to FTP and Gopher sites, as well as newsgroups that provide information and discussions on the tragedy.

Where

http://www.csl.sony.co.jp/earthquake/index.html

Links

A huge assortment of links to choose from.

This Museum Is an Internet Natural

The Natural History Museum in Berne, Switzerland, is open to Internauts interested in learning more about the animals (St. Bernards), vegetables (chocolate bars), and minerals (watch fobs) of Switzerland and other parts of Europe.

From St. Bernards to butterflies, you'll find a wide assortment of exhibits at the Natural History Museum.

FREE $TUFF from the World Wide Web

Founded in the early part of the 19th century, this internationally renowned museum is famous for its exhibits of birds and mammals in their natural surroundings. It also houses an outstanding collection of minerals, including rare gems and rock crystals from the Swiss Alps.

While still a work in progress, the museum's Web site is quickly adding to its extensive online collection with exhibits like:

- Vertebrate Animals
- The Canine Collections
- Swiss Dog Breeds
- The History of The Saint Bernard Dogs
- Invertebrate Animals

Also, look for lots of other useful science-related links to Web sites around the world.

Where

http://www-nmbe.unibe.ch/index.html

Links

Current Events/Exhibits

Albert Heim Foundation

Canine Collection

Biology, Earth Sciences & Scientific Museums

She's Gonna Blow!

At first, I thought this might be the newest theme park from Disney, but scientists and students alike will find something of value at VolcanoWorld. Whether you're a serious student of vulcanology (this has absolutely *nothing* to do with Spock) or just a geologic rubbernecker looking for thrills, VolcanoWorld delivers. This Web site, funded by NASA, provides a wide variety of information about volcanoes to schools around the world, visitors at Hawaii Volcanoes National Park and Mt. St. Helens National Monument, and Web cruisers like yourself.

360

Rock the Volcano. Who says vulcanologists don't have a sense of humor?

You'll find reports and pictures of the latest eruptions, photos of volcanoes on every continent, and a virtual walk through an active volcano. You can even get your questions answered by linking to the Ask the Volcanologist (and yes, you can spell it both ways). Is it getting warm in here or is it just me?

Where

http://volcano.und.nodak.edu/

Links

What is VolcanoWorld?

Ask a Volcanologist

How to become a Volcanologist

Current and Recent Eruptions

Images of Volcanoes

When it comes to loading this site, it moves about as fast as day-old lava. Don't blow your top, though. Once it's up, you'll find some great info on volcanic activity around the globe.

Have You Hugged a Tree Today?

Spotted owls and red squirrels alike will appreciate what's happening at the Natural Resources Conservation Service Web site. Formerly the Soil Conservation Service, the NRCS is a federal agency created to teach the American people how to conserve natural resources on private lands.

Bruce Babbitt and Al Gore are both rumored to spend a lot of time at this site when Bill lets them play with the computer. Drop by to get answers to your environmental and conservation questions on:

- Soils
- Plants
- Water
- Air

You'll also find links to dozens of other government agencies that deal with the environment and conservation. Some of these links were down last time I checked, but this site is still taking shape and shows a lot of potential for delivering valuable conservation info to Internauts.

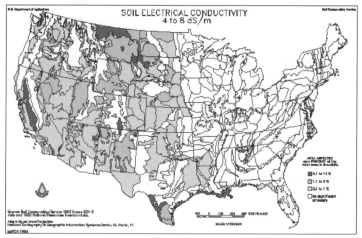

A soil salinity map of the U.S. And you probably didn't even know there was such a thing.

Where

http://www.ncg.nrcs.usda.gov

Links

WWW Servers (U. S. Federal Government)

The Federal Web Locator

Earth and Environmental Science Internet resources

Energize Me

So you think it's a long wait at the gas pump when there's a car or two ahead of you. Oh, let me slit my wrists! You ain't seen nothing till you've sat for hours in a rationing line from circa 1974. Never again! You'd be surprised at how open you suddenly become to alternative energy sources when you're staring at the back of somebody's Pinto for several hours waiting to fill 'er up.

This site from the University of Oregon provides a wide variety of terrific links on energy-related issues and some historical perspective on the energy crisis of the 1970s. There's also an alphabetical listing of energy resources on the Net, lots of information on ozone depletion, and archives from *Home Power* magazine. Plus, if you're able to view MPEG movies, check out the animated wind farm and the animation showing the dissipation of the ozone holes at the earth's poles.

Where

http://zebu.uoregon.edu/energy.html

Links

Brief Fossil Fuel Primer

Solar Radiation Database

Homepower Magazine

A Day Without Sunshine...

Anyone interested in learning how to be a little less reliant on dinosaur remains to heat their homes may want to stop in at the Solstice home page to learn about some of the alternatives. This electronic clearinghouse provides state-of-the-art information on RE/EE (that's renewable energy and energy efficiency for you non-governmental types—you'll see those letters a lot at this site), particularly information on the relationships among RE/EE, the environment, and sustainable development.

You'll find loads of useful information on streamlining your energy usage, different types of renewable and alternative energy resources (like

The sun'll come out tomorrow.

solar and wind), and government policies and legislation that could affect the fledgling alternative energy industry.

Where

http://solstice.crest.org/

Links

Answers to Your Energy Efficiency Questions

Case Studies

Efficiency

Renewables and Alternatives

Education and Social Issues

Tonight's Forecast: Dark

What's it going to be tomorrow: rain, snow, or sunshine? Here in Arizona, we pretty much count on sun, with any extreme variation considered to be a direct intervention by God. If it ever snows in July, I'd say it's a fair bet it'll be standing room only in every church, mosque, and synagogue within 100 miles. But I digress.

Here's a Web site that lets you get your local forecasts without having to sit through 30 minutes of local happy-talk from guys named Stu, Brandy, and Dewey. Bring up these satellite weather photos from Plymouth State

College to see weather disturbances throughout the United States, Mexico, and Canada, updated continuously. Just click on the area you're planning your next picnic in and you'll get the local forecast, up-to-date highs, lows, current temperatures, and more.

Residents of our 49th and 50th states (that's Alaska and Hawaii to you non-U.S.ers) may feel slightly snubbed at not being included here, but their weather doesn't vary much anyway. Alaskans can pretty much assume it's going to snow, unless it's July, then it'll probably rain. The only variation I've ever seen in Hawaii is that it gets dark at night.

Of course, if you miss that "local *newsie* feel" when you access this site, just bring up the weather map, stand in front of your screen, and wave your arms a lot while talking about high pressure disturbances that will cause either rain or no rain. Chatting about your plans for the weekend and wearing a cap and T-shirt from a local charity will also lend to the realism.

Where

http://vortex.plymouth.edu/usamap.html

Links

Fifty of 'em, including Canada and Mexico

Weatherphiles who like to give as much as they get will want to check out another great weather site at:

http://www.ems.psu.edu/wx

This site includes a place to enter your own weather observations.

Gardening Tips Galore

The Complete Guide to Garden Stuff from Books That Work is a veritable online encyclopedia of over 500 gardening tips for weekend gardeners. Author Steve Ettlinger includes information on everything from the basic tools that you'll want in your arsenal to the best pesticides.

But this site includes more than information on plants and fertilizer. You'll also find hundreds of links to information on the best gardening-related items like bird feeders, lawn statues, fencing materials, patio equipment, and much more.

Where

http://www.btw.com/garden_archive/book_toc.html

Links

Way too many to list. Access this site and start pointing and clicking.

Let Me Map It Out for You

One of the more primitive maps you'll find at this site.

My experience with maps doesn't go much further than using them as makeshift tablecloths on weekend picnics or trying to figure out how to refold them so they'll fit back into the glove box. But kids looking for a good overview of the study of maps (and what kid isn't!) will want to check out this site devoted to cartography (that's the study of maps in case you're geographically challenged like me).

This site takes you on a humorous, imaginative, and historical journey of map-making, starting with the ancient Egyptians. You'll learn about the different types of specialized maps used today and their purposes, along with some good examples. Now let's see, that's back and forth, back and forth, right?

Where

http://loki.ur.utk.edu/ut2Kids/maps/map.html

Links

Suggested reading list and other WWW resources

Other UT Science Bytes articles

When It Rains It Pours

Although only covering around eight percent of the Earth's land, the rain forests of Central and South America, Asia, and Africa comprise about 50 percent of all growing wood on the planet and over 40 percent of the Earth's plants and animals. Of course, if you're a developer, you'd probably be more inclined to think of these forests as mammoth strip malls and theme

Macaws in one of the rain forests of Central America.

parks waiting to happen. But did you know that those same rain forests also provide the majority of the oxygen we breathe? So, the more we pave, the deeper you'll have to breathe. I think I'll start that oxygen mask franchise now.

This site includes lots of rain forest facts and figures, along with pictures of the huge variety of plants and animals that call these tropical jungles home. Find out about the alarming destruction of the rain forests, the efforts being waged to stop it, and what you can do to help.

Where

http://mh.osd.wednet.edu/

Links

Amphibians

Birds

Mammals

Searchable List of Threatened Species

Documents and Treaties

Have a Yabba Dabba Doo Time

Who needs a time machine when you've got Web sites like Chicago's Field Museum of Natural History to send you on this blast to the past—way back to the age of dinosaurs? This exhibit beams you back 245 million years, give or take a day, into a multimedia world of prehistoric proportions. Starting in the Triassic period, this exhibit follows the glory days of the dinosaurs through the Jurassic and Cretaceous periods, right up to when they became 40-weight for your father's Edsel.

Monsters among us at Chicago's Field Museum.

This site is slow to load to be sure, but definitely worth the wait, and you'll find plenty of sites, sounds, and animation to carry you through, along with links and pointers to interesting information about a large variety of dinosaurs.

Where

http://rs6000.bvis.uic.edu:80/museum/Dna_To_Dinosaurs.html

Links

Lots of audio links and pointers to more information about each prehistoric period.

This site is a little short on instructions, but just click on the Tour button to move through the exhibit.

Birds of a Feather

At my house, attracting birds has never been much of a problem. Currently, I've got a small family of enterprising Cactus Wrens on my back porch setting up a commune the size of a small trailer park. And every morning, an army of sparrows comes for an all-you-can-eat buffet from my dog's food dish.

But if your house is avianally scarce, check out this site for three free booklets to teach you how to attract, feed, and shelter different species of birds.

Where

http://www.gsa.gov/staff/pa/cic/trav&hob.htm

Download

For The Birds

Pulling the Net Over Environmental Destruction

Ol' Mother Earth must be one tough lady to put up with the kind of punishment we dish out. When you consider acid rain, deforestation, smog, chemicals in the water tables, and nuclear waste, I'm amazed we haven't all turned into five-eyed mutants by now.

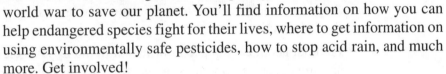

EcoNet's Environmental Directory is trying to help. This guide will point you to a huge assortment of online organizations fighting a world war to save our planet. You'll find information on how you can help endangered species fight for their lives, where to get information on using environmentally safe pesticides, how to stop acid rain, and much more. Get involved!

Where

http://www.igc.apc.org/igc/www.eco.html

Links

Agriculture & Trade

Biodiversity

Climate

Endangered Species

Energy

Environmental Education

Environmental Justice & Environmental Racism

Environmental Law

Forests

Mushrooms & Mycology

Pesticides

369

Population
Seas and Waters
Sustainable Development
Toxics, Hazards & Wastes
Transportation
Wildlife

Where to Find More Goodies

This section only scratches the surface of the environmental information available on the Web. Try these sections to go a little deeper:

- Check out *History* for some beautiful pictures from turn-of-the-century Yosemite National Park.
- Anyone with a penchant for environmental law can get his or her fill in the *Law* section.
- Find out about earthquake information in the Los Angeles area and conserving the environment using electric cars in *Science and Technology*.

FREE $TUFF

The wages of sin are
death, but by the time
taxes are taken out,
it's just sort of a tired
feeling.

Paula Poundstone

Religion

Christian Resources

The Internet and Web have been given a bad rap by many in the media who've hyped the relatively minute portion of cyberspace devoted to sex and debauchery. Sure it's out there, but you can find much of the same thing either in your local bookstore or public library. Less often reported is the enormous amount of educational, religious, and inspirational material waiting for your perusal.

A great place to start your cyber-pilgrimage is the Christian resources page, which includes links to many other areas of the Internet for anyone interested in learning more about Christianity. For instance, you'll find links to online versions of the King James Bible in English, German, and French; links to European sites devoted to Christianity; information about the history and culture of Christianity; and lots more.

In addition, there are lots of links to:

- Christian books and documents
- Christian organizations and churches
- Commercial Christian Web servers
- Other Christian-related Web servers and information
- Christian newsgroups

Where

http://saturn.colorado.edu:8080/Christian/list.html

Links

Bible Study

What is a Christian?

Bibles

Biblical Contradictions

Christian Organizations and Churches

Other Lists of Christian Net Resources

Amy Grant Archive

If you're in Europe and find things running a tad slow, try accessing this site's U.K. mirror at:

http://www.csv.warwick.ac.uk/~phujd/resources.html

Catholic's Guide to Internetting

I was born and raised Catholic and *I* don't understand three-quarters of what's contained at this site, but for those who paid a little more attention in Sunday school than I did, here's the Catholic's Guide to Internetting.

This site is a treasury of Latin prayers, a directory of Latin masses still being conducted in the U.S. and Canada, and a lesson on how to pray the Rosary. If there were only a nun to rap your knuckles with a ruler, this site would have it all.

Was this the burial cloth of Jesus? Come explore this link to the fascinating and controversial Shroud of Turin Web page.

You'll also find interesting writings from the early Church (A.D. 1 through 500) like the Confessions of St. Augustine, as well as writings from Vatican II (Son of Vatican?) from 1962 through 1965, and a fascinating link to a Web site devoted to the Shroud of Turin.

Where

http://www.cs.cmu.edu:8001/Web/People/spok/catholic.html

Links

Dominican Web

Free Catholics Web

Shroud of Turin Page

bit.listserv.catholic newsgroup

Wiretap collection of Catholic source documents

Give Us This Day...

My morning ritual includes the consumption of at least two cups of coffee (one for each eye) as I wade through the E-mail I've accumulated since the previous evening. I also go online to check the latest news, wondering if we may have gone to war sometime in the late hours while I slept. The news is rarely good, so I find myself going into rant mode before the sun has even completely risen.

OUR DAILY BREAD

February * March * April

Praise the LORD from the earth, you great sea creatures and all the depths.
Psalm 148:7

Need a little inspiration? Try one of these daily pick-me-ups.

This site offers a welcome breather for anyone wanting to start his or her day on a better note. Our Daily Bread is a Web site updated daily with a Bible verse, brief discussion of the passage du jour, and a daily prayer to inspire you.

Where

http://unicks.calvin.edu:80/woh/

Links

Our Daily Bread

Today's

Archive Page

A World Full of Religion

Which religion has the most devotees around the world? If you said Christianity, you'd be absolutely...*wrong*. The title belongs to Buddhism. Other big players include Hinduism, Judaism, Islam, and Baha'i, and all are represented at the Facets of Religion Web page.

In addition to information on the history and dogma of these religions, this site includes links to some of their major writings and other Web sites devoted to each religion.

Where

http://www.biologie.uni-freiburg.de/~amueller/religion/

Links

Hinduism

Judaism

Buddhism

Christianity

Islam

Sikhism

Baha'i Faith

Blessed Be the Card Catalog

Did you know that librarians have their own patron saint? Yep, St. Jerome, patron saint of bookworms. Remember that next time you're a little late returning those dusty volumes. It's not too surprising really when you consider that the same goes for hairdressers (St. Martin de Porres), writers (St. Francis de Sales), and even tax collectors (St. Matthew, who obviously had last pick), all of whom have someone pious watching over them.

Now, the Vatican has ventured onto the Web. While online confessions are still in the future (at least serious ones), they've created an online exhibit of books and manuscripts to help keep you a little closer to the straight and narrow. Rome Reborn: the Vatican Library and Renaissance Culture includes over 200 of the Vatican Library's most precious manuscripts, books, and maps.

According to this site, the exhibition presents the untold story of the Vatican Library as the intellectual driving force behind the emergence of Rome as a political and scholarly superpower during the Renaissance.

Originally displayed in the Library of Congress, this online exhibit includes not only objects from the Library of Congress exhibit, but also the alternate objects (brought from Rome to be used in case there was a problem with any of the primary objects) and items omitted later in the planning process.

Where

http://sunsite.unc.edu/expo/vatican.exhibit/exhibit/Main_Hall.html

Links

Vatican Library

Archaeology

Humanism

Mathematics

Music

Medicine and Biology

Nature Described

Orient to Rome

Rome to China

An early engraving of the Sistine Chapel, circa 1578.

Be sure to take the virtual shuttle bus to connect with other fascinating exhibits curated by the Library of Congress, including the Soviet, 1492, and Dead Sea Scrolls exhibits. Blessed be your tax dollars!

A Message of Unity

Originally founded as a splinter group of the Muslims, Baha'i teaches unity of mankind, equality between men and women, and freedom from prejudice. Pretty controversial stuff at the time of its founding in the early 19th century.

From its humble beginnings, Baha'i has grown to include nearly 4.5 million followers worldwide. Here's a Web site devoted to the teachings of the Baha'i faith, providing a good overview of its philosophies, including:

• Peaceful resolution of conflicts

• Harmony between science, religion, and reason

• The avoidance of alcohol and drugs

376

Where

http://sunsite.unc.edu/Bahai/

Links

Introduction to the Baha'i Faith

Baha'i Resources on the Internet

Some Information about the Baha'i Faith

Baha'i News From South Africa

Repent Your Cybersins

Well, it had to happen sooner or later. With everything else being wired up, automated, streamlined, and customized, an online confessional was just a matter of time. No real word from Upstairs on whether this site is "officially sanctioned" (though I haven't seen any lightning bolts), but even if not, it's still a lot of fun.

Confession Booth

Bringing the net to its knees since 1994

Digital Priest: How long has it been since your last confession, my child?

Days: [_____]

And what is it you wish to confess?

I committed the following sin:

(○ Murder) (○ Adultery) (○ Sloth) (○ Lust) (○ Avarice) (○ Deception) (○ Gluttony) (○ Pride)
(○ Anger) (○ Covetousness) (○ Misplaced Priorities) (○ Big-Time Kludgy Hack) (○ Fish in Microwave)
○ Didn't put printouts in bin)

Confessions are a snap now with this handy online confessional.

Sinners enter the number of days since they last came clean, and a handy check box helps to streamline the process a bit. You can even add more details of your sin in a dialog box at the bottom of the screen.

Religious voyeurs can read the sins of others by clicking on the Scroll of Sin hyperlink. Please don't take it too seriously.

Where

http://anther.learning.cs.cmu.edu/priest.html

Links

The Scroll of Sin

'Cause the Bible Tells Me So

While certainly one of the most fascinating and inspiring books ever written, the King James Bible is no easy read. Here are some programs for those who like their old-time religion mixed with a little high-tech gadgetry:

- Morning and evening readings by C. Spurgeon
- Proverb-A-Day for Windows
- Screen saver with Bible verses for Windows
- Windows sermon database and management system
- Windows in Time Bible Timeline

You'll find programs that offer inspirational verses, screen savers that pop Bible verses onto your screen, a database to help missionaries manage their sermons, and a timeline that helps make sense out of Biblical events.

Where

http://www.acs.oakland.edu/oak/SimTel/win3/bible.html

Download

me_v11.zip
provaday.zip
psaver11.zip
sfilea.zip
witbtl.zip

A Hebrew Luach? Oy Vay!

According to this calendar, the year is already 5755. I'm later than I thought! But if you're running on Hebrew time, everything is still kosher. Here's a program that provides an in-depth look at the Hebrew "luach" (that's calendar to the rest of us). You'll get all the important (and a few less significant) dates celebrated by Jews around the world, as well as the classic dates from the Luach's Gregorian counterpart.

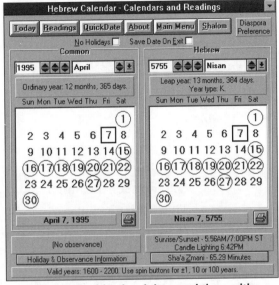

Get important Jewish-related dates and times with Hebrew Calendar 7.2.

This calendar lets you select cities from around the world to determine the sunrise and sunset times for daily prayer intervals, Shabbat times, and much more. Mazel tov!

Where

http://www.acs.oakland.edu/oak/SimTel/win3/calendar.html

Download

hbcl72.zip

Anglicans Online!

While this site includes online versions of the *Book of Common Prayer*, *The 39 Articles of Faith*, and other Episcopalian, Anglican, and Church of England books of worship, the scope of Anglicans Online! is much broader. You'll find religious software for the Mac and PC, a Bible dictionary, and other general Christian-related sources of interest.

You'll also find more specific topics related to the Anglican Church, including links to the Anglican Church of Canada's General Synod in 1995, an online searchable Bible, links to related newsgroups, an easy link to subscribing to the Episcopal mailing list (or to search its archives), and much more.

Where

http://infomatch.com/~haibeck/anglican.html

Links

Software for Theologians

Easton's Bible Dictionary

U.S. Episcopal Church

Thirty-Nine Articles

Comic Relief for Priests

The Scrolls That Rocked the World

Found near the Dead Sea along the Jordan River in 1947, the Dead Sea Scrolls have proven to be one of the greatest archaeological, historical,

Here's one of the many scrolls found near the Dead Sea along the Jordan River.

and religious discoveries ever. These scrolls include copies of the Old Testament *one thousand* years older than any others previously known to be in existence.

For decades after their discovery, these documents were a closely guarded treasure, available to only a few select examiners. But their contents are now being displayed to millions around the world via the Internet. This online exhibit examines the historical context of the scrolls and the community from which they originated. You can also read the fascinating story of their discovery 2,000 years after they were hidden.

Where

http://sunsite.unc.edu/expo/deadsea.scrolls.exhibit/intro.html

Links

Introduction — The World of the Scrolls

The Qumran Library

The Qumran Community

Today — 2,000 Years Later

Old-Time Religion Meets New-Time Cyberspace

In the beginning, ARPANET created the Internet and it was good. But the Internet was without form, and void of 25 million people. And the Spirit of Progress said let there be TCP/IP connections, and that was even better.

Maybe that quote isn't covered at this site, but here's the place to go for a great melding of old time religion and realtime technology. This online version of the King James Bible is fully searchable, so just type in a keyword and get hundreds of hits from thousands of biblical verses.

Bible, King James Version

Word: [   ]

(ex. "adam " or "word of god" or "man " near.10 "woman ")

To submit the query, press this button: [Submit Query]

Searching for salvation on the Web.

Where

http://etext.virginia.edu/kjv.query.html

Links

As many links as there are verses in the Bible, and then some.

Better Latter Than Never

Founded by Joseph Smith in 1830, the Church of Jesus Christ of Latter Day Saints has grown to a worldwide membership of around 6 million followers. This Web site, which takes pains to stress that it's "unofficial," provides a wide assortment of information on the Mormon religion.

You'll find a fully searchable online version of the *Book of Mormon*, as well as *Teachings of the Prophet Joseph Smith* and other sacred Mormon texts. In addition, there are interesting links to such favorite Mormon pastimes as genealogy and BYU sports.

Where

http://wings.buffalo.edu/~plewe/lds.html

Links

A good introduction to the LDS Church

The Articles of Faith

Teachings of the Prophet Joseph Smith

Brigham Young University

Genealogy/Family History

Gimme Eternal Salvation, and an Order of Fries

McChurch is a hybrid of serious religion and religious spoofing. The folks here seem to have a healthy respect for religion, but enjoy lampooning the money-grubbing, hair-brushed, TV evangelism that's essentially the fast-food version of religion. The icons of religious icons are especially humorous.

McChurch uses the McDonald's metaphor to spread its word (over 3,200 saved), but also provides some serious religious speed by providing numerous links to dozens of religious sites scattered around the Web. Whether you're seeking for truth or laughter, you'll find some help here, but you *do* have to make sure you have a sense of humor about the almighty before you poke around at this site.

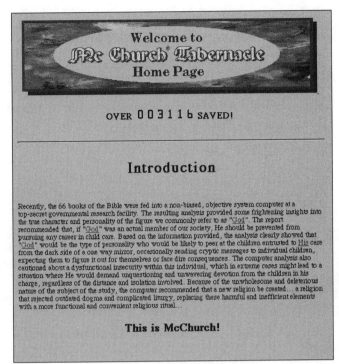

Welcome to MacChurch. May I take your order?

Where

http://McChurch.org/

Links

God

Check out the art icons too.

I'm not sure whether this site's located on a server that offers limited access or part-time access, or if this just an especially crowded site. In any case, it sure can be difficult to get into. Keep trying; it'll be worth the wait.

UU Got That Right

Following a tradition that's more than 400 years old (with roots a thousand years older), Unitarian Universalism is made up of a wide variety of members with an even wider assortment of religious beliefs and creeds. But the common bonds its members share are the belief in:

- The inherent worth and dignity of every human being regardless of religious affiliation
- Using reason and conscience as a guide to what is moral
- Religion as a personal philosophy
- Universal salvation
- The unity of God

Once viewed as heretical, contemporary UUism—with its melting pot of religious ideas—has evolved into an alternative to creed-based religions. The Unitarian Universalist Resource List provides information about UUism, its history, and links to dozens of other Web sites, mailing lists, and newsgroups.

Where

http://www.qrd.org/QRD/www/UUA/uu-toc.html

Links

What is Unitarian Universalism?

UU Organizations and Contacts

UU Resources - General

UU Theology

Where to Find More Goodies

Two of the livelier topics you'll find amply represented on the Web are politics and religion. Look in these other sections for more information on what's out there:

- Christian literature in the *Books, Magazines, and Literature* section.
- Dare I mention the mountain-biking links in *Sports, Recreation, and Hobbies*? Nah, better not.

FREE $TUFF

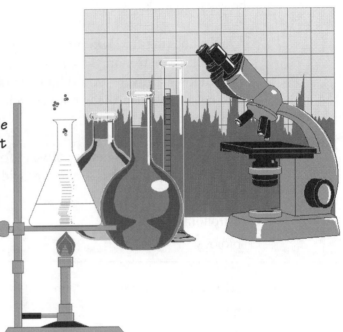

In studying the science of yesteryear one comes upon such interesting notions as gravity, electricity, and the roundness of the earth—while an examination of more recent phenomena shows a strong trend towards spray cheese, stretch denim, and the Moog synthesizer.

Fran Lebowitz

Science and Technology

The University of Michigan Does Science

I could fill a book by just describing all of the science- and technology-related software at the University of Michigan archives. But I can save both you and me some time just by pointing you to this archive and letting you do the rest. Whether you're searching for science software for DOS, Windows, or the Mac, this is (literally) one of the best places in the world to look.

If you're looking for DOS programs, go to the site I've specified below and check the astronomy, electronics, math, and programming folders. For Windows software, you'll find several programs at the site I've indicated below, but also check out the "science" folder for additional Windows programs on science.

If you're looking for science software for the Mac, this is definitely the place to be. Try the Mac site I've provided below, then check out these folders:

- astronomy
- biology
- chemistry
- compsci
- math
- medical
- olbio
- physics

Where

http://www.umich.edu:80/group/itd/archive/Public/html/msdos/windows/science/   (DOS)

http://www.umich.edu:80/group/itd/archive/Public/html/msdos/windows/science/   (Windows)

http://www.umich.edu:80/group/itd/archive/Public/html/msdos/windows/science/   (Macintosh)

Links

You're on your own from here.

According to My Calculation...

While the well-dressed scientist may have a little trouble fitting this overblown abacus into her pocket protector, it *will* fit nicely onto her hard drive. Though I don't even pretend to understand all the bells and whistles on this scientific calculator for Windows (heck, I don't even pretend to understand just the bells), I go by that time-tested rule of the more buttons, abbreviations, and formulas, the better. Based on these highly critical criteria, I'd say this program is one of the greatest scientific discoveries on the Web. Try it out, figure it out, and try not to hurt yourself with it.

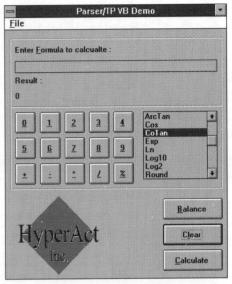

Let's see: Take the square root of the hypotenuse of the right triangle, multiplied by the temperature of dirt....This is starting to sound like the royalty formula for my last book contract.

Where

http://www.acs.oakland.edu/oak/SimTel/win3/calc.html

Download

scicalc1.zip

Spare the Frog and Spoil the Child

What's the first repressed memory that surfaces when you think back to 8th-grade biology and frog dissection? If you said the number of chambers in the heart and a detailed image of the digestive system, you obviously didn't attend my school. If, on the other hand, you said finding the

FREE $TUFF from the World Wide Web

frog's head in your purse, I've been waiting 20 years to apologize. Send me the bill for any subsequent therapy you had to go through.

Fortunately—especially for the frogs—those days of dissecting the real things are fading quickly. Kids and adults alike can now experience the thrill of virtual frog dissection—odor free and from the comfort of their computers—courtesy of the Lawrence Berkeley Laboratory. You select the view you want (top or bottom), the parts of the frog you want to dissect (maybe *want* isn't the right word), and then the fun begins.

This little fella gave his cyberlife in the name of science and tasteless practical jokes.

You can display the dissection sequence as a series of still pictures or you can view MPEG movies that rotate the entire frog or the various organs currently being sliced and diced. (Sorry Mac users, a QuickTime version is not yet available. I suggest you register your displeasure with the authors of this site so that something gets done to change the situation pronto.) There are 24,000 possible movie sequences, four for every combination of organs.

Where

http://www-itg.lbl.gov/vfrog/dissect.html

Links

"Whole Frog" Project
Virtual Frog Builder Game
Tutorial
Overview
Paper
FAQ

This site is both fun and educational, so it probably won't surprise you to learn that it's also a very busy place. Access may be denied or may be slow during peak traffic hours. For a good mirror site, try:

http://george.lbl.gov/vfrog

The site is also wildly popular among real frogs, who no doubt favor the idea of sparing them and using animated stunt doubles in their place. Also, the site is now available in Spanish, French, German, and Dutch.

Time for Your Physical

Physics, for anyone who may have overslept that semester, is that insignificant branch of science concerned with the laws that govern the basic structure of the universe. While that may very well be true, back in high school we didn't get much further in the physics of the universe than studying the effects of placing marshmallows in a vacuum tube. Presumably, this was to test the viability of serving astronauts hot cocoa in deep space, or maybe to complement their weenie roasts.

Maybe your physics experiences are a little different, or maybe you don't have any physics experiences at all. If not, download this Windows-based, hypertexted physics tutorial to find out what you missed.

Where

http://www.acs.oakland.edu/oak/SimTel/win3/educate.html

Download

physicst.zip

Better Living through Chemical Engineering

The School of Chemical Engineering and Materials Science, University of Oklahoma, offers information on research in the areas of bioengineering, polymer science and engineering, environmental engineering, and energy studies—and no, I don't understand what I've just written.

Except for the Institute for Gas Utilization and Processing Technologies page (try saying *that* five times fast), most of the related pages here just offer information on the programs and research being conducted at the school. The IGUPT page, on the other hand, offers plenty of information on the use of natural gas for innovative purposes. It's actually pretty interesting. No, really.

The School of Chemical Engineering and Materials Science at the University of Oklahoma

Welcome to the School of Chemical Engineering and Materials Science World Wide Web server at the University of Oklahoma. Please exlpore our departmental information regarding the graduate and research programs in chemical engineering. We are involved in many areas of chemical engineering research including bioengineering, energy, polymer science and engineering, and, environmental engineering. Feel free to contact us via e-mail if you have any questions regarding our research or graduate programs.

Chemical Engineering Departmental Information

But the real value of this site is as a launching pad to

"Oooooooohhh! Klahoma, where the polymers come sweeping down the plains!" Hmmm. Doesn't quite have the ring I expected.

several other great science pages. There are links to major employers of individuals who have a degree or background in chemical engineering, and there are links to some of the best general-interest science Web sites available.

Where

http://www.uoknor.edu:80/cems/

Links

For employment opportunites in the field of chemical engineering, check out:

AT&T

General Electric

IBM Corp.

Motorola

Monsanto

Schlumberger

For links to other outstanding science-related Web pages, try:

The National Science Foundation

The Department of Energy

The Environmental Protection Agency

The National Institute of Health

Bug Off

Named for the Caribbean island in which the feasibility of eradicating bugs by sterilization was first demonstrated in 1955, Curacao is a computer program that simulates the release of sterile insects into an area and then estimates how long it takes the little buggers to mate, become frustrated with their infertility, develop feelings of inadequacy, and die out.

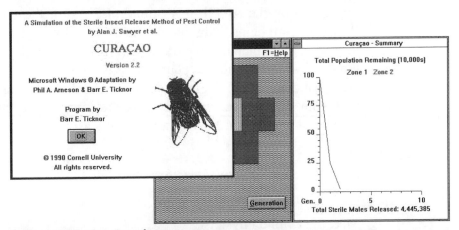

Going, going, gone. But what a way to go.

Talk about your repressed minorities! I mean, it's not bad enough that scientists have all but destroyed the little guys' sex lives, or even that they want to eradicate the poor devils, but graphing their demise with this simulation program is just sick and wrong. Besides, I didn't understand it all that well in the first place. But I'm sure there's a student out there that could impress the heck out of his biology professor with this program. Extra credit, anyone?

Where

http://www.acs.oakland.edu/oak/SimTel/win3/biology.html

Download

cura22.zip

Let's Get Physical

Word has it that British physicist and mathematician Stephen Hawking, author of *A Brief History of Time*, was actually thinking of a career in the shoe business until he came upon this site. Good thing—Dr. Scholl's loss was physics' gain. If you're thinking of taking the same road, but don't know where to start, check out the Physics Careers Bulletin Board for help.

Sponsored by the American Institute of Physics, the Physics Careers Bulletin Board helps fledgling physicists—or physicist wannabe's—get their start. Each month, six physicists are featured—each from a different job sector—who can answer your questions about how they got where they are, what courses and degrees you'll need, and how to combine physics with your other career interests. This site's new, it's exciting, and like physics, it's *really* hard to explain. But at least it's not just theoretical.

Where

http://www.aip.org/aip/careers/careers.html

Links

Meet the Online Physicists

Visit the Archives Section

Physics Careers Information Center

Forget Pizza—Order a Museum Tonight

One of the features of the Web that continually amazes me is the willingness for non-English-speaking Web sites to provide their information in English. I'm almost embarrased by this privilege. Almost. Since English is the only language I speak with any degree of coherency, I'm mostly relieved that English has become the language of the Web.

Anyway, a great example of this eagerness to entice the English-speaking world can be found at the Institute and Museum of History and Science, a Web page located in Florence, Italy. All of the information at this site is available in either English or Italian.

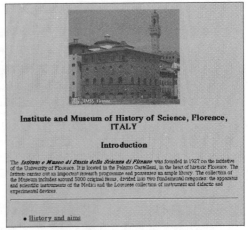

Institute and Museum of History of Science, Florence, ITALY

Introduction

The *Istituto e Museo di Storia della Scienza di Firenze* was founded in 1927 on the initiative of the University of Florence. It is located in the Palazzo Castellani, in the heart of historic Florence. The Istituto carries out an important research programme and possesses an ample library. The collection of the Museum includes around 5000 original items, divided into two fundamental categories: the apparatus and scientific instruments of the Medici and the Lorenese collection of instrument and didactic and experimental devices.

● History and aims

If you're planning to take a trip to Italy soon, make sure you stop at the Institute and Museum of History of Science, in Florence. Come to think of it, even if you're not planning to take a trip to Italy, you can still visit here—courtesy of the Web.

Most home pages for museums, planetaria, zoos, botanical gardens, and other tourist destinations do little more than provide their hours of operation and a listing of what you'll find when you visit. But this site offers a wealth of information about the collections housed at the museum, along with enough information about how museum operates that you'll probably be able to start your own—provided you have access to a couple of hundred- or thousand-year-old collections of artifacts.

Where

http://galileo.imss.firenze.it/

Links

The Medici Collection

The Lorraine Collection

The Library

PenWorld Gets Personal

"Pen," in this case, stands for *Personal Electronics News*, a publication that's devoted to providing up-to-date information for consumers who use personal computers, PDAs, games, and other personal electronic

If you're a consumer electronics buff, this site's for you.

devices. Businesses need not apply, since this site is more devoted to entertainment and pure fun rather than productivity.

This site provides current and back issues of *Personal Electronics News*, along with links to other sites that will interest consumer electronics buffs. The last time I checked this site, its authors were stressing its newness as a "site under construction." But I found a lot of information, and the links I checked were all stable. So, the authors of this site are clearly an overly worrisome bunch. Pay them no heed, and just enjoy what you find here. If you love using high-tech gadgets for fun and other home uses, this is the site to explore.

Where

http://www.penworld.com/

Links

This Weeks Feature Articles - Introduction

Back Issues

Industry News

Net News

Politics

Real World

Talking Heads

Periodic Table

Anybody who has ever taken a chemistry class will remember this laugh-a-minute chart they were required to memorize. This shareware program displays the periodic table of the elements as a Windows 3.1 help file. Simply click on any box to bring up detailed information about that element. There are even hyperlinks to related information.

Where

http://www.acs.oakland.edu/oak/SimTel/win3/chem.html

Download

ptable10.zip

This site has a lot of other science-related programs that you'll probably need a Ph.D to understand, including a molecular viewer, a mass calculator, and one that displays atomic coordinates. I'm convinced that if you were to somehow combine these programs, you could cause the universe to begin collapsing back in on itself. Not wanting to be saddled with that kind of responsibility, I left them alone. If you're more adventurous, have at it, but don't say I didn't warn you.

L.A. Rocks, Rolls, and Shakes

It used to be that when you thought of L.A., visions of sun, beaches, mountains, great weather, and all-around state-of-the-art living came to mind.

My, how times can change. Today, L.A. is literally awash in floods and mudslides, along with earthquakes, fires, and several other natural and unnatural disasters.

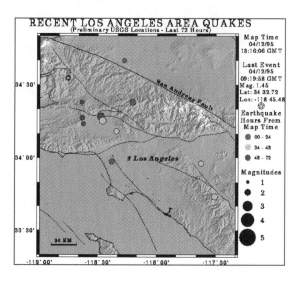

Los Angeles County is massive, so either you live there or you know somebody who lives there (or at least you know somebody who knows somebody who lives there). The eyes of the world are on L.A., along with the eyes of the Web. Specifically, you can track the earthquake activity in L.A. County from the map provided at this site. What's next for these folks? A plague of locusts?

Where

http://quake.wr.usgs.gov/QUAKES/CURRENT/los_angeles.html

Links

Click on any of the circled earthquake sites for more information.

You're Not Going to Believe This

The Skeptics Society, whose mission is to examine every claim made by pseudoscience, pseudohistory, and the pseudonormal, and then stomp the claim in the dust, is now on the Web. This gang provides an important service in doing research to separate "real" science from the charlatans. You'll find links to selected articles from *Skeptic Magazine*, transcriptions from discussion forums, and reviews of skeptics books and tapes. Don't believe me? Come see for yourself.

Where

http://www.skeptic.com

Links

Skeptic Magazine

Skeptics' Books and Tapes
Skeptics Society HyperNews Discussion Forum
Other Skeptical Resources on the Net

Dictionary of Computing

Stumped about the meaning of such cryptic acronymns as SMTP, ISDN, and IBM? Well, here's a site that provides some realtime answers to your questions. This site doesn't provide any graphics—but then, its mission isn't visual, it's verbal. If you want information about a computer term or some other technical phrase, this is the place to look.

The Free On-Line Dictionary of Computing provides a search engine that you can use to look up any word or phrase relating to the technically obtuse world of computing. Just enter your word or term in the search box, and let the Dictionary of Computing do the rest.

Where

http://wombat.doc.ic.ac.uk/

Links

There are some links here, but they're all pretty arcane. You'll be best served by sticking with the Dictionary of Computing search engine.

NSF Online

The National Science Foundation is an agency of the U.S. Government whose mission is to promote the development and progress of science and engineering. But for Web surfers, the more important news is that the NSF home page has been on the Web since August of 1994 and provides some great links to available grants, publications, research information, and other topics on science and engineering.

One of my favorite links is "News of Interest," which connects you to news articles about recent events and upcoming happenings in the field of science. This is a great service for educators and students, but professional scientists will also find valuable information here.

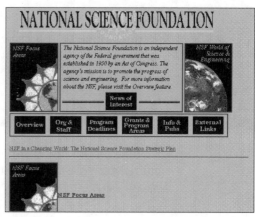

Where

http://www.nsf.gov/

Links

NSF Focus Areas

News of Interest

NSF World of Science & Engineering

Grants & Program Areas

Info & Pubs

External Links

Come On Baby, Do the Eco Motion

What you'll find here is positively electrifying—everything you've ever wanted to know about electric cars: how far they can go, how fast, how efficient they are, how affordable they are, how goofy they look.... Just kidding, electric-car people.

To tell you the truth, these folks are pretty serious about evangelizing the use of electric cars in the 21st century (if not sooner). One of the points they keep making is that, even though an electric car can't go as far as its gas-sipping counterparts, half the people in the world don't *need* to travel 40 or more miles per day.

The point: Electric cars are more efficient than gas vehicles for day-to-day commuting. I found the information here to be informative and thought-provoking, so I suggest you poke around here. The environment is a terrible thing to waste.

Where

http://cyberzine.org/html/Electric/ecomotion.html

Links

Sample Vehicle Conversions

Other Sources of EV information

Eco-Motion Classifieds

Where to Find More Goodies

The Internet was founded by scientists, and those roots are still firmly planted in all niches of the Web, including:

- Information on *Discover* magazine's online version is provided in *Books, Magazines, and Literature*, as well as a good selection of science-fiction books and magazines.
- Learning about the science behind weather is made fun in the *Education and Teaching Tools* section.
- Look for back issues—way back to 1835—of *Scientific American* and other 19th Century science journals in the *History* section.

 # FREE $TUFF

THE CREATION OF THE UNIVERSE was made possible by a grant from Texas Instruments.

PBS

Space and Astronomy

They're Heeeeerrrre

If E.T. had known about this site, he wouldn't have had to phone home. He could have just sent E-mail and browsed through the family album while waiting for a ride. This site has some fascinating pictures, stories, and chilling interviews with surprisingly credible witnesses of UFOs.

There is also lots of interesting information on such UFO hot spots as Groom Lake, Area 51, and The Gulf Breeze—as well as theories of coverups purportedly engineered by the National Security Administration, NASA, and the Department of Defense. Just what in the world's going on out there?

Where

http://www.bgsu.edu/~jzawodn/ufo

Links

NASA Astronauts Who Have Seen UFOs

Extraterrestrials Discussion List

List of UFO Books

The U.S. Air Force doesn't want you snooping here. Think they're hiding some little green guys nearby?

Astronomy Software (PC Users)

When it comes to finding great planetarium, telescope, and night sky simulation software on the Internet, the sky's the limit. You'll find at least 10 freeware, shareware, or demo programs at this site alone that will satisfy even the most discerning of astro observers.

There are programs that simulate your view of the evening sky regardless of your longitude or latitude, solar system calculators that plot the position of stars a thousand years ago or a thousand years from now, gravitational simulators, and utilities that list astronomical events for any date in history.

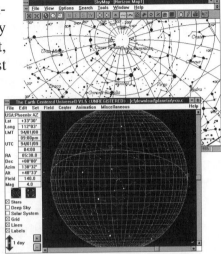

Look! Up in the sky! Here are just two examples of the software that amateur astronomers can download.

Where

http://www.acs.oakland.edu/oak/SimTel/win3/astronmy.html

Download

ecu15.zip

galileo1.zip

hubble14.zip

nbodyd16.zip

skymap22.zip

skytim11.zip

Astronomy Software (Mac Users)

Astronomy programs for Macintosh users are definitely *not* in short supply at the University of Michigan's Macintosh archives. In fact, the selection here is downright astronomical. Here, you'll find a total of 23 (at this writing) software packages for astronomy buffs.

Some of the programs here are more than four years old, and do seem to show their age. But there are also some recent software postings that are so good they'll likely have you running eagerly to your telescope (or to the store to *buy* a telescope). Two of my favorites are Stars to Harp By (also known as Harpstars) and MPj Astro.

Both of these are great, versatile, planetarium programs, and both offer different options and unique opportunities for planetary study for astronomy buffs. "Harpstars" is available on the Web as either a 68K Mac version (floating-point unit recommended) or as a native Power Mac version (download either harpstars2.1fpu.sit.hqx or harpstars2.1ppc.sit.hqx). MPj Astro is another great planetarium program, and frankly, it's my favorite. The author (to my knowledge) hasn't made a native Power Mac version available, but the existing version runs well on both 68K and Power Macs and offers an impressive number of display options for users (download mpjastro1.3.sea.hqx).

Harpstars and Mpj Astro are just the tip of the universal iceberg. Here's a complete description of the programs you can download from this archive:

- **3dgalaxyccollisions.cpt.hqx** Enter your date and the application shows you how the galaxy collision would look like.
- **coords2.3a.cpt.hqx** Converts coordinates from geodetic to Cartesian coordinate systems, and vice-versa.
- **earthplot3.01.sit.hqx** Enter the latitude, longitude, and altitude, and the program draws you a map of the Earth view.
- **gravitation4.0.cpt.hqx** A graphic, two-dimensional orbital simulation that you can customize.
- **harpstars2.1fpu.sit.hqx** or **harpstars2.1ppc.sit.hqx (for native Power Mac systems)** One of my favorite Macintosh planetariums—lets you view stars by date and time and shows constellations.
- **macastrol1.6.cpt.hqx** An impressive shareware package that shows you what the sky looks like at any place in the world between the years 1500 and somewhere in the next century.

- **moonclick1.21.sit.hqx** Produces a continually updated, real-time image of the moon for any place, date, time, and other variables.

- **moonphaser1.0.sit.hqx** Calculates the phases of the moon, colorfully.

- **moontool1.01.cpt.hqx** Displays details about the current moon phase and related matters.

- **mpjastro1.3.sea.hqx** A great planetarium program that lets you display the universe for any date and time from the year 1 to 4000 (in case you're around that long). Includes many, many other features.

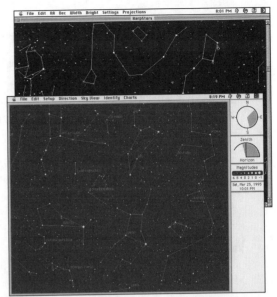

The Harpstar and MPj Astro planetarium programs are only two of the more than 20 astronomy programs you can download from the University of Michigan Macintosh archives.

- **orbitrack2.15.sit.hqx** An artificial satellite tracking program that calculates angles of satellites, plots current satellite positions on a world map, and more.

- **planetcolor51.cpt.hqx** Computes the locations of the planets for any time and any place on earth, along with lunar and solar eclipses.

- **planetfacts1.6sit.hqx** A HyperCard stack that displays vital statistics about the planets. Requires HyperCard 2.0.

- **planetplus5.0.cpt.hqx** Plots the positions of seven solar bodies, their magnitude, and more.

- **sattrak1.02cpt.h1x** Follows and plots locations of satellites circling the planet.

- **shadow.sit.hqx** Draws a map of the world and overlays a nightside version in shadow.

- **skycharttwothou1.02.sit.hqx** Calculates and displays the appearance of the night sky, and more.

- **solsneighbors.sit.hqx** A catalog of information on all stars within 16 light years of Earth (HyperCard stack).

- **spacestation.cpt.hqx** Elementary-level introduction to space and space exploration.

- **staratlas0.8.cpt.hqx** A star charting application that allows you to set declination and latitude to view, set the magnitude of stars to view, and more.

- **telescopes1.02.sit.hqx** An introduction, for high school or college students, to the instrumentation of astronomers. Good graphics are used to explain such tools as the Hubble telescope, Keck telescopes, and many others.

Where

http://www.umich.edu:80/group/itd/archive/Public/html/mac/misc/astronomy/

Links

Each file name is a link to the downloadable file.

All files are encoded with BinHex and compressed either with StuffIt or Compact Pro. If you have StuffIt 3.5 or higher, you can use it to decode and uncompress all of these files.

NASA's Newest Launch

Did you know that NASA's headquarters are *not* located at the Kennedy Space Center in Florida, nor at the Johnson Space Center in Texas? After a quick tour of this home page, you'll learn that NASA's headquarters aren't at any of its space centers, they're in Washington, D.C.

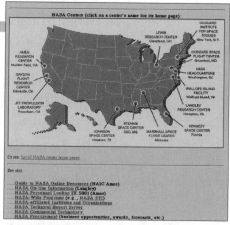

Cleveland may be the heart of rock and roll, but it's also home to a major NASA research facility.

"So what?" you say? Well, you'll also learn that the Jet Propulsion Laboratories in Pasadena, California is a NASA research facility and that this fantastic Web site was created by the staff of NASA's Network Applications and Information Center (NAIC). What, you didn't even know the NAIC existed? Neither did I, but I'm pretty darn thankful for their efforts, and you will be, too.

At this site, you can learn everything you ever wanted to know about NASA, as well as a few hundred NASA facts you didn't even know you wanted to know. Perhaps more important, though, is the mind-numbing collection of links to hundreds of sites of additional space information. For instance, the Guide to NASA Online Resources link takes you to such diverse information sources as The Catalog of Galactic Supernova Remnants and the International Solar-Terrestrial Physics Information Center. Whew! This site provides a mother lode (or maybe that's the mother ship) of information for serious researchers, students of all ages, educators, and all space and science buffs.

Where

http://www.gsfc.nasa.gov/NASA_homepage.html

Links

NASA's Strategic Plan

NASA Educational Programs

NASA Online Educational Resources

NASA Information Sources by Subject

Guide to NASA Online Resources

NASA-Wide Programs

NASA-Affiliated Institutes and Organizations

NASA Technical Report Server

NASA Commercial Technology

Other Space Agencies

Other Aerospace Sources

Simply SPACESIM

SPACESIM is an electronic newsletter published monthly by the National Association of Space Simulating Educators (NASSE), and is devoted to the development of telecommunicated educational space simulations. Previous issues contain announcements of simulations organized by NASSE and the National Educational Simulations Project Utilizing Telecommunications (NESPUT), lesson plans, software reviews, simulator construction techniques, simulation primers, and much more.

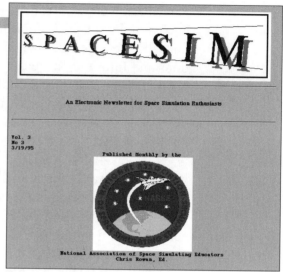

Hop in and take this baby for a spin around the solar system.

This organization isn't a bunch of graduate-college Ph.Ds droning on about physics and space arcanery; it's mostly composed of elementary-to-high school educators who want to open the minds of students to real-world problems, real-world solutions, and real-world excitement.

If you're searching for a teaching method that:

- Integrates curricula
- Motivates students
- Challenges *you*
- Uses relevant technology
- Uses Internet resources

—you'll want to visit this site.

To get a feel for some of the origins and objectives of NASSE, take a look at this excerpt from one of the online newsletter's third-issue articles:

It all started one day as Don Weatherby and I were discussing our students over lunch. Don was our metal technology teacher and listened rather intently as I was "singing the blues" about my 4.0 students who could memorize anything, but had no common sense and could not do any meaningful work with their hands.

"You know, my kids are just exactly the opposite...many of them struggle in the traditional classroom, but put them in a room with a car engine, and they will have it pulled, pistons out and placing new rings in a couple of hours," he commented.

We both looked at each other with a gleam in our eyes.

"I wonder what would happen if we put those two kind of students together into cooperative groups and forced them to depend on each other," I said with a smile slowly creeping across my lips.

"Let's talk to the boss and see!" replied Don.

And with that humble beginning, Space Technology Class at Gahanna Lincoln High School came about. Team taught with emphasis on astronomy and space exploration and making tools to accomplish science tasks, the course quickly became one of the most popular on campus. It is taught with an outcome based slant. Foundational information and/or skills are taught or discovered by students in a lab type setting. Once these foundational skills are taught, they are practically applied to new situations. Finally, some type of authentic integration or evaluation event is held to give the students a "real world scenario" of how those skills are actually used in life.

Where

http://chico.rice.edu/armadillo/Simulations/ssimv1n2.html

Links

Links change with each issue. Look for links to other issues as well.

Our Tour's Next Stop: The Planets

Quick, how many moons in the galaxy can you name?

I thought so. If names like Europa, Leda, Himalia, and Elara don't ring a bell, you may want to browse this site at the University of Arizona.

The Nine Planets home page is your trajectory into our solar system. (Or maybe you think you've been beamed down from a *different* solar system, hmm?) And once you've left Earth's orbit, you probably won't want to return. This is an impressive, interactive multimedia tour of the solar system, complete with sound clips and very rich graphics.

For each planet, comet, and other major body you visit, you'll get:

- an inline picture
- some facts about the body
- a list of pictures that can be found elsewhere on the Net
- data on any satellites the object might have, plus links to information about those satellites
- links to more information about the object elsewhere on the Web
- a list of open issues about the object for which scientists currently have no answers

Where

http://seds.lpl.arizona.edu/nineplanets/nineplanets/nineplanets.html#toc

Links

Introduction

Express Tour

Mercury

Venus

Earth

Mars

.

.

.

You get the idea.

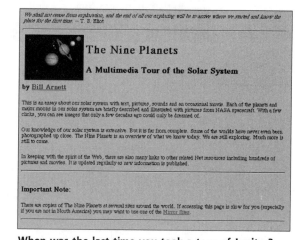

When was the last time you took a tour of Jupiter?

Because this site is so graphics-intensive, access to its pages might be slow at times. If you find this to be the case—especially if you're accessing the site outside of North America—the site's author (Bill Arnett)

recommends that you use one of its mirror locations. Just click on the Mirror Sites link on the home page for a list of mirror addresses.

Welcome to the National Air and Space Museum

One of the favorite tourist stops in Washington, D.C. is the Smithsonian Institution's National Air and Space Museum. You can truly let your imagination fly in this building, with two levels of displays of actual aircraft—from early Goddard rockets to Lindbergh's Spirit of St. Louis to Apollo spacecraft and beyond. A little-known additional level in this massive building contains a library and archive of photos and other information that never made it into the public displays. There's only so much room in the real world. But that's not the case in cyberspace.

Now you don't have to travel to the Nation's Capital to see these mind-dazzling displays and photos. Museum staffers are in the process of creating a virtual tour of the National Air and Space Museum on the Web. Included will be all the text and photos from "Beyond the Limits," the gallery that showcases the history of aviation and space technology. This project is still under construction, but it's definitely worth a visit or two, or three, or four....

Where

http://ceps.nasm.edu:2020/NASMAP.html

Links

Click on any exhibit shown in the floor plan at the home page

At this writing, Exhibit 213 (The Beyond the Limits exhibition) appears to be the only completed presentation, but even this is impressive. Check back frequently, because as this Web site grows, you can expect it to grow in popularity as well, and it'll no doubt be tough to access when it matures.

Take a virtual ride on the Space Shuttle Simulator at the Smithsonian's National Air and Space Museum Web site.

Online Planetaria

Okay, so maybe that heading is just a little deceptive. The truth is, most of the planetaria on the Web simply provide details on schedules, programs, directions to the planetarium and other visitor information. At most sites, you won't actually find any online presentations or graphics. Two exceptions are the planetarium at the Community College of Southern Nevada and the Northern Lights planetarium in Breivika, Norway.

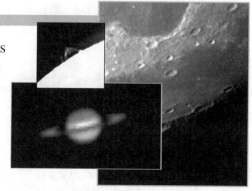

The sun, the moon, and Jupiter all make appearances any time of day at the planetarium at the Community College of Southern Nevada.

The planetarium at CCSN is rich in graphics of heavenly bodies, and includes good descriptions of the photos displayed there. The Northern Lights planetarium includes several presentations; however, at this writing, they're mostly text. The planetarium staff promises more graphics as the Web site progresses.

All the other planetaria listed below simply provide visitor information, although some sites also include links to other astronomy information on the Web.

Where

http://star.arm.ac.uk/ (Armagh, Northern Ireland)

http://www.nscee.edu/~drdale/ (Community College of Southern Nevada)

http://tfnet.ils.unc.edu/~dataman/ (Morehead, North Carolina)

http://130.183.24.194/fdt_e.html (Munich, Germany)

http://www.uit.no/npt/homepage-npt.en.html (Breivika, Norway)

http://ids.net/~cormack_pl/museum.html (Providence, Rhode Island)

Links

Varies for different sites.

EROS Data Center

The EROS Data Center is in the process of making available recently declassified satellite photographs collected by the U.S. intelligence community during the 1960s. This page has some sample images, including the Executive Order commanding the images be made public, a blurb from the acting CIA director, and a historical fact sheet with information on mission dates and statistics. An Internet catalog and image browser capability for the entire collection is planned, at no charge. They used your money to get these, so go take a look.

Where

http://edcwww.cr.usgs.gov/eros-home.html

Links

Who We Are and What We Do

National Satellite Data Archive

Declassification of Intelligence Satellite Photography

Landsat Data Available from U.S. Geological Survey

I don't want to mislead you: Although all of the information provided at EROS and related links is free, the satellite images themselves are *not* free; in fact, they're way expensive ($400 apiece). Even so, there's a wealth of satellite and geological information to be found here. I should also mention that it's easy to get lost among these links.

Simulate the Senses

This NASA page was "hit" (or accessed) over 200,000 times during a recent shuttle mission, which actually brought down the server. But the Astro-2 page, dedicated to an experiment on the shuttle flight, was quickly back up; you can't keep a good thing down, and this is one of the best Web sites you'll find. There's lots of great mission information, live views of the shuttle, up-to-the-minute MPEG movies, and more. It's this kind of innovation that's bringing the excitement back to the space program. Come see for yourself.

Where

http://astro-2.msfc.nasa.gov

Links

Hardware and Science

Flight Crew

NASA Team

Flight Log

Come Aboard!

Visitor's Port

Whoaaaah! It's a long way down from here.

 I highly recommend taking the virtual tour around the shuttle as it orbits the Earth. Start with the **Come Aboard!** button, then click on the **virtual reality** link, and then click on **fly around**. It can take awhile to work through all of the graphics, but the simulation images here are excellent. In fact, this is perhaps the best online simulation I've seen on the Web. You can also take the tour offline by downloading either the Macintosh or Windows version of the software.

Where to Find More Goodies

Here are a few more interesting space-related sites you'll find in this book:

- *Education and Teaching Tools* is the place to go for classroom projects in astronomy.

- Try *Kid Stuff* for links to NASA.

- *Nature and the Environment* includes links to satellite photos of the fault lines from the Kobe earthquake in Japan, as well as pictures from weather satellites.

FREE $TUFF

I think that the team that wins
game five will win the series.
Unless we lose game five.

Charles Barkley

Sports,
Recreation,
and Hobbies

You Don't Stand a Snowball's Chance in...

And now for something completely pointless. But first, some personal background: I grew up in Alaska, and still have clear memories of snowball fights that made the Battle of Gettysburg look like a barn dance. I live in Arizona now, though, so I rarely have the opportunity to relive those moments of glory.

Holy incoming, Batman! Duck!

Aha! Modern technology again comes to the rescue. The Rome Laboratories in Rome, New York, have developed the latest in stealth snowball technology: a virtual snowball launcher that lets you fire away at the all-too-real human targets who dare walk in front of the camera mounted in the lab.

The camera records your shot, digitizes the picture, then transmits it back to you, along with your score. Workers (potential victims) have even been ranked according to their speed, agility, and vertical leap (watch out for the wily and elusive RLSBC-TRANSIENT-X—he's a tough one). There's even a Batman cardboard cutout you can practice on when workers are out of season (home for the evening, that is). I practiced this site on a Sunday afternoon, and I couldn't even hit the broad site of the Caped Crusader, which shows you just how out of practice I am.

Where

http://www.rl.af.mil:8001/Odds-n-Ends/sbcam/rlsbcam.html

Links

Lots of links to provide you with the what's, how's, and who's of this site.

Sports Thrills for Couch Potatoes

Okay, you're not a kid anymore. But you still miss your high-school glory days of touchdown passes, slap-shot goals, grand-slam home runs, and just all-around sports-induced adrenaline and camaraderie. Well, this site might not provide much camaraderie, but the games you'll find here are guaranteed to revive those memories of you and your teammates playing 'til it hurts (and hurts, and hurts).

Currently, six links are provided to PC sports games you can download.

Where

http://wcl-rs.bham.ac.uk/GamesDomain/directd/pc/dos/sport/sport.html

Links

One-Nil

Cunning Football

Goal

Solar Hockey League

Soccer

Y.A. B. Baseball

On Top of Old Smooookeeey...

Ever wondered whether anything good came out of the Great Depression? While the Tennessee Valley Authority hardly compensates for the hard times way back when, the results are truly a national treasure.

The efforts of our parents and grandparents are now bearing fruit in the great outdoors, and the University of Tennessee Canoe & Hiking Club's Web server showcases many of the activities you can enjoy, thanks to the

This fun bunch at the University of Tennessee provides you with a gateway to outdoor recreational opportunities in the Southeastern U.S., including maps, images, stories, and upcoming events.

417

pioneering work of the TVA. This club's server contains links to many outdoor clubs in the Southeast and across the country, along with maps of Southeastern recreational areas, including the Great Smokies, and images for outdoor recreational destinations as far south as Panama.

Where

http://feeder.oac.utk.edu/utchx.html

Links

Sports Club

Stories

Events

Lots of Pictures

Satellite and Weather Links

I Think I Can, I Think I Can

The Atlas Model Railroad Company—designers, manufacturers, and sellers of N and HO scale model railroad trains, books, and manuals—is now chugging through cyberspace.

One of the model railroad layouts available for viewing at this Web site.

Model railroading tycoons will find a boxcar load of information here about model layouts, track, accessories, model buildings, and software for designing track layouts. The Atlas catalog is online, as well as several books on model railroading. All abooooaaard!

Where

http://www.atlasrr.com/atlasrr/

Links

Getting Started in Model Railroading

Atlas Online Catalog

Put Your Layout on the Web!

Other Railroading Resources on the Internet

Because It's There

If your interest in climbing is limited to an occasional dash up a flight of stairs, you probably won't find this site at Edinburgh University in Scotland to be your cup of tea—the picture on the home page alone will be cause for ver-

Next step: Splaaaattt!

tigo. While this site deals mainly with Scotland and other parts of the UK and Europe, there's enough information here on climbing to help anyone who's interested in this activity.

In addition to an extensive archive about climbs in Scotland, there's info on ice climbing, mountaineering clubs, where to get avalanche forecasts by E-mail, and mountains of information about Scottish mountaineering books and climber's guides.

Where

http://www.ucs.ed.ac.uk/~p91152/climbing

Links

The Climbing Archive

Rock Climbing In Europe

The UK Climbing Pages

Hill Walking and Mountaineering

A Coaster Compendium

Here's a great collection of roller coaster pictures, coaster-related events and news, and answers to frequently asked questions for roller coaster buffs. Want to know which coaster is the highest, the fastest, the longest, or the twistiest? You'll find the answers here, along with detailed information about some of the greatest, most gut-busting coasters in the U.S.

Where

http://sunsite.unc.edu/darlene/coaster/coaster.html

Links

List

ACE

Search

rec.roller-coaster

FAQ

Oompph!
Waaaahhh! Anybody... seen...
my....
stooooommmmacccchhh??!!!

The Running Page

Planning on running a 5K soon? Maybe a 10K? Gearing up for a marathon? If you're serious about using your legs for intense pain and pleasure, you'll find that information about your running obsession is well represented here. This is arguably the best international Web site for hardcore runners. You'll find information on international races, races in your area, and links to publications for the serious runner.

Where

http://sunsite.unc.edu/drears/running/running.html

Links

Running Clubs

Upcoming Races

Personal Bests

Exercise Trails Network

Running Related WWW Servers

Running Publications (Print)

Cross Country Analysis

Endure This!

This is a great site for anybody who loves to pump their ticker to the max. You'll find state-of-the-art information for optimizing your performance in cycling, running, or swimming. Links here will take you to clinics on nutrition, optimal training techniques, running clubs throughout the world, and listings of upcoming events worldwide. If you do cardio sports to the limit, this site's for you.

Where

http://s2.com/html/etj/etj.html

Links

Running Clubs

Upcoming Races

The Running Scene in Different Areas

Personal Bests

United States of America Track and Field

Exercise Trails Network

Running Related WWW Servers

Running Publications

Your Source for Outdoor Adventure

Currently, the Sport Source appears to be a fledgling Web site, and probably needs a little more time to mature. Maybe by the time you read this, the site will be close to a finished state. In the meantime, the Sport Source provides links to several online sports-related magazines, including *The Endurance Training Journal, Climbing,* and *Inline.* These folks clearly cater to outdoors types; armchair sports enthusiasts need not apply. The Cruzing button takes you to some great links to other outdoors-related Web sites, and the What's New button keeps you abreast of major sports events around the world.

Where

http://s2.com/

Links

What's New

News Group

Cruzing

The Newsstand

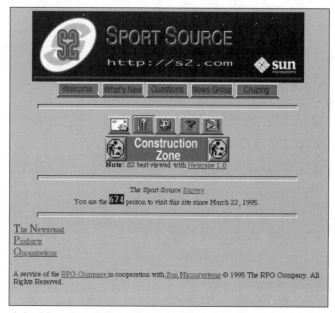

If the idea of spending your weekend outdoors conjures up the image of raking leaves, you don't belong here. But if your idea of fun includes sleeping on top of a windy mountain or jumping out of a perfectly safe airplane, this site's for you.

 When I last tried Products, Organizations, and some of the other links on this page, my Web browser came up empty. But things change quickly on the Web, so you might have better luck.

Time for Football

With this program, any time you log on to your computer is football time. This clock utility allows you to display your favorite gladiator of the gridiron's logo on your Windows.

Where

http://www.acs.oakland.edu/oak/SimTel/win3/clock.html

Download

fbclck24.zip

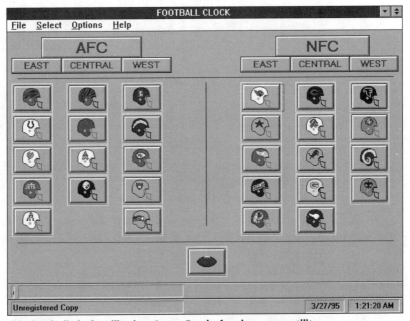

This football clock utility is a Super Bowl of a shareware utility.

Sports Card and Stamp Collection Catalogers

Sports card collectors, stamp collectors, or collectors of stamps about sports (did I miss anyone?) will appreciate these programs to help them keep track of their inventories. These two windows programs let you search, sort, and print summaries of your collection, as well as let you keep track of lots of other information. You'll never actually have to look at your cards or stamps again.

Where

http://www.acs.oakland.edu/oak/SimTel/win3/entertn.html

Download

am_sp13.zip

am_st13.zip

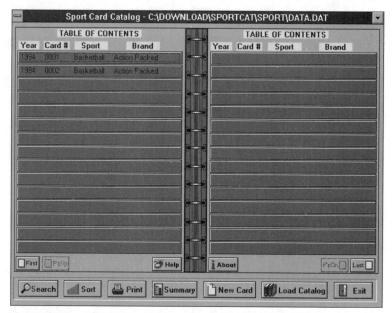

Those who can, do. Those who can't, collect cards of those who can—but hey, that's most of us.

Rocky Mountain Biking

If the acronym NORBA sounds to you like an evil organization from a James Bond flick, you'll probably want to bypass this site. On the other hand, if you get a thrill by hopping on your fat tire machine and pushing your heart, lungs, and leg muscles to the limit, you'll want to take a rest stop here.

Colorado Mountain Bike Racing provides detailed information about the North American Off Road Bicycle Association's (NORBA) Colorado Off-Road Point Series—including the Iron Horse Classic, Rage in the Sage, Melee in the Mines, and the Monarch Mountain Challenge (the highest mountain bike race in the country).

At this site, you'll find a calendar of this year's races, course descriptions, contacts, team rosters, and last year's results. I found the course descriptions to be so detailed and inspirational, I could hardly stay in front of my computer to finish this chapter. Life's short, ride hard!

Where

http://www.tcinc.com/mtbike/co_mtb.html

Links

Iron Horse Classic

Rage in the Sage

Steamboat Springs Classic

Melee in the Mines

Fat Tire Bike Week

Riders Del Norte

Monarch Mountain Challenge

King of the Rockies

Grand West Outfitter's Gear Grinder

Fall Classic

And many more

You won't find any mountain biking graphics here, but who wants to look at a picture of a hamburger when they're hungry? Besides, it just means accessing this site and its links will be as fast as riding a downhill singletrack with no brakes.

Go to the Net!

Here's a great site for the truly tennis obsessed. The Tennis Server home page includes everything you ever wanted to know about tennis and a little bit more. Here, you'll find worldwide tennis tournament news, the ATP Tour Electronic Newsletter, monthly player and equipment tips, graphics of players and equipment, an online service called The Racquet Workshop, hyperlinked versions of the Rules and Code of Tennis, an HTML Version of the Tennis FAQ...hey, I'm outta breath!

The Tennis Server also sponsors an E-mail newsletter containing notification of updates to the Tennis Server, as well as other tennis information of general interest. Mailings occur about once a month. Periodically, tennis-related polls and surveys are also direct mailed to people on this list.

Where

http://arganet.tenagra.com/Racquet_Workshop/Tennis.html#Courtside

Links

Racquet Workshop Entrance

Player Tip of the Month

Equipment Tip of the Month

The Rules and Code of Tennis and Tennis FAQ

Other Tennis Info on the Information Superhighway

And dozens more

The original Tennis Server is located in Houston. However, a mirror site is also available in West Virginia at:

http://www.mountain.net/Pinnacle/Racquet_Workshop/Tennis.html

Use the site that's fastest for you. And be sure to join the E-mail list if you want to receive regular tennis news or if you want to participate in the surveys.

Soccer Comes to the U.S. (on TV, at Least)

Forget six-point touchdowns and mucho padding. That's for weenies. If the word "football" conjures up images of guys in shorts banging a checkered ball against their heads, not to mention banging against each other, you'll feel at home here. The Soccer on US TV page provides extensive (exhaustive might be a better word) listings of upcoming soccer matches that will be broadcast on TV in the U.S.—including ESPN, ESPN2, Prime, Univision, and many other cable services. If you're visiting the U.S. from elsewhere in the world (where people *really* appreciate soccer), or if you just love soccer, you'll want to visit this site.

Where

http://www.best.com/~olivert/soccer/tv-info.html

Links

Links to other interesting soccer-related WWW sites

World-Wide Collectors Digest

If you collect it, it's probably included here. This site is an exhaustive clearinghouse of information for collectors of trading cards, comic books, memorabilia, model trains, planes, and more. You'll find out where all the trade shows are located and you can find out what your mint condition 1965 Mickey Mantle Topps card is *really* worth.

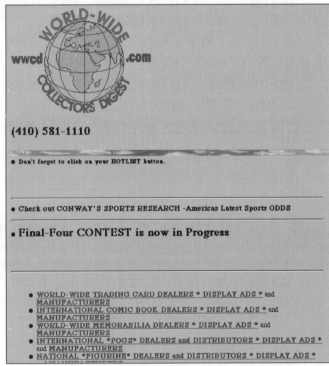

Trading cards! Comic books! Getcher red hot comic books!

These guys like real sports, too. They've included complete 1995 schedules for the NBA, NFL, NHL, and even major league baseball. And if you want to put a few dollars down on Sunday's game, be sure to check out the CONWAY's Sports Research link, which provides the odds for upcoming games in several pro and college sports.

Where

http://www.wwcd.com

Links

WORLD-WIDE TRADING CARD DEALERS * DISPLAY ADS * MANUFACTURERS

INTERNATIONAL COMIC BOOK DEALERS * DISPLAY ADS * MANUFACTURERS

WORLD-WIDE MEMORABILIA DEALERS * DISPLAY ADS * MANUFACTURERS

INTERNATIONAL *PGS* DEALERS and DISTRIBUTORS * DISPLAY ADS * MANUFACTURERS

NATIONAL *FIGURINE* DEALERS and DISTRIBUTORS * DISPLAY ADS * MANUFACTURERS

INTERNATIONAL TOY TRAINS and PLANES DEALERS * DISPLAY ADS * and MANUFACTURERS

SUPPLIES-Trading Cards-Comic Books-Memorabilia-Trains/Planes

PROFESSIONAL SPORTS SCHEDULES and Archives

CONWAY'S Sports Research

General Aviation Site Flies High on the Web

If you have *any* interest in flying, you'll want to add this site to your hotlist or list of bookmarks. It's a list of aviation sites on the Web, maintained by numerous aviation server administrators. You'll find everything from gliding in Poland to aerobatics, skydiving, hang gliding, hot air ballooning, air racing, and beyond—including photos and weather information.

Actually, I can't recommend this site highly enough. Want to know what the German Aerospace Research Organization is studying these days? It's here. Need to find a flying club in your neck of the skies? Go here.

Want to dogfight in a Mig 29? You'll find out where to get in the cockpit. Want to build your own plane? You guessed it. This site will link you to the Experimental Aircraft Association and the Homebuilt Homepage.

Okay, suck in that gut and get ready to do a few negative Gs.

In short, anything you want to do in the air you can find out about here. You'll even find scheduling and reservation information for major airlines. The links alone are breathtaking in scope. So go catch up on your FARs or simply fly vicariously. Happy landings!

Where

http://adswww.harvard.edu/GA/ga_servers.html

Links

I couldn't even *begin* to list 'em.

SPORTS ILLUSTRATED Online

Know why Michael Jordan wore number 45 when he returned to the NBA, not his former number 23? Jordan said his father saw the last game he played wearing number 45, and he wants to keep it that way, and 45 is the number he wore while playing for the Chicago White Sox's farm team, which he wants to honor. The story's in *Sports Illustrated*,

Air Jordan's back on the floor.

but even more interesting, it's free to read on the Web, complete with the great photos this magazine's known for.

Apparently, *SI* is one of those rare publications that believes putting its issues online won't sacrifice street sales. Take advantage of their goodwill, good writing, and great photos.

429

Where

http://www.timeinc.com/si/

Links

They Said It

Classics

Images

Dirt Heads, Dirt Heads, Roly Poly Dirt Heads

This is *the* page to check out if you're a fat-tire fan. Count me in. I'm the kind of lunatic who actually has considered trading in my mortgage for a full-suspension, totally tricked out titanium roller. Fortunately, my wife doesn't share my enthusiasm, so the house is still ours. If you love mountain biking, you'll love this site, *the* online center of the universe for mountain bikers.

Calvin's dad is obviously dialed in.
How about you?

The emphasis here is on trails in the San Francisco Bay area, but there are links to trails throughout the U.S., Canada, Europe, even New Zealand

(I've already got my next vacation idea). You'll also find information on upcoming races, along with the results of recent ones.

Where

http://xenon.stanford.edu/~rsf/mtn-bike.html

Links

Too numerous to list

At first, my editor, Ron (totally loaded Manitou hard-tail aluminum wonder bike) Pronk, wanted to include this site in the *Religion* section. If you knew him, this brash display of obsessiveness wouldn't surprise you. Alas, calmer heads prevailed.

Hey, Let's Go Cyber Cycling!

If you love two-wheeling without benefit of a motor, you've got to check out this Web site. Currently, you'll find information regarding resources available on the Internet for cycling enthusiasts, and a relatively comprehensive list of manufacturers phone numbers.

And by the way: The guy who maintains this page gives equal time to mountain bikers and road bikers. Whether you bike for recreation or for competition, this site has a lot to offer. You'll find information on:

- Bicycle product lines
- Original and after-market componentry and accessories
- Information regarding tour operations and vacation destinations

I especially enjoyed the articles available from the links to online cycle magazines. Here's one of my favorite excerpts, from *MTB Pro*:

> Men are interested in one thing—themselves. Mountain bikers, though, are interested in themselves and their mountain bikes—and then maybe a woman. In that order. Or that's how it seems, sometimes. So what do women think about them? Jenny Press reveals a few home truths every male MTBer should know...
>
> For the woman who goes mountain biking the problem can be even worse. While men become exhausted, mountain biking gives the female a new lease

on life. As Sarah puts it: "Give me a decent saddle, take me out on a ride and that's it—my hormones are all over the place. Put a man on a mountain bike for a couple of hours and when he gets home all he wants to do is eat a bowl of pasta, have a bath and go to bed."

Where

http://www.cyclery.com/

Links

Internet Bicycling Links

Racing Information

Phone Numbers & E-mail

Bicycling Magazines

Mazda Miata Home Page

Okay, so maybe this site isn't for everybody, but the Mazda Miata is rapidly gaining cult status worldwide, so I figured I should point the way to the Miata on the Web: It's the Mazda Miata Home Page, produced by Gary J. Fischman of Menlo Park, California, which offers tons of information about the Mazda MX-5 Miata—the '90s recreation of a classic roadster from the '60s. The Miata page provides infor-

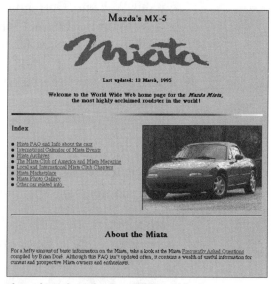

If you love the Miata, you'll love this site.

mation on the car, archives of the listserver devoted to it, information on local and regional events and clubs, and a marketplace for after-market products and services.

Where

http://www.catalog.com/miata/miata.html

Links

Miata FAQ and Info about the cars

International Calendar of Miata Events

Miata Archives

The Miata Club of America and Miata Magazine

Local and International Miata Club Chapters

Miata Marketplace

Miata Photo Gallery

Pick a Card, Any Card

The secret's out; this Web page is for magic buffs, and includes links and information for magicians of all ages. You'll find access to all things magical on the Web, including information about magic in movies, TV, magic clubs, and individual magician appearances worldwide.

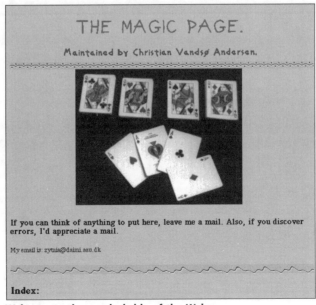

Welcome to the magical side of the Web.

Where

http://www.daimi.aau.dk/~zytnia/eg_html

Links

Too numerous to include here

Where to Find More Goodies

You'll find links to sports, recreation, and hobbies in some of the unlikeliest places, including:

- You can get excerpts of selected articles from *Sporting News* in the *Books, Magazines, and Literature* section, as well as lots of sports factoids like the complete list of NBA number one draft picks.

- Gun enthusiasts will find lots of NRA information in the *Law* section.

- Auto enthusiasts will want to try the *Television* section for links to the U.K.'s *BBC Top Gear* television program, which caters to the autophile crowd.

FREE $TUFF

I find television very educating. Every time somebody turns on the set, I go into the other room and read a book.

Groucho Marx

Television

Let's Get Serious

If you want to get beyond your favorite TV shows and you're ready to delve into the full spectrum of TV and other broadcast-related sites on the Web, then this is *the* place to check out. The INFOSEARCH Broadcasting Links page contains an excellent alphabetical list of links to Web pages and other Internet sites that involve broadcasting.

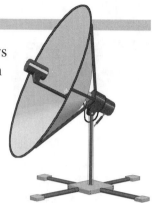

The intriguing feature of this site is its dedication to broadcast technology, which means you'll find links to sites that provide radio and satellite information, including some fairly technical sites, but you'll also find links to sites that deal mostly with TV show trivia and gossip. This page is both serious and fun, and provides an alphabetic listing that's easy to view and to use.

Where

http://www.xmission.com/~insearch/links.html

Links

You'll find an extensive alphabetical listing here; the sites are too numerous to list.

TVNow Cable TV Schedule Software

Way back in the dark ages, it used to be easy to keep track of what was on television and when it was on. In my house, Disney always followed Lawrence Welk. If you timed it just right, you'd miss the polka stuff and get to see the bubble machine as the credits rolled. Life was simple.

These days, you just about need to have a degree in theoretical physics to keep track of the cable, satellite, pay per view, super stations, and national networks. By the time you've finished reading the listings, you've missed everything anyway.

But now you can use the speed of your computer to search for TV shows, specials, movies, sporting events, and much more, on over 70 National cable channels, including:

- Premium Movie Channels like HBO, SHO, DIS, CIN, and STARZ
- Pay Per View Channels like VC1 and REQ
- National Networks (ABC, NBC, CBS, FOX, PBS)
- Superstations like TBS, WGN, and TNT
- Cable Networks like A&E, USA, FAM, LIF, NIK, and FXM
- Sports Networks like ESPN, PRIME, and MSG
- Music Channels like MTV, VH1, and TNN

Download the shareware Windows or DOS version of TVNow as well as the current cable television schedules from this site to get started.

Where

http://www.vnet.net/tvnow/tvnow.html

Links

Windows (tvnwin28.zip)

DOS (tvnowdos.zip)

The registered version of TVNow has TV listings for movies, sports events, concerts, specials, and children's programming on over 70 cable channels, and also lets you choose only channels that you want. The shareware version only has TV listings for the movies on over 70 cable channels.

The Ultimate TV Listing for Couch Potatoes

Ultimate isn't really the ultimate description for this site. Comprehensive, exhaustive, unabridged, obsessive, bottomless, and couch-potato heaven are a few other words that come to mind. To tell you the truth, this is the type of site that makes my job as a writer more difficult. See, I've got to fill a certain number of pages per chapter. But after I've mentioned this site, there's not much left to say about TV on the Web, because links to virtually all TV-related sites are represented here. So, after you get over feeling sorry for me, head on over to this Web page.

Sites are broken into categories based on genre (sitcoms, drama, soaps, and so on), but you can also access a complete list of all shows represented on the Web. When you do, you'll get a set of links for each show.

For some shows, all you'll find is a link to a newsgroup; for other shows, you'll get links to one or more Web sites devoted to the show, where you'll find episode information, bios on the show's stars, photos, and more.

Inexplicably, *Mystery Science Theatre 3000* is the clear Web winner in terms of site numbers, with 11 links to different MST-3K Web sites. *Star Trek* Web sites are almost as numerous, but these links cover all three generations of the show. You'll also find lots of links to perennial ratings losers, like *Parker Lewis Can't Lose* (obviously, he did), the *Powers of Matthew Star*, and *T.J. Hooker.* Let's all do a group snore.

Other links take you to shows I've frankly never heard of, and I'm not sure I want to, like *Blakes' 7*, *Gargoyles*, *Shortland Street*, and (I'm almost afraid to ask) *Pig Sty.* From what I've been able to determine, this site covers all shows presented in English, but that includes programs from the U.S. as well as Canada, Great Britain, Australia, and a few other locales—so the list is truly huge and I have to plead ignorance where shows originating outside the U.S. are concerned.

You'll also find links to nostalgic favorites, including *All In The Family*, *The Andy Griffith Show, Bewitched, The Brady Bunch*—hey, I'm not even out of the "B" listings and I'm already getting teary eyed. The point is: If the show is a favorite of yours—past or present—it's probably represented here. However, I must admit I was disappointed to discover that one of my all-time favorites, *Hogan's Heroes*, is absent from the list. Schultz would not consider this a jolly joke.

For many shows, you'll see EPG links, which take you to "episode guides," brief descriptions of a show's episodes—from first episode to the last in the series. For an ever-increasing number of shows (as I've already indicated), you'll also find links to Web sites devoted to the show. Makes you wonder about the lives of some of these Web-page authors, or if they have one at all. But I shouldn't be too critical since this is one of my favorite sites to visit. It's entertaining, it's brain numbing, it's overwhelming—hey, it's television!

Here's a list of shows reperesented at this site:

Watch the cast of "Frasier" on NBC   NBC

The A-Team
Absolutely Fabulous
Aculpulco H.E.A.T.
The Adventures of Pete and Pete
Alf
All In The Family
American Computer Enthusiasts
The Andy Griffith Show
Animaniacs
Are You Being Served
Automan
The Avengers
Babylon 5
Barney and Friends
Batman: The Animated Series
Baywatch
Beakman's World

Beavis and Butthead
Beethoven
Beverly Hills, 90210
Bewitched
Blackadder
Blakes' 7
Blossom
Bob
The Bold and the Beautiful
Bottom
The Boys Are Back
The Brady Bunch
The Adventures of Brisco County, Jr.
The BBC Home Page
Bump in the Night
Cheers
Chicago Hope
Clarissa Explains It All
Combat!
Cybill
Darkroom
Days of our Lives
Deep Space Nine
Doug
Dr Quinn Medicine Woman
Dr. Who
Duckman
Due South
E.R.
Earth 2
EastEnders
Eerie Indiana

Ellen
The Equalizer
Fawlty Towers
Flying Blind
Forever Knight
Frasier
Friends
Full House
Future Quest
Gargoyles
General Hospital
Get A Life
Get Smart
Gilligan's Island
Going for Gold
Gold of Gaia
The Heights
Hercules: The Legendary Journeys
Herman's Head
High Tech Heroes
Highlander
Home Improvement
Homicide
Howard Stern
I Love Lucy
The Incredible Hulk
The Invaders
The Kids in the Hall
Knight Rider
Kung Fu: The Legend Continues
Late Night with Conan O'Brien
Late Show with David

439

Letterman
Liberty Street
Liquid TV
Logan's Run
Lois and Clark: The New
    Adventures of Superman
Lost in Space
Law and Order
MacGyver
Mad About You
Magnum P.I.
Man from U.N.C.L.E.
Married with Children
M*A*S*H
Max Headroom
Melrose Place
Miami Vice
Mighty Morphin' Power
    Rangers
Mike & Maty Show
Mission: Impossible
Models, Inc.
The Monkees
Monty Python's Flying
    Circus
The Muppet Show
Murphy Brown
MTV
My So Called Life
Mystery Science Theatre
    3000
The Nanny
Northern Exposure
NYPD Blue
One Life to Live
The Outer Limits
Parker Lewis Can't Lose
Party Of Five
Picket Fences
Pig Sty
Planet Of The Apes
Platypus Man
The Powers of Matthew
    Star

The Price is Right
The Prisoner
Probe
Quantum Leap
Quatermass
Rat Patrol
The Real World
Reboot
Red Dwarf
The Red Green Show
Remington Steele
The Ren and Stimpy
    Show

Full House

Renegade
Road to Avonlea
Robotech
Roseanne
ROX
Rush Limbaugh
Sailor Moon
San Diego Rocks
Saturday Night Live
Saved By The Bell
The Scenic Route:
    Adventures From My
    Home Page
SCTV
SeaQuest
Seinfeld
Shortland Street
Silk Stalkings
SIM-TV
The Simpsons
The Six Million Dollar
    Man
Sledge Hammer!

Slider
Soap
Something Is Out There
Space: 1999
Star Trek
Star Trek: Deep Space
    Nine
Star Trek: The Next
    Generation
Sar Trek: Voyager
The StarLost
The State
Stingray
Street Cents Online
Subculture
T.J. Hooker
Tales From The Darkside
Taz-Mania
Tekwar
Theodore Tugboat
This New House
The Tick
The Time Tunnel
Tiny Toon Adventures
The Tomorrow People
The Tonight Show with
    Jay Leno
TV Nation
Twilight Zone
Twin Peaks
UFO
Unhappily Ever After
V
VR-5
The Wild Wild West
Wings
Wiseguy
The Wrong Trousers
The X-Files
XUXA
You Can't Do That On
    Television
Young and the Restless
The Young Ones

Where

http://www.tvnet.com/UTVL/utvl.html

Links

I think I've already covered that.

And For the Truly Interactive Couch Potato...

Put down your nuclear channel changer for a minute and check out this site, where you can *really* voice your opinion of what you like and don't like on the tube. Brought to you by the same folks who gave you the Ultimate TV home page, the Interactive TV Index provides you with a few creative ways to fight back against bad TV and encourage (at least what *you* consider to be) good TV.

One of the most useful links here, TV Internet Resource Guide, isn't interactive at all, but it *will* take you to additional links that access addresses

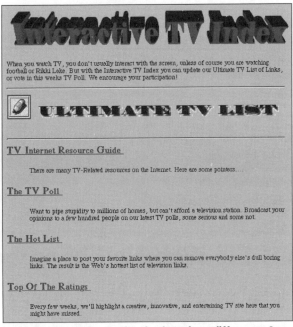

Don't just sit there. Get involved. Make a difference. Say something stupid. After all, it's only TV.

and home pages for local TV stations and national networks, along with links to weekly TV listings by region and ratings information.

The other links here are more fun than they are useful (but then, this is TV, not rocket science). For instance, The TV Poll link lets you view and participate in the current TV Poll question. The answers get pretty ridiculous and R-rated at times, but this is still basically good, clever fun. When I checked in, the poll request was to suggest the name for the next sequel to Star Trek. According to the current standings, the winner was probably going to be "Star Trek—The Final Conflict: Kirk and the Slaphead slug it out to see who gets to wear Shatner's rug," but running a close second was "Star Trek: Another Show Better Than Howard Stern." You can also view results to previous poll topics, which include "New alt.tv Newsgroups We Would Like to See," "Best Ways to Have Gotten off Gilligan's Island," and my favorite, "Faces We're Sickest of Seeing on TV."

Another interactive link, The Hot List, is almost too hot to handle. Here you can add your favorite URL for a TV-related link, or delete a link that someone else has included but that you think is pretty lame. It's a good thing the participants here don't get to meet each other in person....

Where

http://www.tvnet.com/ITVG/itvg.html

Links

TV Internet Resource Guide

The TV Poll

The Hot List

Top Of The Ratings

Television Free For All

PBS Joins the Web Neighborhood

Mister Rogers Neighborhood just got bigger. In fact, the entire PBS neighborhood may need a few additional ZIP codes simply by becoming a member of the Web. As the American Express motto goes, "Membership has

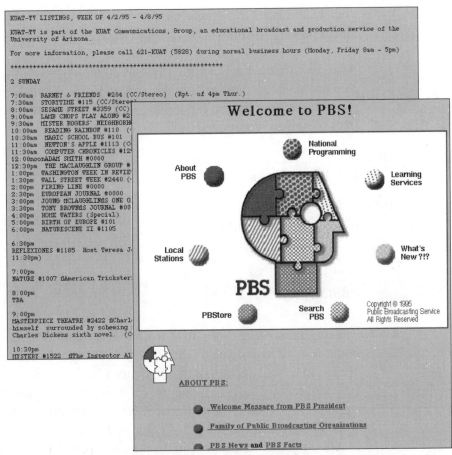

```
KUAT-TV LISTINGS, WEEK OF 4/2/95 - 4/8/95

KUAT-TV is part of the KUAT Communications, Group, an educational broadcast and production service of the
University of Arizona.

For more information, please call 621-KUAT (5828) during normal business hours (Monday, Friday 8am - 5pm)

++++++++++++++++++++++++++++++++++++++++++++++++++++++++++++

2 SUNDAY

7:00am  BARNEY & FRIENDS #204 (CC/Stereo)  (Rpt. of 4pm Thur.)
7:30am  STORYTIME #115 (CC/Stere
8:00am  SESAME STREET #3359 (CC)
9:00am  LAMB CHOPS PLAY ALONG #2
9:30am  MISTER ROGERS' NEIGHBORH
10:00am  READING RAINBOW #110  (
10:30am  MAGIC SCHOOL BUS #101
11:00am  NEWTON'S APPLE #1113 (C
11:30am  COMPUTER CHRONICLES #12
12:00noonADAM SMITH #0000
12:30pm  THE MACLAUGHLIN GROUP #
1:00pm  WASHINGTON WEEK IN REVIE
1:30pm  WALL STREET WEEK #2440 (
2:00pm  FIRING LINE #0000
2:30pm  EUROPEAN JOURNAL #0000
3:00pm  JOUNG MCLAUGHLINflS ONE O
3:30pm  TONY BROWNflS JOURNAL #00
4:00pm  HOME WATERS (Special)
5:00pm  BIRTH OF EUROPE #101
6:00pm  NATURESCENE XI #1105

6:30pm
REFLEXIONES #1185  Host Teresa J
11:30pm)

7:00pm
NATURE #1007 flAmerican Trickster

8:00pm
TBA

9:00pm
MASTERPIECE THEATRE #2422 flCharl
himself  surrounded by scheming
Charles Dickens sixth novel.  (C

10:30pm
MYSTERY #1522  flThe Inspector Al
```

For local PBS programming information, start from the PBS logo guy's head, select your state, then see if your local station provides detailed program logs.

its privileges." And, you'll find lots of privileged PBS information when you log onto this site.

When I was a kid (way back when "black and white" didn't refer to a patrol car), I was always getting the Public Broadcasting System confused with the Emergency Broadcasting System. The first time one of my schoolteachers announced we were going to watch something important on PBS, I thought the Russians were coming.

If you, too, are confused about PBS's mission, programming objectives, or its future, check out this site. If you just want program listings for your local PBS TV or radio station, you'll also probably find this Web site to be very useful.

Also, be sure to check out the PBStore, which lets you order videotapes of popular shows and series, such as Ken Burns' *Civil War* and *Baseball* programs. Okay, maybe the videos aren't free, but everything else from PBS *is*, so why complain?

Where

http://www.pbs.org

Links

National Programming

Local Stations

Learning Services

PBStore

The program listings are one of my favorite features here. I started at the home page, which displays the PBS "head" logo. Then, I clicked on the "Local Listings" portion of the logo guy's brain to get a U.S. map. Next, I clicked on my state, Arizona, to get information and links to local TV stations. In Arizona, there are two: KAET (Phoenix) and KUAT (Tucson). The information for KUAT, located at my alma mater (University of Arizona), included a hot link to complete programming schedules and other local-station information. Very useful stuff. Except...

I live in Phoenix now, and was disappointed to discover that the information for the local KAET PBS affiliate did not include a hot link to any more-specific programming or other station information—other than an address and phone number. Get with the program, guys!

Anyway, your experience here might be similar. Some stations have their own Internet server, in which case you'll be able to find tons of information about your local PBS station's programming, goals, and other info. But other stations aren't yet on the Net, so you might not find much info for your local station. In any case, if you (or your kids) enjoy PBS, this is a good site to check out. As I write this, the site's very new, so you can expect it to offer more information and services as the months progress.

Get Caught Up in the TV Net

TV Net serves as a good example for the Web community because it offers one of the most graphically attractive home pages you'll find anywhere on the Web. But aside from physical beauty, this site offers some great links for boob-tubeophiles as well.

TV Net is as attractive as it is useful. Whether you love TV or hate it, you'll find a home at this page.

The Highlights link tunes you in to home pages and other Internet sites available for both local stations in the U.S. and worldwide, and networks (including cable networks). But the truth is that most stations (and even several major networks) haven't yet hopped on the Web.

TV Net is still acommodating these somewhat dark-age broadcasters: You'll find snail-mail addresses for virtually all local affiliate and independent stations in the U.S. and many stations worldwide. So if you

want to write to your local station of choice, either to complain or to praise, this is a great place to go for addresses and contact names.

If you're interested in broadcasting-industry news, gossip, and insider info, be sure to check out the Shoptalk link.

Where

http://www.tvnet.com/TVnet.html

Links

Just click on any of the links on the home page to explore some of the diverse information available on TV and TV-related issues.

Where to Find More Goodies

Web potatoes will find lots of a-peeling (groan) TV-related sites, like:

- The *Twilight Zone* episode guide, in *Books, Magazines, and Literature.*
- Fans of '70s television should check out the not-so-ancient history of some of your favorite shows in the *History* section.
- David Letterman's latest Top Ten lists are available in *Humor.*
- Information on the latest soccer games are coming to a sports channel near you in the *Sports, Recreation, and Hobbies* section.

FREE $TUFF

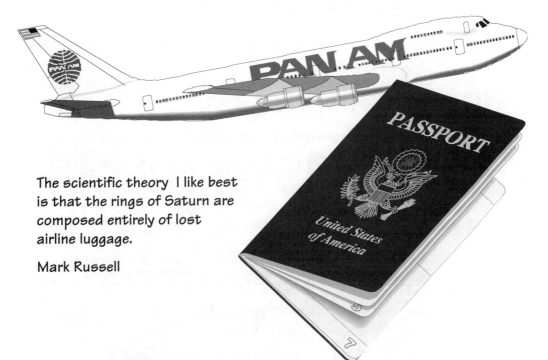

The scientific theory I like best
is that the rings of Saturn are
composed entirely of lost
airline luggage.

Mark Russell

Travel and

Geography

Hong Kong, Here We Come!

Cathay Pacific CyberTraveler is giving away a trip for two, each month, to Hong Kong. If you live in the U.S. (everyone else: sorry!) and are registered with CyberTraveler, you're eligible to win. Registration only takes a couple of minutes and doesn't cost anything, so what have you got to lose, except maybe your luggage?

In addition, by registering with Cathay Pacific CyberTraveler, you have the option of receiving E-mail announcing great opportunities to earn American Airlines bonus miles, award sales, or even special offers from hotel or car rental companies. Start packing!

Flying high on Cathay Pacific Airways.

Where

http://www.cathay-usa.com/register2.html

Links

See Internet Faststart contest rules for full details

Great Tours, Low Prices

Southeast Asia Links

Tourist Guide to Hong Kong

448

If you're looking for pictures of Hong Kong to fatten your online scrapbook, try the Hong Kong picture archive at:

http://sunsite.unc.edu/hkpa/

Onward and Upward

Before you hit the highway, hit this site to read about the road trips, pilgrimages, journeys, and quests of others bitten with wanderlust. ONWARD includes real stories from real people about real places and their unreal experiences.

At ONWARD, you'll experience the same sights and sounds the authors are writing about as you read their stories. The next best thing to being there? Maybe—but it's a distant second. Don't worry, it's nothing like sitting through Uncle George's slide show of his trip to Yosemite, but you'll find yourself itching to pack up and get motoring.

Particularly touching and interesting is Philip Greenspun's *Travels with Samantha*, a multimedia-filled online journal of his tour across North America.

One of the many incredible views you'll see in Travels with Samantha at ONWARD.

FREE $TUFF from the World Wide Web

Where

http://sunsite.unc.edu/onward/home.html

Links

Megaloop94

The Crash Network

Travels with Samantha

Big Bend

GNN's Travel Pages

Remembering Jack

No Simple Highway

Geography the European Way

Quick, what's the capital of Latvia? If you said Riga, you might be right. To tell you the truth, I'm not really sure. I could take a stab at answering, but with all the political unrest these days, what's here today is often overthrown tomorrow.

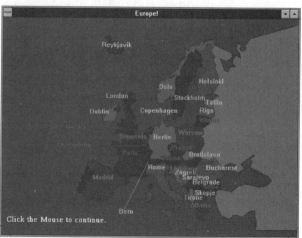

So many countries, so little time.

But you don't need *me* to help you, now that you can download a copy of Europe!, a fun and colorful freeware game that teaches you European geography while you play. Learning while you *play?* What's next, losing weight while you sleep? Test yourself on European countries, capitals, exports, and geography.

Where

http://www.acs.oakland.edu/oak/SimTel/win3/educate.html

450

Download

eurwin20.zip

Once you've learned where all these countries are, point your browser to this site to get a collection of world flags:

http ://www.adfa.oz.au/CS/flg/col/Index.html

Viva Las Vegas Travel Kit

Before you cash in all your traveler's checks for nickels or practice drawing to an inside straight, you'll want to load this handy freeware program onto your laptop computer. Travel Bag for Windows provides easy access to the most needed travel information—provided your destination is Las Vegas, that is. Just point and click to get:

- Toll-free numbers for airlines and car rentals
- A complete list of major hotel chains
- Las Vegas information and phone numbers
- International travel information
- Local online access numbers in all U.S. cities for CompuServe and America Online

It's rumored that Wayne Newton even makes his travel plans with this handy freeware program.

Where

http://www.acs.oakland.edu/oak/SimTel/win3/entertn.html

Download

tbag20.zip

You're On Shaky Ground

Whether you're just visiting or are making San Francisco your home, here's a site that links you to the best that San Francisco has to offer. For

work or play, eating or drinking, shopping or sleeping—the San Francisco Bay Area Web Guide links you to hundreds of places to get information on:

- Weather and road conditions
- Concert and other event listings
- Museums and other attractions
- Cities and community organizations
- Job openings and available housing
- Newspapers
- Radio and television stations
- Shopping, dining, and lodging
- Sports schedules and outdoor activities

You can even get loads of information on San Francisco's surrounding areas, including:

- Central Valley
- Lake Tahoe and Reno
- Monterey Peninsula
- North Coast
- Santa Cruz
- Yosemite

Where

http://www.hyperion.com/ba/sfbay.html

Links

Arts & Entertainment

Attractions

Events

Shopping, Dining & Lodging

Sports & Recreation

Cadillac Tastes on a Subaru Budget

Traveling on a shoestring doesn't have to mean living out of a backpack and eating Top Ramen for breakfast every morning. The Student and Budget Travel Resource Guide provides tons of links to Internet sites devoted to traveling on the economy plan and other resources for low-budget—and no-budget— travelers.

You'll find links to travel-related Net newsgroups, geographical information, how to get where you're going, what to wear, where to stay once you're there, even how to get out of jail (just kidding about that last one). Learn how to get cheap air fares, how to pack, and even how to get bumped off a flight for fun and profit. There are train schedules, information on avoiding jet lag, and where to find jobs that will send you packing.

Where

http://asa.ugl.lib.umich.edu/chdocs/travel/travel-guide.html

Links

Comprehensive Travel Guides: For the Big Picture

Armchair Travel: For the True Budget Traveler

North America

Europe

Asia

Surf's Up!

Aloha from Internet Island, Hawaii's newest tourist trap—at least in cyberspace. This fun peek at America's tropical paradise provides tourists with historical information about Hawaii, its culture, and current news from our 50th state.

The Coconut Boyz, Mo'o and Lolo, hanging ten off the coast of Internet Island.

You can also register to enter lots of online contests (with prizes given each month), get up-to-the-minute surf reports from the islands, and even learn to say your name in Hawaiian. Just call me Patalanahoahatrick Vincanetamooieroni. Rolls off the tongue, doesn't it?

Where

http://hisurf.aloha.com

Links

Island Happenings

Aunty Leilani's Culture Caves

Coconut Boyz Beach House

Historic Park

Learn Your Name in Hawaiian

Island Buzz On Line

For Hawaii travel information with a little more of a mainstream bend, check out Hawaii's Visitor Bureau page at:

http://www.visit.hawaii.org/

The New Age Capital of America

Just two hours north of Phoenix is Sedona, home to crystal mongers, extraterrestrial tourists, and ancient sacred vortex undergarments—In other words, new age paradise. So what if you're 3,000 miles from Phoenix? No problem. You can still transport yourself (bilocate is the politically new-age-correct term) directly to Sedona via the Web. Fill out the online form

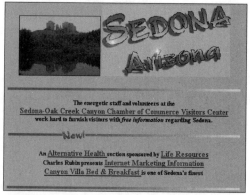

Welcome to Red Rock country, where even some of the locals claim to be billions of years old.

at the Chamber of Commerce Visitors Center to receive brochures and information about Sedona through your snail mail.

In addition, this link is a hiker's paradise, with information on dozens of day hikes in the Sedona-Oak Creek area. If you lean more toward ancient history, find out about the Indian ruins of Tuzigoot National Monument and Montezuma Castle National Monument.

Where

http://www.sedona.net/sedona.html

Links

Calendar of Events

Golf Courses

Hiking Trails

Hotels & Motels

Indian Ruins

Map

Other Interesting Locations

Resorts

Restaurants

Reservations

Tours

All kidding aside, this site is arguably one of the most attractive as well as informative tourist sites on the Web. Don't miss it.

George Washington Slept Here, and Here...

Visiting TravelWeb is like having your own personal travel agent. In fact, it's more like *being* your own personal travel agent. You can access online brochures on hotels, motels, inns, resorts, and more from some of the industry's major chains, including Hyatt, Hilton, and Best Western. Just click on a hotel you're interested in to get phone numbers, locations, credit card and currency information, and more. You'll even find check-in and check-out times. All that's missing is the mint on your pillow.

In addition, you'll get information on the services offered (babysitting, whether rooms have modem lines, whether pets are allowed, and so on), and what kind of rating the hotel has earned. Considering the number of places ol' George slept, he could have really used this service.

Where

http://www.travelweb.com/

Links

Best Western International Search Page
Hilton Hotels and Resorts Search Page
Hyatt Resorts Search Page
John Gardiner's Tennis Ranch
Le Mirador Resort and Spa
Traveler Safety Tips
Currency Exchange

The Conrad London, a five-star hotel you can access at this five-star Web site.

This site is growing fast, so check back often for the latest additions.

That's a Fact, Jack

Produced annually by the good guys at the Central Intelligence Agency for a very exclusive audience of U.S. Government officials (and 20 million of their closest Internet friends), *The World Factbook* contains detailed information on over 250 countries, continents, regions, and territories around the globe. And I do mean detailed. We're talking *minutiae*.

Interested in vacationing in Bermuda? It's here. How about France? Oui. And never again will you find yourself embarrassingly unprepared when you're in Antarctica. A sampling of the information you'll find here includes:

• Location and size
• Boundaries and terrain

- Climate and natural resources
- Population and birth rate
- Religions and ethnicity
- Government and economy
- Head of state's horoscope and shoe size

So whether you're interested in overthrowing a government or just want to know a little more about a country before you get there, nothing else on the Internet compares to this site for the sheer volume of information available. There's even a wide assortment of world maps in both GIF and JPEG formats.

Where

http://www.ic.gov/94fact/fb94toc/fb94toc.html

Links

You don't really expect me to list them all, do you? In addition to a link for each country, here's a smattering of other links:

Reference Maps

Selected International Environmental Agreements

Weights and Measures

Cross-Reference List of Geographic Names

We Strongly Advise You

Before you book that super-saver vacation to Haiti, you might want to invest a couple of minutes at this Web page. This is the place to go to find up-to-the-minute postings on travel warnings and advisories from the U.S. State Department.

You'll also get the latest information on the local economy, entry requirements, U.S. Embassy locations, medical facilities, crime, and too much more to list. You can even download maps and flags for each country.

Where

http://www.stolaf.edu/network/travel-advisories.html

```
STATE DEPARTMENT TRAVEL INFORMATION - Mexico
=================================================================
Mexico - Public Announcement
 March 17, 1995

U.S. DEPARTMENT OF STATE
 Office of the Spokesman

For Immediate Release

The U.S. Embassy in Mexico City has advised its employees to use
only taxis from authorized taxi stands "sitios" at the airport and
throughout the city.  Several Embassy employees were recently
abducted, assaulted, and robbed after hailing taxicabs in the
streets of Mexico City.  Travelers may consult their hotels or local
telephone directories for telephone numbers and locations of
authorized taxi stands or the U.S. Embassy in Mexico City for
further information.
```

A recent advisory for Mexico.

Links

From Afghanistan to Zimbabwe and all points in between, you'll find hundreds of links here, including:

World Tourist

The Travelers' Tales Resource Center

MCW International Travelers Clinic

CIA World Factbook

Don't Drink the Water

The greatest risk to international travelers isn't terrorist bombings, kidnappings or hijackings, it's diarrhea, malaria, and hepatitis (though those afflicted would probably give anything for a terrorist bombing to put them out of their misery). Here's a site that contains useful information on the health risks that come with traveling abroad and what you can do to minimize your chances of contracting these maladies, like:

- Standard food and water precautions can reduce the risk of diarrhea, and antibiotics can rapidly cure it if it occurs
- Taking malaria medications and using insect repellents to avoid bites from malaria-infected mosquitoes
- The chance of getting Hepatitis A can be reduced by vaccination or an injection of immune serum globulin
- An oral vaccine is now available for protection against typhoid
- Vaccinations against polio, meningitis, and yellow fever

Visit this site to find out more about staying healthy enough to enjoy your stay.

Where

http://www.intmed.mcw.edu/ITC/Health.html

Links

Travel Medicine Kit

Traveling While Pregnant

Altitude Sickness

Auto Accidents

Motion Sickness

Get Outta Town

Planning a vacation in the U.S.? You and 200 million others. But this year don't leave it to your cousin Arnie to make all the arrangements. I mean, how many times in one person's life do you need to see every slice of roadside Americana between Duluth, Minnesota and Orlando, Florida?

Instead, let the U.S. Department of the Interior make things easier for you. While you won't find any mention of "The World's Largest Ball of String" or "Mummified Space Aliens" here, they do publish some great booklets to help get you where you're going—no matter where Cousin Arnie sends you.

You'll find lots of information on national parks, government travel offices throughout the United States, and what your rights are when flying (in an airplane). You'll also find out how you can receive free maps, calendars of events, travel guides, and brochures to help get the most out of your trip. And if you're planning a trip abroad, be sure to check out the valuable passport and customs information.

Where

http://www.gsa.gov/staff/pa/cic/trav&hob.htm

Download

Discover America: A Listing of State and Territorial Travel Offices of the United States

Fly-Rights

Lesser Known Areas of the National Park System

Passports & Customs

Planes, Trains, and Automobiles

Regardless of where you're going for your vacation, you can bet that somebody else has already "been there/done that." Better to learn from the mistakes of others than from your own. So get past the hype from the travel brochures and find out the truth about those destinations *before* you get there.

Welcome to the **Rec.Travel Library**, the most comprehensive travel and tourism information source on the Internet. We maintain specific information on destinations around the world, as well as general travel tips.

Please send us your comments or suggestions!

Internet Solutions

rec.travel Library

Country Collections

Africa - Asia - Caribbean - Central America - Europe - Middle East - North America - Pacific - South America

Make the rec.travel Library your first stop come vacation time.

The rec.travel archive is a great place to find out from others just how good that cruise was, which hotels and hostels to avoid, and what to do once you get there. Vacations come but once a year; don't spend the next 50 weeks grumbling about the two you wasted.

Where

http://www.digimark.net/rec-travel/

Links

Airlines on the Internet

Railroad Timetables on the Internet

Car Rentals - Rent-a-wreck

Health

Hostels

Round-the-World Travel

Where to Find More Goodies

To paraphrase Jim Stafford, the Web lets you take a trip and never leave the farm. So pack your cyberbags, then check out these sections that contain other travel-related sites:

- Turn to *International* for help with your travel plans to other countries, including India, Norway, and the U.K., as well as thousands of cities around the world.

- If you're really into traveling, take a tour of the planets with software and sites provided in *Space and Astronomy*.

Index

Invest
235

Car 240